The Sporting Chef's Favorite

WILD GAME RECIPES

By
Scott Leysath

Arrowhead Classics Publishing Co.

Newcastle, California

| All recipes | Scott Leysath |
| Edited | Maureen McCarthy |

Cover Photography	William Karoly
Cover design and Graphics	The Graphics Company, P. O. Box 1247, Newcastle, CA 95658
Page Layout and Typography	The Graphics Company (www.egraphicscompany.com)

Back Cover Artwork: Joe Garcia. Color prints available from Spinetta Winery And Gallery, 12557 Steiner Road, Plymouth, CA 95669. 209-245-3384

This edition published by Arrowhead Classics Publishing Company
P. O. Box 1247, Newcastle, CA 95658 www.arrowhead-classics.com

ISBN 1-886571-23-6
EAN 978-1-886571-23-5
Library of Congress Catalog data pending

First Softcover Printing. Printed in USA

Cover photo: Scott Leysath cooks his favorite grouse recipe at Sardine Lake, below the California Sierra Buttes mountain range north of Downieville, and Sierra City.

Some additional recipes in this book are posted at Scott's Web site. Plus, you can find more great recipes from The Sporting Chef at
www.SportingChef.com.

Scott Leysath – The Sporting Chef

Since the late 1980's Scott Leysath has been recognized as a leading authority on proper preparation of fish and game. Building on a corporate restaurant management background, Leysath opened his own Sacramento, California restaurant in 1987. Along with innovative fish and game items on the daily menu, he invited sportsmen to bring in their bagged fish and game so he could show them how it is supposed to taste. His reputation for extraordinary fish and game cooking led to the beginning of his catering enterprise, Silver Sage Caterers. Silver Sage provides exceptional meals for Northern California sporting groups such as Ducks Unlimited, California Waterfowl Association, National Wild Turkey Federation, Mule Deer Federation, Rocky Mountain Elk Foundation, California Deer Association and Safari Club International. Scott Leysath has found his niche in gourmet fish and game cooking.

Writer and Media Personality

Scott is a regular contributor for a handful of outdoor publications and websites, including Western Outdoor News, California Waterfowl, ESPNOutdoors.com Ducks.org and Realtree.com. He spent four years on *HGTV's Home Grown Cooking with Paul James*. When not in front of the camera giving useful cooking tips or preparing dishes, Scott scripted, coordinated and directed the show's cooking segments. His first show, The Sporting Chef, earned Excellence in Craft honors from the Southeastern Outdoor Press Association as well as accolades from outdoor writers across the U.S. His current show, HuntFishCook, is a co-hosted with the legendary Donny McElvoy. For more on the show, visit www.HuntFishCook.com. Scott also appears on numerous weekly outdoors television and radio programs such as Ducks Unlimited TV. He is also a charter member of Ducks Unlimited's Culinary Council.

Corporate Chef/Entertainer

Beginning in 1997, Scott began working for corporate entities - conducting wild game cooking demonstrations and wild game dinners. He appears at numerous restaurants, hunting and fishing lodges, private residences, country clubs and banquet facilities. Scott has established relationships with chefs, caterers and restaurant operators throughout the U.S., especially in the southeast, Texas and the Rocky Mountain states.

Chef Leysath is featured at outdoors/sportsman and food expositions where he entertains attendees with his subtle wit and culinary mastery. He practices what he calls "short attention span cooking", knowing that learning is an active process and that guests not entertained will move on to other venues. In a period of less than one-hour, Scott will prepare up to ten fabulous fish and game dishes, encouraging guests to devour each one as it is prepared. He adds the special celebrity touch to any event or product campaign.

SportingChef.com

Scott's website, SportingChef.com, receives tens of thousands of visitors each month. This is testimony to the fact that many hunters are at a loss as to what to do with their game. Too often, those that hunt do not eat that which they harvest. Part of being a responsible sportsman requires making the best use of our bagged fish and game.

Catch Scott's HuntFishCook TV Show and other Sporting Chef shows on-line anytime at MyOutdoorTV.com. or SportingChef.com

Contents

Wild Game Cooking

Few experiences compare to the exhilaration of a successful hunting or fishing adventure. After much planning and anticipation, we who hunt set out in search of a limit of big game, trophy sized fish or game birds. It's amazing how we are able to wake up before our alarm clocks sound when the day's activity promises an outdoor adventure rather than a day at the office.

While the taking of game during the outdoor experience is what motivates most of us to brave otherwise intolerable weather, marshes, high mountains and a long hike through pant-ripping briar thickets, too few of us enjoy the cooking and eating of game. Too often you may hear expressions of dislike for wild game dishes. There's a reason. Many people have had an unpleasant experience with improperly prepared or handled game. They have been operating under the misconception that game is tough, when in reality it is often the lack of good care, and sometimes poor preparation that has made it so. Another reason could be that recipes handed down from generation to generation may not satisfy today's more sophisticated palates. The recipes in this book, are contemporary and money saving in that you use little fuel energy and fewer fats, and develop a lot more flavor and enjoyment. Those who have not tried wild game for years are usually surprised to discover how incredibly delicious properly prepared game dishes taste. I know. I have been cooking game for public palates for years, and I've fed many converts.

Still, on numerous occasions, I have had disheartening discussions with hunters regarding the preparation of wild game. One gentleman explained how he removes the unpleasant taste from pheasant by soaking the bird in buttermilk for twenty-four hours before deep-fat frying it. After that, he smothers it with brown gravy. Unbelievably to me, the birds he spoke of had been plump farm-raised versions that could hardly have tasted much different than chicken. I believe that given the choice between the aforementioned dish and a pheasant deftly prepared, the diner will choose the latter. Try one of my recipes for pheasant in this book. You'll find yourself returning to this book more and more.

Introducing Wild Game Meals to Friends

Introducing newcomers to wild game meals requires some careful planning. For instance, you can't plop a whole roasted duck down in front of a guest and expect anything less than apprehension from them. Remember, we eat with our eyes as well as our mouths. To help make the visual part of the meal more appetizing, try removing the breast from the carcass and letting it stand for a moment to allow the juices to drain. Then, slice the meat at an angle and fan out the slices from a focal point as you would a work of art. Finish the dish with a rich and flavorful sauce and serve with a complementary side dish or two. Along with presenting game in an attractive manner, two main principals of game cooking will guarantee great meals: All game must be handled properly and please, don't over cook your game.

1. All Game Must Be Handled Properly.

When you purchase meat, poultry or fish at a market, it usually comes neatly packaged and labeled. For instance, if you notice that one package of beef looks a little discolored from the others, you will probably opt for the "healthier" appearing one. The discoloration of the package you reject results from exposure to oxygen. The same thing happens to your game when it has been exposed to heat or air, or when it has not been properly cleaned, dressed and stored.

Care of Hunted Meat

At the hunt, or immediately upon taking large game, it is important to clean and cool it as soon as possible. Rinse with cold water and either get it to the butcher, (my usual recommendation), or butcher it yourself. I do not recommend hanging or aging game for extended periods of more than a week or two, unless you have access to a temperature-controlled aging locker. Your best bet is to cool it and wrap it carefully before clearly labeling each package with a permanent marker. Include the type of animal (deer, elk, moose), the cut of meat (chop, roast, stew) and the date of packaging.

Storing Wild Game

Plan ahead before storing game birds and small game. In many instances, you can make more judicious use of freezer space by removing the meat from the animals and wrapping the disjointed carcasses separately for use in game stocks. Once I have enough carcasses to make a hearty stock, I remove them from the freezer and undertake the task of preparing a variety of stocks that are then frozen in small quantities in concentrated form for use throughout the year.

Regardless of how you wrap your game before freezing, do so carefully. Exposure to oxygen is the worst enemy of all meats. Make certain that all packages are wrapped tightly.

One of the greatest inventions designed to help us with preserving food that we want to save for future cooking, is the home vacuum packaging system Vacuum packaging insures that stored game is not exposed to oxygen when used with the proper storage bags. This eliminates spoilage and freezer burn, which occurs no matter how well a product is wrapped. Vacuum packaged fish and game are more easily stored; the packages take up less freezer space and they can be thawed by simply placing the sealed packages in cold water. I vacuum package even those items I do not intend to freeze, but need to keep fresh for up to a week. I prefer the FoodSaver™ unit for its ease of operation, affordability and durability. FoodSaver™ patented VacLoc® bags don't leak, and the contents remain significantly fresher than those stored in plastic containers or zipper-lock type bags, usually extending shelf life 3 to 5 times longer than traditional storage methods. The modest cost of one of these handy units is outweighed by its utility. Freezing small game, waterfowl and game birds in milk cartons filled with water also works well. I have found that they can be frozen for a year or so with good results. The biggest drawback of this method is the amount of space necessary to store frozen milk cartons. Thawing is also cumbersome.

I rarely freeze big game backstraps or tenderloins. Assuming they make it to my kitchen, I refrigerate them for only a day or two before cooking. The same goes with large drake mallards or other large ducks. They do seem to taste better within the week they were shot.

Although certain precautions will guarantee that your game has the best chance of retaining the most flavor during prolonged freezing, properly handled fresh game will almost always taste better than frozen game. The only exception would be an animal that has been feeding on unsavory items that may affect the flavor of the meat. Sometimes we can do all the right things in terms of preparation, yet unpleasant flavors prevail. Such is the chance one takes when cooking wild game.

Fat and sinew should be trimmed from all large game animals. Most unpleasant flavors can be attributed to the fat of the animals. Replace the natural fat from game animals with commercial substitutes, such as bacon or butter.

2. Do Not Overcook Your Game

If you want the very best flavor and tenderness from your wild game, do not cook it past medium-rare. Beyond medium-rare, game will toughen up and develop the dreaded "gamy" flavor and texture. Game meats are extremely lean, making them unforgiving when they are overcooked. Meat can turn from being perfect to having the texture of shoe leather in a matter of minutes. Therefore, it is recommended that you remove the meat from the heat source just before it reaches the desired temperature. If you should miss the mark, the only way to rescue overcooked game is to cook it for an hour or two in liquid until the meat becomes tender and starts to fall apart. The finished product will certainly be edible, but the flavor and texture will be more reminiscent of stewed meat than the delicious flavors you would have had otherwise.

A good meat thermometer will help you get a feel for when to remove game from the flame. Game birds should not be cooked past 150°F degrees. Antlered game is medium-rare at 135°F. Ducks and geese should be removed at 130 - 135° F for medium-rare. Because of possible risk of exposure to trichinosis, bear and wild boar should be cooked to a safe internal temperature of 140°F. After using the meat thermometer a time or two, learn to trust your judgment when cooking wild game. As the meat cooks, apply pressure to the flesh with your fingers. The meat will yield to pressure less and less as it cooks. When in doubt, pull it out of the oven or skillet and test for doneness. Most meats, especially large cuts, will continue to cook a bit after they have been removed from the heat. It is far better to remove game that has been slightly undercooked than to overcook it.

When The Fat Is Gone

The nutritional benefits of wild and farm-raised game are superior to commercially-raised beef, pork and poultry. Game is usually seven to ten times lower in fat and cholesterol than comparable cuts of domestic meats. Wild game is truly free-ranging and devoid of antibiotics, steroids and hormones. Properly prepared game dishes will tantalize the senses with rich, intense flavors not found in even the finest quality beef steaks and roasts.

Some of these recipes specify high-fat ingredients such as butter and cream. If you prefer lower-fat dishes, you can achieve similar results by substituting beef or chicken broth or wine combined with a thickening agent. Cornstarch, mixed with an equal amount of cold water, wine or stock will thicken any sauce without adding appreciable amounts of fat or cholesterol. Bring the liquid to a boil and whisk in the cornstarch mixture a little at a time until thickened. A paste made of arrowroot and cold water, added to the sauce while it is still hot, but not boiling, will enable you to achieve similar results.

The addition of fats to game dishes is designed to add moisture to lean meats. Game meats may also be protected from drying out by covering with copious amounts of fresh herbs and vegetables, thus avoiding the addition of high-fat bacon or butter. When preparing a venison roast for example, thinly slice root vegetables such as carrots, potatoes and onions. Lay them over the roast with an assortment of fresh herbs. Not only will you preserve the low-fat benefits of wild game cooking, but you will add flavor and moisture from the herbs and vegetables.

Many of my recipes specify the use of fresh herbs and vegetables. I am fortunate enough to live in an area where fresh herbs and a wide variety of vegetables are in abundance either in my own garden, or at local supermarkets. Should you live in an area where fresh herbs and vegetables are not readily available, it will be necessary to adjust quantities accordingly. Fresh herbs in particular have a distinctly different flavor than dried herbs. Therefore, the finished dish may vary somewhat when dried herbs are substituted for fresh. As a rule of thumb, use about three to four times less quantity of dried herbs when substituting for fresh ones. If you want the very best flavors, consider planting a small herb garden in the sunniest part of your yard during the summer. Herbs are typically hardy and require little care. They can easily be grown in a sunny location indoors in pots as well. You'll want to avoid growing herbs in pots outdoors in direct sun since the soil would dry out quickly and stress the plants. Harvested fresh herbs can be washed, dried and vacuum packaged in FoodSaver VacLoc bags, and stored in your freezer. You can also use zip lock type bags, but watch out for freezer burn. Make sure if you use the zip lock instead of the vacuum bags to push as much air out as possible before sealing the bag. Your fresh herbs will keep for a long time in the vacuum bags. The flavors are in the natural oils of the herb and are superior in flavor to dried herbs.

It is advisable to avoid buying the least expensive ingredients, unless they are available in good quality. I have discovered that lesser-grade cooking products such as inexpensive olive oil or soy sauce often result in an unremarkable meal. If a product is available in a "low-salt" version, buy it. You can always add more salt, but it takes a miracle to reverse an oversalted dish.

What If Wild Game Is Not Available?
All recipes in this book can be adapted wonderfully for cooking with non-game

meats. Since game meat is a bit more dense, (less fat) you should increase the quantity of meat by about ten percent when using beef, pork and poultry. It will shrink more than game animals due to the increased fat content. Substitute chicken, game hens or commercially-raised rabbit for upland game recipes. Beef will work well with any of the antlered game recipes, and lean trimmed pork will suffice as a substitution for wild boar. I have provided a short list of exchanges at the end of this introduction.

You will discover that I have a penchant for garlic. Game and garlic work together like a hunter and a good bird dog. Although the flavor is not nearly as pronounced, you can substitute minced garlic found in jars, for fresh garlic cloves. In many areas, peeled garlic cloves may be purchased at supermarkets and specialty stores. To peel a fresh garlic clove, set it on a firm flat surface. Place the flat side of a chef's wide blade knife on the garlic and give the knife a firm rap directly above the clove. The skin will peel easily. To mince garlic, repeat the procedure with the chef's knife, except now, you'll want to smash down on the knife with a little more force to flatten the clove. Use the knife to chop up the smashed garlic. Then, sell your garlic press at the next yard sale.

Innovative wild game and non-game preparation requires the cook to invoke the spirit of the pioneer. Go forth boldly into the kitchen and throw caution to the wind. Mix and match flavors with reckless abandon. I am quite certain that our early settlers learned to eat a great many previously unknown animals, fish and plants, prepared in seemingly unorthodox ways, as they made their way across virgin America.

Armed with a good quality chef's knife, a boning knife, and a variety of sauce pans, skillets, roasting pans and stock pots, you're well-prepared to attack magnificent game preparation with the same tenacity that was employed to bag your game. Make liberal use of good wine, fresh herbs and seasonal fruits and vegetables. Experience, creativity, and experimentation will pave the way for you to become a more confident sporting chef.

For those who don't reoutinely have a bag of squirrels in the freezer, there are a number of online resources for farmed game. Give www.HouseofWildGame.com a try.

WEIGHTS AND MEASURES
Used In This Book

3 teaspoons = 1 tablespoon
2 tablespoons = 1 fluid ounce
4 tablespoons = 1/4 cup
8 ounces = 1 cup
1 pint = 2 cups (or 16 fluid ounces)
1 quart = 2 pints (or 32 fluid ounces)
1 gallon = 4 quarts (or 128 fluid Ounces)

SUBSTITUTIONS YOU CAN MAKE

UPLAND GAME

Wild Turkey, whole	Domestic turkey, not pre basted
Wild Turkey, pieces	2 Quartered pheasants
	4 Chukar or Hungarian Partridges
	Domestic turkey pieces, skin, fat removed
Pheasant, whole	2 grouse
	2 Chukar or Hungarian Partridges
	Small domestic turkey, fat removed
Pheasant, cutup	Wild turkey legs and thighs
	4 grouse, quartered
	4 Chukar or Hungarian partridges, quartered
	8 to 12 quail breasts
	Domestic turkey legs and thighs
	Chicken legs and thighs
Quail	Pheasant, cut up
	Ruffed grouse
	Chukar
	Chicken, skin, fat removed
Dove	Quail breasts
	Pheasant, cut up
	Chukar, cut up
Cottontail Rabbit	Squirrels
	Parts of domestic rabbit
	Pheasant or one of its substitutes

BIG GAME

Elk, Caribou	Moose, tenderloin
	Venison, loin portion
	Lean Beef, sirloin, fat removed
Venison	Moose, Elk or Caribou, usually the tenderloin portions
	Lean Beef tenderloin, fat removed
Boar	Shoulder roast from any big game
	Rib roast from moose or elk
	Lean domestic pork tenderloin, fat removed

STARTERS

I cannot think of a better way to begin a wild game dinner than with a tempting wild game appetizer or salad. A well-prepared first course whets the appetite for the main course to follow. Appetizers can be served in portions at tableside or on platters while partaking of a glass of good wine as the chef puts the finishing touches on the entrée. For a casual dinner, prepare an assortment of appetizers in place of a single main dish.

Many of the main dishes found elsewhere in this book make suitable appetizers. For example, prepare Mallard Breast Stuffed with Mushrooms and Gorgonzola Cheese (see page 20) as per the recipe. Cut the finished rolled breasts into thirds and skewer with a toothpick. Small upland birds such as quail and dove make excellent finger food and can be served right off the grill at game barbecues.

When serving appetizers, make an effort to present them in an attractive manner. Garnish with a sprig of fresh herbs or a thin slice of a colorful vegetable. Avoid serving starter courses in large quantities as you will want your guests to comfortably enjoy the main course.

ASIAN RABBIT MINI-CALZONE

Although you may make four large entrée- sized calzones with this recipe, I prefer the miniature version as a unique appetizer. Substitute upland game birds, if desired.

12 Servings

1	pizza dough (see page 9)
¼	cup sesame seeds, lightly toasted in a 325° F oven
½	cup fresh cilantro, minced
2	cups boneless rabbit, cut into 1/2 inch cubes
1	tablespoon cornstarch
2	tablespoons soy sauce
2	tablespoons dry sherry
1	tablespoon seasoned rice vinegar or white wine vinegar sweetened with a pinch of sugar
1	garlic clove, minced
1	tablespoon peanut oil
⅔	cup snow peas, strings and ends removed and sliced into fourths
1	cup mung bean or soy bean sprouts
2	teaspoons fresh ginger, minced
¼	cup red bell pepper, diced
1	cup fresh mushrooms, sliced thinly
⅔	cup fresh or canned pineapple, diced
½	cup apricot preserves
1 ½	cups Monterey Jack cheese, grated

Prepare dough as per recipe, but add sesame seeds and cilantro before mixing.

Combine rabbit with next 5 ingredients, toss and marinate 15 minutes at room temperature. Strain rabbit from marinade. Reserve marinade. In a skillet or wok over medium-high heat, heat peanut oil and add rabbit pieces. Cook until medium brown. Add marinade and cook 2 - 3 minutes more, bringing to a boil. Remove from heat & cool. Place cooked rabbit in a large bowl with remaining ingredients.

Once dough has risen, knead on a lightly floured surface for 2 minutes and form into a roll. Cut roll into 12 equal portions. Roll or press each piece into a 4 inch circle. Place an equal amount of filling into each dough circle and fold over, turning up edges with your fingers to seal in contents. Arrange calzones

BARBECUED DUCK PIZZA

The variations possible for this appetizer are limited only by your imagination. Experiment with other game meats, cheeses and other toppings to add a personal touch to your pizza.

6 - 8 servings

2   large duck breast halves, skin removed and sliced diagonally into very thin strips
2   cups tomato-based barbecue sauce
2   tablespoons red wine vinegar
4   tablespoons olive oil
2   garlic cloves, minced
4   ounces spicy Italian sausage, casing removed and crumbled
¼   portion pizza dough (see below)
1   cup gruyére or swiss cheese, grated
1   cup parmesan cheese, freshly grated
1   cup mozzarella cheese, grated
¼   red onion, cut into thin rings
4   roma tomatoes, cut into about 5 slices each
¼   cup fresh cilantro, chopped

Combine barbecue sauce and vinegar, place in a container with the sliced duck and mix well. Cover and refrigerate for 4 to 6 hours. In a large skillet over medium-high heat, heat 2 tablespoons of the olive oil, add garlic and cook for 1 minute. Add duck with sauce and cook for 3 to 4 minutes, or until duck is just cooked and still tender. Remove duck, set aside to cool and add sausage. Cook until well browned and remove from heat.

Place the dough on a pizza pan, prick several times with a fork and brush with remaining olive oil. Spread cheeses and then duck and sausage evenly over pizza. Top with tomatoes and onion rings. Bake in a 500° oven for 12 to 15 minutes or until crust is golden brown. Sprinkle cilantro over pizza and slice.

Pizza Dough

Makes two 12 inch pizza crusts

1   pkg active dry yeast
1   cup warm water mixed with 1-tablespoon sugar
3   cups all-purpose flour
1   teaspoon salt
⅛   cup olive oil

In a large mixing bowl, sprinkle yeast over water and stir until dissolved. Place in a warm location for 5 minutes to activate yeast. Add remaining ingredients, one at a time, mixing in each. Place dough on a floured surface and knead until smooth and elastic. Form into a ball, brush top with a little olive oil and place in a greased bowl. Cover and set in a draft-free, warm location for about 1 1/2 hours or until dough has doubled. Shells may be frozen by cooking at 325° for 10 minutes before cooling, wrapping and placing in freezer.

SMOKED DUCK TOASTS
WITH RED CHILI AIOLI

A tempting appetizer with a spicy hot finish.

24 - 28 toasts

1	large smoked duck, breast meat only (see page 145)
6-8	thin slices sourdough or rye bread
½	cup olive oil
6	garlic cloves, minced
½	teaspoon chili flakes
¼	teaspoon salt
1	egg yolk at room temperature
2	teaspoons fresh lemon juice
2	teaspoons fresh lime juice
½	teaspoon cayenne pepper
1	teaspoon chili powder
⅔	cup olive oil
24-28	fresh cilantro leaves

Slice breasts diagonally across the grain into very thin strips. Combine next three ingredients and brush one side of bread slices. Trim crusts and cut bread into 4 triangles per slice. Lay triangles on a sheet pan and toast in a 325° F oven until lightly browned. In a food processor or blender, combine next 6 ingredients and process until blended. While processor is running, add oil in a very thin stream until aioli thickens. Spoon a small dollop of the aioli on the center of each toast. Fold each duck slice to fit the toast and place the folded slices on the aioli. Garnish each with a fresh cilantro leaf.

ELK CARPACCIO

You will get a true appreciation for the choicest cut of elk by sampling a lightly marinated slice or two of raw tenderloin. Even if you shy away from raw meat, you owe it to yourself to try just a bite.

4 servings

12	ounces elk tenderloin, carefully trimmed of all fat and sinew and sliced paper thin with a very sharp thin-bladed knife or electric slicer.

NOTE: Before slicing, place the meat in the freezer until very cold, but not frozen. You should be able to get at least 12 slices from a 12 ounce tenderloin.

2	tablespoons freshly squeezed lemon juice
2	tablespoons extra virgin olive oil
1	tablespoon red wine vinegar
1	garlic clove
1	tablespoon freshly ground black pepper
2	tablespoons fresh basil, minced

Arrange equal portions of sliced meat on 4 plates. Combine remaining ingredients and drizzle over meat. Let stand 3 to 4 minutes before serving.

VENISON CARPACCIO
with Figs

I often begin my wild game cooking demonstrations by eating a small piece of raw deer or elk. Some will exit immediately. Many stick around just to see if I'm going to keel over and die. It's like watching a wreck on the freeway.

If you're trying to disarm some lurking wild game viral strain as yet undiscovered, you may decide that it's best to cook your meat at least to medium temperature. That's the way your Daddy ate it and, by golly, that's the way you like it, too. To kill bacteria, etc., you'll need to cook your meat to at least 160 degrees. In terms of cooked venison, that's the stuff baseball mitts are made of. Keep in mind that, as a rule, we don't take three-legged deer with mange. We hunt healthy animals free of disease, added steroids, antibiotic and hormones. They graze on grasses, seeds and, hopefully, corn.

This recipe is simple and delicious, but it requires an open mind. You can change your eating habits at least for one bite. Trust me. That bite will be followed by more. It's that good.

4 appetizer servings

8	ounces venison tenderloin, silver skin removed
	pinch Lawry's seasoned pepper
	pinch coarse salt
3	tablespoons extra virgin olive oil
2	tablespoons balsamic vinegar
1	lemon, juice only
1	clove garlic, minced
6-8	fresh figs, each thinly sliced widthwise
2	ounces freshly shaved parmesan cheese
2	green onions, thinly shredded lengthwise; green part only

Place venison in the freezer until the meat is very firm, but not completely frozen. Remove from freezer and slice across the grain into as thinly as possible without shredding. Arrange slices on four plates. Season meat with pepper and salt. Arrange fig slices over meat. Combine olive oil, lemon juice, vinegar and garlic in a container with a tight-fitting lid. Shake vigorously to blend. Drizzle over venison and figs. Let stand at room temperature for 10 minutes. Top with shaved parmesan cheese and green onions.

MARINATED GOOSE
WITH CITRUS AND HERB VINAIGRETTE

Those who shy away from the distinctive flavor of goose will be pleasantly surprised with this delightful first course.

6 servings

2   Canada geese breast halves, skin removed and sliced diagonally across the "grain" into ¹/₄ inch strips
1   cup olive oil
¼   cup orange juice
2   tablespoons lime juice
½   cup white wine vinegar
2   garlic cloves, minced
3   tablespoons red onion, minced
¼   cup sugar
¼   cup fresh basil, minced
3   tablespoons fresh oregano, minced
2   tablespoons fresh mint, minced
1   teaspoon salt
1   teaspoon ground mustard
½   teaspoon freshly ground black pepper
4   cups green cabbage, shredded
2   cups red cabbage, shredded
1   tablespoon caraway seeds
6   slices from a large ripe tomato

In a large skillet or wok over medium-high flame or setting, heat 3 tablespoons of the oil and stir-fry goose until just rare. Remove goose from oil and drain well on paper towels. In a large bowl, combine remaining olive oil and next 12 ingredients. Mix well. Add goose to bowl, toss well, cover and refrigerate for 12 to 24 hours, tossing occasionally.

Remove goose from marinade and form into six mounds. Combine green and red cabbage and caraway seeds and toss with marinade. Place equal portion of cabbage on each plate. Place tomato slice on the center of the cabbage and top with marinated goose.

ENSALADA AY CARAMBA

This spicy salad calls for rabbit, but the dish works equally well with light-fleshed game birds such as quail, chukar or pheasant.

4 servings

2	cottontail rabbits, boned and cut into 1/2 inch cubes
2	tablespoons fresh lime juice
2	tablespoons fresh lemon juice
3	tablespoons tequila
1	teaspoon sugar
1	tablespoon chili flakes
1	tablespoon ground cumin
½	teaspoon cayenne pepper
½	cup peanut oil
2	large corn tortillas, cut into 1/4 inch strips
1	medium head iceberg lettuce, shredded
1	ripe, but firm avocado, sliced into 12 slices
1	cup cooked black beans
½	cup sliced black olives
½	cup pepper Jack cheese, grated
2	cups pico de gallo salsa (see page 88)
¼	cup sour cream blended with
1	teaspoon fresh lime juice

In a medium bowl, combine rabbit with the next seven ingredients. Cover and marinate in refrigerator for 2 hours, turning 2 or 3 times. Remove rabbit from marinade and drain. In a large skillet over medium-high heat, heat 3 tablespoons of the oil and cook rabbit pieces until well-browned and fully cooked, about 5 minutes. Remove rabbit and set aside to cool. Add remaining oil. When oil is hot, add tortilla strips and cook until crisp. Drain on paper towels.

For each salad, on a large plate, arrange a layer of lettuce, then evenly distribute black beans and olives. Place a small mound of rabbit on the center of the lettuce. Arrange 3 slices of avocado around base of rabbit mound. Mound salsa on rabbit. Place a dollop of sour cream on salsa mound. Distribute cheese evenly and garnish with tortilla strips.

GRILLED PHEASANT SALAD

A delicious main course salad in the fall or winter when navel oranges are available.

4 servings

- 4 pheasant breast halves, skin intact
- ½ teaspoon ground coriander
- ½ teaspoon dried basil flakes
- 2 tablespoons honey
- ½ cup orange juice
- 1 tablespoon soy sauce
- 2 teaspoons balsamic vinegar
- 4 tablespoons brown sugar
- 4 teaspoons water
- ⅓ cup slivered almonds
- ½ medium red onion, peeled and sliced into very thin rings
- ¾ cup navel orange segments, skin removed
- 1 head butterleaf lettuce, torn into 2 inch pieces
- 1 head romaine lettuce, hearts only with large leaves torn in half
- ½ cup balsamic vinaigrette
- ⅓ cup bleu cheese crumbles

Combine dry seasonings, honey, orange juice, soy sauce and vinegar in bowl. Place pheasant breasts in marinade, cover and refrigerate for 3 to 4 hours, turning breasts occasionally. Grill or barbecue pheasant breasts over medium heat until just cooked. Remove from heat and allow to cool. Once cooled, remove skin and cut breasts into 3/4 inch cubes.

Pre-heat oven to 375°F. In a small, oven-safe non-stick skillet over medium heat, add water, sugar and almonds. Stir frequently while sugar caramelizes and coats almonds. When caramel starts to thicken, place skillet in oven until almonds are lightly browned, spreading out almonds to brown evenly. Remove skillet, let cool. After almonds cool, break up large pieces.

In a large bowl, toss pheasant, almonds and remaining ingredients, reserving a few bleu cheese crumbles. Place equal portion of salad on four plates, topping each with reserved bleu cheese crumbles.

Balsamic Vainaigrette

Makes 1/2 Cup

- 2 tablespoon balsamic vinegar
- ⅓ cup olive oil
- ½ teaspoon dijon mustard
- ⅛ teaspoon black pepper
-    pinch salt

In a small jar with a tight-fitting lid, combine all ingredients and shake vigorously. Can be refrigerated for up to 1 week.

PHEASANT TIMBALES
WITH LEMON VINAIGRETTE

A delightful appetizer with extraordinary flavor and eye appeal. Serve with baby lettuces for a delicious salad.

6 servings

2   pheasant breast halves, skin removed, poached in chicken broth, cooled and
        hand-pulled into small strips
1   large red bell pepper, roasted, peeled, seeded and cut into 6 strips
        (see page 167 for directions for roasting bell pepper)
2   cups fresh spinach, steamed for 1 minute and drained well on paper towels
½   cup feta cheese, crumbled
1   cup half and half
2   large eggs
2   tablespoons butter
1   tablespoon shallot or green onion bulb, minced
2   tablespoons red wine vinegar
1   teaspoon dijon mustard
    juice of 1 lemon
⅓   cup olive oil
1   egg white
    salt and pepper
2   cups green or Nappa cabbage, shredded
1   medium tomato, seeded and diced into 1/4 inch cubes

For vinaigrette, combine shallot, vinegar, mustard and lemon in a medium bowl. While whisking, add oil in a thin stream and then egg white. Whisk until emulsified. Season with salt and pepper.

Bring the half and half to a boil in a sauce pan over medium-high heat. Lightly season with salt and pepper. In a bowl, beat the eggs, and then whisk the hot half and half into the eggs. Add the cheese and stir to blend. Grease 6 individual ramekins or 6 sections of a muffin tin with the butter. Fill each ramekin with equal amounts of cheese, half and half and egg mixture, making sure that the cheese is equally distributed. Lay equal amounts of well-drained spinach in ramekin, followed by red bell pepper and shredded pheasant. Liquid should "bleed" throughout ramekin. Place timbales in a baking dish filled with water 1/2 inch below the rim of ramekins. Bake in a 350°F oven for 30 minutes. Remove from oven and run a sharp knife around the inside of the ramekin and remove timbales. On six plates, distribute cabbage, place one timbale on each portion of cabbage and drizzle over with vinaigrette. Top with diced tomato.

PAN-FRIED QUAIL
AND NECTARINE SALAD

Quail season starts early while you can still take advantage of late-season nectarines. Peaches may be substituted for nectarines if they are more plentiful in your part of the country.

4 servings

6	quail, skin intact and cut in half
¼	cup dry sherry
½	cup flour
1	teaspoon garlic powder
½	teaspoon salt
¼	teaspoon black pepper
¼	teaspoon dried basil flakes
½	teaspoon paprika
¾	cup vegetable oil
4	handfulls mixed baby lettuce or a mixture of red leaf, butter leaf and romaine lettuce, if baby lettuce is unavailable
1	cup dry roasted and salted peanuts
¼	cup medium red onion, peeled and diced fine
1 ½	cups celery, diced
1	cup jicama, peeled and julienned
2	ripe, but firm nectarines, cut into wedges

Soak quail in sherry for 20 minutes, turning often. In a plastic bag, combine the next 6 ingredients. Place quail in bag to coat with seasonings and flour. In a large, heavy skillet over medium-high heat, heat oil until hot. Brown quail evenly on each side, about 2 - 3 minutes per side. Remove quail and set on paper towels to drain excess oil.

In a large bowl, toss remaining ingredients, reserving a little dressing. Arrange salad mixture on 4 large plates and distribute 3 quail halves per plate. Drizzle remaining dressing over quail.

Dressing

1	each egg white
¼	cup seasoned rice vinegar
¼	cup peach preserves
1	each garlic clove, minced
2	teaspoons dijon mustard
	juice of 1 lemon
¼	cup sour cream
¼	cup olive oil
	salt and pepper to taste

Place above ingredients except oil, salt and pepper in a blender or food processor and blend until smooth. While blending, add olive oil in a thin steady stream until emulsified. Season with salt and pepper.

PHEASANT TEMPURA

Great finger food to begin a game feast with an Asian flair. Choose your favorite vegetables and serve with an assortment of dipping sauces such as Plum Sauce (see page 89) or Chinese Hot Mustard.

6 - 8 servings

Batter
4	eggs
2 ⅔	cups flour
2	teaspoons salt
2	cups flat beer

Preparation
2	boneless pheasant breast halves, skin removed and sliced diagonally into 1/2 inch thick strips
2	carrots, peeled and cut into 1/2 inch by 3 inch sticks
2	zucchini, cut into 1/2 inch by 3 inch sticks
10	fresh mushrooms, whole
1	large red bell pepper, cut lengthwise into 8 strips
1	quart peanut oil

To prepare batter, beat eggs in a bowl and then add 2/3 cup flour and salt. Add beer and remaining flour, a little of each at a time, beating after each addition. Do not overbeat. Batter should be a little lumpy. Allow batter to stand for 1 hour.

Heat oil in wok, deep fryer or deep sauce pan to about 375° F.

Using tongs or chopsticks, dip each piece in batter, fry both sides until golden brown and serve immediately.

DUCK LEGS CORNELL

Inspired by my long time hunting buddy and business partner, Greg Cornell, during a fundraiser for the California Waterfowl Asoociation. Remove duck legs and freeze them throughout the season until you have enough for this unbelievably tender appetizer.

5 - 8 servings

25-30	assorted duck legs and thighs, skin intact
2	cups pineapple juice
1	cup soy sauce
½	cup cider vinegar
6	garlic cloves, minced
1	tablespoon Tabasco sauce
2	teaspoons chili flakes
½	teaspoon ground dried ginger
1	tablespoon coarse grind black pepper
2	tablespoons sesame seeds
1 ½	cups brown sugar

Pre-heat oven to 450°. Spray a deep baking pan with pan coating spray, then place legs in pan. Combine remaining ingredients and pour over legs. Cover with lid or foil and place in oven. Bake for 1 hour and then rearrange legs in pan. Repeat after baking one more hour. Check legs every 20 minutes or until meat almost falls off of the bone. Remove from pan, place on a serving tray, sprinkle with sesame seeds and allow to cool slightly before serving.

Note: Oven temperatures vary. As the legs cook, the liquid will cook off and thicken. Don't allow the liquid to completely cook off or the legs, and your baking pan, will burn. Add additional liquid if necessary.

GRILLED VENISON SKEWERS
WITH DIPPING SAUCE

Grilling time is critical as prolonged cooking will result in something more closely resembling beef jerky. Any antlered game will suffice.

6 - 8 servings (20 skewers)

2 ½   pounds venison top round or rump roast, sliced across the grain
into 1/4 inch thick strips (about 2 ounces each)

Note: Slicing with the grain will make the skewers chewier

½   cup Worcestershire sauce
½   cup game stock or beef broth
¼   cup soy sauce
2   tablespoons balsamic vinegar
4   garlic cloves, minced
2   tablespoons cracked black pepper (or 1 tablespoon table ground)
20   bamboo skewers, soaked for 30 minutes in water
2   cups Mustard Dipping Sauce (see page 170)

Combine Worcestershire sauce, game stock, soy sauce, vinegar, garlic and pepper in a large bowl. Add sliced venison, mix well, cover and marinate in refrigerator for 3 to 4 hours, turning occasionally. Remove meat and skewer lengthwise on bamboo skewers. Place on a well-greased barbecue over white-hot coals and sear on each side, about 2 minutes per side. Arrange on a platter around a bowl of dipping sauce.

DUCK EGG ROLLS

You can stuff just about anything into an egg roll, deep fry it and it will taste pretty good.

4 appetizer servings

1 ½ cups boneless and skinless duck breast, sliced thinly across the grain
2 tablespoons soy sauce
1 teaspoon fresh ginger, minced
2 garlic cloves, minced
2 tablespoons peanut oil
¼ cup dried apricots, thinly sliced
1 ½ cups green or Nappa cabbage, shredded
8 egg roll wrappers
1 tablespoon cornstarch mixed with 1 tablespoon cold water
   oil for frying

Dipping Sauce
¼ cup soy sauce
1 tablespoon hoisin sauce (Asian section of your grocery store.)
1 tablespoon brown sugar
2 tablespoons rice vinegar or white wine vinegar

Combine sliced duck with next three ingredients and marinate for 30 minutes. Drain ducks. Stir-fry duck in hot peanut oil for 45 to 60 seconds over high heat in a wok or skillet. Transfer to paper towels to cool. For each egg roll, lay the wrapper on a flat surface. Place about 2 to 3 tablespoons of the cabbage on the lower third of the wrapper forming an area of about 1 inch tall by 3 inches wide. Arrange apricots and cooked duck on top of cabbage. Turn in sides of wrapper to just overlap stuffing. Begin rolling egg roll by starting at the edge nearest you and rolling away from you, like a burrito. When you get to the edge, moisten it with a little or the cornstarch mixture to help it seal. Place egg roll in hot oil, enough to submerse it and fry until golden brown and crispy. Drain fried rolls on paper towels.

Combine sauce ingredients and serve with fried egg rolls.

SMOKED TROUT APPETIZER

6 – 8 appetizer servings

- ¼ cup kosher salt
- 1 ¼ cups firmly packed brown sugar
- 1 teaspoon onion powder
- 1 teaspoon garlic powder
- ½ teaspoon cayenne pepper
- 3 1-pound trout, cleaned (of course)

Combine salt, sugar, onion powder, garlic powder and cayenne pepper. Rub fish inside and out with mixture. Place in dish, cover and refrigerate for 12 hours.

Remove trout from dish. Place on rack. Air-dry in refrigerator until shiny, about 2 hours.

Place trout in low-temperature smoker for 1 - 2 hours or until firm.

RED AND GREEN PEANUT SLAW

- ½ head green cabbage, outer leaves removed; cored and sliced thin
- ½ head green cabbage, outer leaves removed; cored and sliced thin
- 1 cup mayonnaise
- ¼ cup white wine vinegar
- 2 tablespoons granulated sugar
  Red bell pepper, julienned, to taste
  Yellow bell pepper, julienned, to taste
- ½ cup dry-roasted peanuts
  salt and pepper to taste

Preparation

In a small bowl, combine 1 cup mayonnaise, 1/4 cup white wine vinegar and 2 tablespoons granulated sugar. Slice 1/2 head green and 1/2 head purple cabbage and place in a large bowl. Add red and yellow julienned bell peppers to taste to the cabbage. Pour in mayonnaise mixture and toss gently. Add 1/2 cup dry-roasted peanuts and season with salt and pepper to taste. Toss to coat evenly. Refrigerate for one half hour before serving. Toss before serving.

RUFFED GROUSE
A LA RUBIO

Dedicated to my boyhood hunting companion, Steve Rubio, with whom I walked miles of logging roads in the Blue Ridge Mountains in pursuit of this elusive bird. Also great served as a main dish with wild rice.

6 - 8 servings

8	ruffed grouse, boned, and cut into bite-sized pieces
1	tablespoon freshly ground black pepper
1	teaspoon onion powder
¼	teaspoon salt
2	tablespoons olive oil
½	cup dry white wine
3	garlic cloves, minced
2	medium zucchini, diced
1	medium carrot, diced
1	large russet potato, peeled and diced
1	tablespoon green peppercorns
1	tablespoon fresh rosemary, minced
1	cup game bird or chicken stock
1	large ripe tomato, peeled, seeded and quartered
2	green onions, diced
1	tablespoon cornstarch mixed with equal part cold water *(optional)*
	salt and freshly ground pepper to taste

Season grouse with next 3 ingredients. Heat oil in a large skillet over medium-high heat and brown grouse evenly. Remove grouse, add wine and cook until liquid is reduced by one-half. Add garlic, vegetables and peppercorns; cook 3 -4 minutes. Add rosemary and stock, bring to boil, reduce heat low and simmer, uncovered, for 15 minutes. Add grouse, tomato and green onions. Simmer 5 minutes more. Thicken with cornstarch mixture, a little at a time, if desired. Season with salt and pepper.

JALAPENO CHEESE HUSHPUPPIES

Be careful when deep-frying these guys. The corn kernels do occasionally pop when they're cooking. It's best to keep a splatter screen over the top.

4	cups self-rising corn meal
¾	cup flour
¾	cup fresh or frozen corn kernels (see note above)
3	tablespoons brown sugar
1	teaspoon salt
1	cup cheddar cheese, grated
	dash or more Tabasco
⅓	cup yellow onion, minced
2	jalapeño peppers, seeded and minced
2	eggs, beaten
¼	cup buttermilk
	oil for frying

Mix first 5 ingredients in a large bowl. Combine remaining ingredients in another bowl and then mix with dry ingredients. Carefully (remember – hot oil can hurt you!) drop ping-pong ball-sized blobs of mix into 325 – 340 degree oil until golden brown. Drain on paper towels before serving.

BARBECUED FROG LEGS

Hey, I usually fry them too, but they don't taste like chicken. This recipe starts with your favorite store-bought barbecue sauce and then you dump a few other ingredients in, just to be different.

Allow 2 – 4 legs per person for an appetizer serving.

	a mess of frog legs
	olive oil
	kosher or sea salt
	freshly ground pepper
	dash or more Tabasco
1½	cups prepared barbecue sauce
2	tablespoons garlic cloves, minced
2	tablespoons lemon juice

Season legs liberally with olive oil, salt and pepper. Add as much Tabasco as you can handle, cover and refrigerate for 1 – 2 hours. Combine barbecue sauce, garlic and lemon in a small saucepan and heat to blend flavors. Slap the frog legs on a well-oiled white-hot barbecue and cook until just done, about 4 – 5 minutes. While cooking, baste with barbecue sauce

SESAME DOVE HORS D'OEUVRE
WITH BACON

Believe it or not, there are other ways to prepare doves than to wrap the breasts with jalapeño and bacon or stewing in a red sauce... oh yeah, and the cream of mushroom soup thing. This preparation is simple, unique and will surprise even those who have decided that they don't like doves. Don't tell them what they are eating they have told you how great they taste. I've allowed for 3 hors d'oeuvres per guest. You may want to increase the recipe a bit, especially the second time around. Don't waste the dove bodies. Use them in your next game bird stock. When pounding the breasts, the idea is to make them of equal thickness, not to pulverize them into oblivion. Don't buy your sesame seeds in the spice section of your market. They're much cheaper in the Asian or Hispanic sections. You can dress these up with some finely diced red pepper and an herb garnish.

4 servings

12	dove breast halves, skin removed; lightly pounded with the flat side of a mallet
2	tablespoons Dijon mustard
1	teaspoon toasted sesame oil
	pinch Kosher salt
$^1/_2$	cup sesame seeds
1	tablespoon olive oil
¼	cup softened cream cheese
1	tablespoon pickled or fresh ginger, minced
12	won ton skins, quickly fried until golden brown and drained on paper towels
2	tablespoons prepared wasabi (optional)

Combine mustard, sesame oil and salt. Coat dove breasts evenly. Place sesame seeds in a shallow plate and press coated dove breasts into seeds to coat evenly. Heat oil in a large skillet over medium heat. Add dove breasts and cook until brown on one side, then flip each over and lightly brown the other side. Remove dove breasts.

Combine cream cheese with the ginger and stir with a fork to blend. Place a dime-sized blob of the cream cheese mixture, about 1/4-inch thick, on the center of each fried won ton. Place a dove breast on the cream cheese. Top with a pea-sized portion of wasabi, if desired.

34

WATERFOWL

During a recent pre-dawn hike through a 70-mile-per-hour rain storm -- so that I could reach a strategically located duck blind in a flooded rice field in northern California -- I was reminded of why I truly love the outdoor experience. While non-hunters may question the sanity of anyone who would seek out such "pleasures" voluntarily, those who have been bombarded by countless ducks in a fierce storm, fully comprehend my affinity for waterfowl hunting. According to labor statistics, nasty weather during duck season is a major contributor to employee attendance problems. Is it any wonder?

If you're not inclined to brave gale force winds, you can purchase commercially raised waterfowl in many markets or from a few 1-800 services.

Armed with a wine glass full of a robust cabernet sauvignon, a skillet and a few select ingredients, you can cook a wild duck that will rival its portly commercially-raised cousin usually found in our nation's finest restaurants. While I have enjoyed several slow-roasted ducks in years past, my favorite method of waterfowl cooking is perhaps the easiest. Start with a hot skillet, add olive oil and fresh garlic. Brown both sides of a pair of duck breasts. Add wine, fresh rosemary, fresh earthy mushrooms, a little butter, salt and pepper and *presto*, a perfectly prepared duck!

The above described technique for cooking ducks specifies duck breasts. While the breasts can best be cooked quickly, legs and thighs require extended cooking to break down the fibrous tendons. I prefer to separate legs and thighs from wild waterfowl and cook separately or use for making stocks. (See: Duck Legs Cornell, Page 10).

Historically, many duck recipes call for the stuffing of the cavity with an assortment of fruits and vegetables. I have yet to taste any discernable flavors with this practice, but I suppose it may help to somewhat prevent drying out the finished bird. Stuffing whole birds will require extended cooking times to cook the meat close to the rib cage, therefore, it should be discouraged.

When wild ducks and geese are in short supply, try these recipes with lean cuts of pork, poultry and veal.

MU SHU GOOSE

Pronounced Asian flavors combine with stir-fried goose for a delicious and unorthodox game dish. Don't forget the Boar Fried Rice (see page 152).

4 servings

- 10 dried black mushrooms, soaked in hot water for 20 minutes, stems removed & caps sliced thin.
- 4 tablespoons peanut oil
- 2 eggs, lightly beaten
- 1 Canada goose breast, both halves, skin removed and cut into matchstick-sized strips
- 1 garlic clove, minced
- ½ teaspoon fresh ginger, minced
- 1 cup sliced bamboo shoots, drained
- 2 cups green cabbage, shredded
- 1 medium carrot, shredded
- 3 green onions with tops, cut into 1/2 inch pieces
- 2 teaspoons soy sauce
- 2 teaspoons dry sherry
- 1 teaspoon sesame oil
- ½ pound bean sprouts
- ¼ cup hoisin sauce
- 8 Chinese pancakes (see below)

Heat 2 tablespoons oil in a wok or large skillet over medium-high setting. Add eggs and cook until just set. Remove eggs, break apart and set aside. Add remaining oil, heat and stir-fry garlic and ginger 1 minute. Add goose, cook 2 minutes. Add mushrooms, bamboo shoots, cabbage, carrots, onions, soy sauce, sherry and sesame oil. Stir-fry 1 minute. Add bean sprouts and eggs and cook 30 seconds to warm. Spread a thin layer of hoisin sauce over each pancake and roll with goose filling.

CHINESE PANCAKES

- 1 cup flour
- ½ cup boiling water
- 2 tablespoons sesame oil

In a medium bowl, add flour. Mix in boiling water until dough is formed. Place dough ball on a floured surface and knead for 5 minutes until smooth. Cover with a moistened cloth and let stand for 20 minutes. Knead for 2 minutes more and roll into cylinder. Cut dough into 8 equal pieces and flatten into same-sized pancakes. Brush sesame oil on one side of each. Put two pancakes together, oiled sides touching and roll with a rolling pin until a 6 inch circle is formed. Repeat process with remaining pancakes. In an ungreased non-stick pan over low heat cook pancakes on each side until lightly browned and slightly puffy. Remove and separate pancakes. Place hoisin sauce and filling on oiled side of pancake and roll. (Use with Mu Shu Goose.)

DUCK
WITH RASPBERRY SAUCE

Served with plenty of raspberry sauce, this dish is an excellent one to initiate those who think they don't like game.

4 servings

4 - 6	large duck breast halves, skin intact
4	garlic cloves, minced
1	tablespoon freshly ground black pepper
2	teaspoons fresh rosemary, minced
¼	teaspoon salt
2	tablespoons brown sugar
2	tablespoons raspberry liqueur
2	tablespoons butter
1	tablespoon olive oil
¼	cup dry red wine
1	cup raspberry sauce (See Page 166)
½	cup fresh raspberries, if available

In a small bowl, combine garlic, pepper, rosemary, salt, sugar and liqueur. Rinse duck breasts with cold water and pat dry with paper towels. Rub seasoning mixture over duck breasts, cover and refrigerate for 4 hours.

In a large skillet heat oil and butter over medium-high flame. Place duck breasts, skin side down in hot butter and oil and cook until skin side is medium brown, about 4 minutes. Flip breasts over and cook other side 3 to 4 minutes more, or until breasts feel just rare. Add wine, cook for 2 to 3 more minutes. Remove duck breasts and let stand for 3 to 4 minutes. Slice diagonally and fan equal portions on each plate. Spoon raspberry sauce over half of each portion and garnish with fresh raspberries.

DRUNKEN DUCK BREASTS

As the name implies, the duck breasts are marinated and then cooked in generous amounts of alcohol. Cheers!

4 servings

8	medium to large duck breast halves, skin intact
1	cup brandy
½	cup triple sec liqueur
¼	cup brown sugar
2	tablespoons freshly squeezed lemon juice
2	tablespoons fresh ginger, grated
2	tablespoon cracked black pepper
3	tablespoons olive oil
1	medium onion, peeled and quartered
½	cup beef broth
3	tablespoons fresh mint, chopped
¼	cup heavy cream
	salt and freshly ground pepper to taste

Rinse duck breasts with cold water and pat dry with paper towels. Combine next 6 ingredients in a non-metallic bowl. Mix well to blend. Add duck breasts, toss to coat, cover and refrigerate for 12 hours, turning occasionally. Remove from marinade, drain well and reserve marinade.

Heat oil in a large heavy skillet over medium-high heat. Place duck breasts, skin side down, and onion into skillet. Cook until skin side is lightly browned, about 3-5 minutes. Flip breasts over and cook other side for an additional 4 minutes or until meat is just rare. Remove breasts and add reserved marinade and beef broth. Cook until liquid is reduced by two-thirds. Reduce heat to medium, stir in chopped mint and cream and heat until sauce thickens, stirring frequently. Season with salt and pepper. Return duck to skillet and heat to serving temperatures. Slice duck breasts and place an equal portion of duck and onion on each plate. Spoon sauce over each portion.

Caution: The marinade contains alcohol and may ignite. Please be careful when adding.

HOLIDAY DUCK
WITH BURGUNDY AND CRANBERRY SAUCE

Forego the turkey on Thanksgiving and try this refreshing duck dish.

6 servings

12	large duck breast halves, skin intact
4	cups burgundy wine
2	tablespoons Worcestershire sauce
4	fresh rosemary sprigs
½	medium onion, coarse chopped
4	garlic cloves, minced
2	tablespoons cracked black pepper
2	tablespoons olive oil
3	tablespoons shallots, chopped
1 ½	cups fresh or frozen cranberries
¼	cup honey
4	ounces butter, cut into 4 pieces
	salt and pepper

In a large bowl, combine 2 cups wine, Worcestershire sauce, rosemary, onion and half of the minced garlic. Place duck breasts in marinade, cover and refrigerate for 6 to 8 hours. Turn duck 2 or 3 times while marinating. Remove ducks, pat dry with paper towels. Pour marinade into a medium sauce pan over medium-high heat. Add shallots and remaining wine. Reduce to approximately 1 1/2 cups of liquid. Pour through strainer and return strained liquid to sauce pan. Add cranberries and honey, reduce heat to medium-low and cook for 10 minutes or until cranberries soften. Remove from heat.

Rub reserved garlic over breasts and coat with pepper. In a large skillet over medium-high heat, brown breasts on both sides (skin side first), about 4 minutes per side. Add 1/2 cup of the sauce and cook for 2 minutes more. Remove ducks and let stand 3 to 4 minutes before carving diagonally into 1/4 inch thick slices. Return sauce to heat until bubbling. Remove from heat and whisk in butter sections, one at a time, until sauce thickens. Season with salt and pepper. On a large platter, arrange duck slices and pour sauce over middle of slices. Serve any leftover sauce on the side.

EASY BARBECUED
ORANGE - ROSEMARY DUCK

Add seasoned vegetables and boiled red potatoes to the grill for a complete outdoor repast. This preparation also works well with all upland game.

6 servings

12	large to medium duck breast halves, skin intact
1	cup dry white wine
¼	cup white wine vinegar
½	cup soy sauce
1	tablespoon pickling spices
6	ounces butter, softened
2	garlic cloves, minced
1 ½	cups orange marmalade
1	tablespoon fresh rosemary, minced
⅔	cup dry white wine
	pinch white pepper

In a large bowl, mix 1 cup wine, vinegar, soy sauce and pickling spices. Place duck breasts in marinade, cover and refrigerate for 24 hours. Pre-heat barbecue coals or gas charbroiler to medium-hot. Combine remaining ingredients. Place breasts on grill, skin side down. Baste with sauce. Cook 4 minutes per side or until breast meat is just firm to finger pressure, basting frequently. Top with any leftover sauce and serve immediate-

MALLARD BREAST STUFFED
WITH MUSHROOMS & GORGONZOLA CHEESE

An elegant dish for a special occasion when you really want to impress your guests.

4 servings

4-6	mallard breast halves, skin removed
¼	cup flour
¼	teaspoon white pepper
½	teaspoon garlic powder
1	pinch salt
4	tablespoons butter
1	tablespoon olive oil
¼	cup dry sherry
3	cups mushrooms, sliced thin
1	garlic clove, minced
6	ounces gorgonzola cheese, crumbled
1	tablespoon fresh parsley, minced
	salt and freshly ground black pepper

Place duck breasts between waxed paper sheets and pound lightly with the flat side of a mallet until meat is 1/4 inch thick or as thin as possible without tearing flesh. Flour 1 side of each breast. In a large skillet, over medium-high flame, heat 2 tablespoons of the butter and brown on the floured side only, about 1 to 2 minutes each breast. Remove breasts, de-glaze pan with sherry, add olive oil and 1 tablespoon butter. Sauté mushrooms and garlic for 2 minutes. Remove from heat. Lay out breasts, browned side down and place equal amount of cheese on the bottom third of each. Spoon 1/4 cup of mushrooms over cheese and begin rolling by grasping the bottom edge of the breast and folding over cheese and mushroom mixture, keeping stuffing in with your fingers. Roll snugly and place, "seam" side down, in a baking dish. Place rolled breasts in a 400° F oven for 6 to 8 minutes, or until cheese begins to run out. Meanwhile, return skillet to medium heat. Add parsley and cook for 3 minutes more. Remove from heat, stir in remaining 1 tablespoon of butter and season with salt and pepper. Place one breast on each plate and spoon mushrooms over each.

MALLARD STIR-FRY
WITH MANDARIN ORANGES

Cook it fast and hot for remarkable flavors! Serve with steamed white rice and cold Asian beer.

4 servings

3 - 4	mallard breasts, skin removed and sliced into 1/4 inch thick strips
2	tablespoons cold water
1 ½	tablespoons cornstarch
2	tablespoons soy sauce
¼	teaspoon sesame oil
2	tablespoons seasoned rice vinegar
2	tablespoons soy sauce
2	garlic cloves, minced
2	tablespoons peanut oil
½	medium red bell pepper, cut in thin strips
½	medium green bell pepper, cut in thin strips
¼	medium red onion, cut in thin strips
1	teaspoon fresh ginger, minced
1	tablespoon brown sugar
1	ounce canned Mandarin orange segments

In a medium bowl, mix cornstarch and water. Add the next 5 ingredients and toss with duck breast strips. Cover and refrigerate for 1 hour. In a wok or heavy-duty deep skillet over high heat, add oil. When oil is hot, add peppers, onion and ginger. Stir-fry 1 to 2 minutes. Add duck, marinade mixture and brown sugar. Stir-fry 3 minutes. Reduce heat to low, add Mandarin orange segments and cook 1 minute more.

BARBECUED DUCK
With HONEY, MUSTARD AND SAGE

4 servings

4	ducks, split
1	teaspoon kosher salt
1	tablespoon cracked black pepper
¹/₂	cup honey
²/₃	cup Dijon or coarse grain mustard
¹/₄	cup yellow onion, minced
4	cloves, garlic, minced
2	lemons, juice only
2	limes, juice only
3	tablespoons fresh sage, minced (or substitute 1 tablespoon dried sage leaves)

Rub ducks with salt and pepper. Combine honey with remaining ingredients in a saucepan. Heat to blend, then cool. Pour half of mixture over ducks, cover and refrigerate for 8 to 12 hours, turning occasionally. Grill ducks over medium barbecue until just cooked, about 130 degrees at the breast. Just before ducks are done, baste with remaining sauce.

GLAZED PEKING-STYLE DUCK

Save this recipe for a pair of large carefully plucked ducks with no breaks in the skin of the breast. Great with steamed rice and stir-fried fresh vegetables.

4 servings

- 2 whole mallard, canvasback or black ducks, skin and neck intact
  (add an additional duck if your guests have particularly hearty appetites)
- 1 cup coffee liqueur
- ¼ cup grenadine syrup
- ¼ cup honey
- 2 teaspoons fresh ginger, peeled and minced
- 2 garlic cloves, minced
- ¼ cup orange juice
- ¼ teaspoon five-spice powder (optional)
- ⅓ cup orange juice
- ¼ cup hoisin sauce
- 3 tablespoons soy sauce
- 1 teaspoon sesame oil
- 1 tablespoon cornstarch mixed with 1 tablespoon cold water

Wash ducks thoroughly with cold water and pat dry with paper towels. Combine next 6 ingredients and pour over ducks in a shallow container. Marinate ducks in refrigerator for 12 hours, turning often to coat evenly. Remove ducks, draining liquid into container with remaining marinade. Pour marinade into a container and reserve.

Tie a cord around the neck of each duck and hang in a cool, dry, well-ventilated area for 4 hours. Place ducks, breast side down on a rack in a roasting pan and bake in a pre-heated 450°F oven for 15 minutes, basting with half of reserved marinade two or three times during cooking. Turn ducks breast side up, baste one more time and bake for 6 to 8 more minutes or until skin is crisp and meat is firm, but still moist. Internal temperature of the duck should not exceed 140°F. Remove duck from pan and let stand for 5 to 8 minutes.

While pan is still warm, carefully add orange juice and scrape pan to loosen any bits of duck or marinade. Add liquid to a medium sauce pan with remaining marinade, hoisin, soy sauce and sesame oil. Heat to boil and thicken with cornstarch mixture, if necessary.

Carve breasts from rib cage, leaving the skin intact. Slice diagonally into 1/4 inch slices. Remove legs and thighs. On a large platter, arrange sliced breasts, legs and thighs. Pour sauce into small bowls for dipping.

DUCK RAVIOLI
WITH LEMON CREAM SAUCE

Won ton wrappers greatly reduce preparation time

4 - 5 servings

3-5	duck breasts (about 8 ounces), cooked rare, cooled and minced
½	cup ricotta cheese
¼	cup dry Monterey Jack cheese, grated
¼	cup Parmesan cheese, grated
2	garlic cloves, chopped
½	cup fresh basil, chopped
¼	cup green onion, chopped
2	tablespoons sundried tomatoes, in oil, chopped
50	won ton wrappers
1	cup flour
¼	cup cornstarch mixed with 1/4 cup cold water
¼	cup freshly grated Parmesan cheese

Place all of the above ingredients except won ton wrappers and cornstarch mixture in a blender or food processor. Pulse until all ingredients are blended into a coarse paste.

On a flat surface, sift flour evenly over. Lay won ton wrappers out as room allows. Form the filling into discs about the size of a 50 cent piece, about 1/4 inch thick. Place a disc on the center of each of the won ton wrappers. Brush cornstarch mixture evenly around the exposed area of the wrapper. Place a second wrapper, centered over the filling disc, atop the first and press firmly, but carefully, sealing all edges. Repeat process for all wrappers, making a total of 25 ravioli. Sift flour over all exposed surfaces, place on floured waxed paper in a container, cover and place in freezer for at least 2 hours. Ravioli can be prepared several days ahead and frozen indefinitely.

Prepare Lemon Cream Sauce (Page 170). Keep warm. In a large stock pot add water, 2 tablespoons vegetable oil and 1 tablespoon salt. Bring to boil. Reduce heat to low and add ravioli, one at a time, stirring gently to prevent sticking. Cook for 4 to 5 minutes or until ravioli are tender and translucent. Spoon warmed sauce onto plates and top with ravioli and grated Parmesan cheese.

PEPPERCORN DUCK
WITH HORSERADISH SAUCE

Reminiscent of carved prime rib. Serve with roasted new red potatoes seasoned with fresh rosemary and lots of fresh garlic.

4 servings

4-6	large duck breast halves, skin intact
½	cup whole grain mustard
¼	cup brined green peppercorns
3	tablespoons pink peppercorns
3	tablespoons black peppercorns
¼	teaspoons salt
¼	cup seasoned bread crumbs
3	tablespoons olive oil
1	cup béchamel sauce (see page167) or substitute heavy cream
¼	cup prepared horseradish
1	teaspoon Worcestershire sauce
2	teaspoons fresh chives, fine diced (or substitute green onion tops)

Coat duck breasts evenly with mustard. With a mortar and pestle, combine peppercorns and grind until peppercorns are crushed. Add salt and bread crumbs and mix thoroughly. You may also crush peppercorns under a heavy flat-bottom skillet on a hard surface, pressing down on the skillet, but it can be a bit messy as the peppercorns escape from the pan. Coat the duck breasts with the peppercorn mixture.

Add olive oil to a large skillet over medium-high heat. When oil is hot, add duck breasts and lightly brown on both sides, about 3 to 4 minutes per side. Reduce heat to low, cover skillet and cook for 2 minutes more. Remove from heat and let stand for 5 minutes.

To make sauce, combine béchamel sauce, horseradish and Worcestershire in a small sauce pan and heat until warm. Slice duck breasts very thinly on a diagonal across the "grain" and fan out equal portions on each plate. Spoon sauce over one-half of each breast portion and garnish with chives.

CUMBERLAND DUCK

Spicy New Orleans style goose best served over white rice. An exception to the "cook it fast and hot" rule, simmer the goose long enough for the meat to become tender.

4 servings

4-6	large to medium duck breast halves, skin intact
1	cup orange juice
3	tablespoons lemon juice
¾	cup port wine
2	tablespoons olive oil
3	strips smoked bacon, diced fine
1	tablespoon shallot, minced
1	rind of 1 orange, white part removed and cut into thin strips
1	rind of 1 lemon, white part removed and cut into thin strips
1	cup red currant jelly
1	tablespoon dijon mustard
1	pinch cayenne pepper
1	pinch ground ginger
1	tablespoon Grand Marnier or orange liqueur
	salt and freshly ground black pepper to taste

Combine lemon and orange juice with 1/2 cup of the wine. Marinate duck breasts for 3 - 4 hours in refrigerator. Turn breasts 3 or 4 times while marinating. In a small sauce pan with boiling water, add sliced lemon and orange rind. Cook for 3 to 4 minutes, remove and plunge into icy water. Reserve blanched rinds.

Remove breasts from marinade. Reserve marinade. Cook diced bacon with oil over medium-high heat for 2 to 3 minutes. Place duck breasts skin side down in skillet, and brown to rare on each side — about 3 to 5 minutes per side — depending on the size of the breasts. Remove breasts, set aside and add reserved marinade, shallots and reserved blanched rind to pan. Reduce liquid by two-thirds. Add duck breasts and all other remaining ingredients except Grand Marnier, salt and pepper. Reduce heat to low and cook, stirring often until jelly is melted. Add 1/4 cup port wine and Grand Marnier. Cook 2 more minutes. Remove duck breasts, let stand for 4 to 5 minutes. Slice thin diagonally across the breast. Season sauce with salt and pepper and spoon equal amount on each plate. Top with sliced duck.

GOOSE LUZIANNE

Pan-seared duck breasts team up with traditional Cumberland sauce for a quick and simple main course.

6 servings

3-4	Canada honker or speckled goose breast halves, skin removed and meat cut into half inch cubes
1	cup red wine
¼	cup red wine vinegar
3	tablespoons Worcestershire sauce
1	tablespoon freshly ground black pepper
1	cup peanut oil
1	cup flour
2	cups celery, chopped
1	cup yellow onion, diced
1	cup green bell pepper, diced
10	fresh garlic cloves, minced
1	teaspoon each cayenne pepper, white pepper, salt and dried basil
1	quart game bird or chicken stock
1	pound andouille sausage, cut into ½ inch slices and sauteed until lightly browned
2	cups fresh oysters and their liquid
1	cup fresh tomato, diced

In a non-metallic bowl, combine cubed goose with next 4 ingredients. Toss well, cover and refrigerate for 6-12 hours. Drain and reserve marinade. In a heavy-duty medium stock pot over medium- high heat, heat 2 tablespoons of the oil, add goose and brown pieces evenly. Remove goose and add a little reserved marinade, stirring to remove bits of meat from the pot. Add remaining oil until very hot and carefully add flour, whisking constantly until flour browns, about 20 minutes. Add vegetables, garlic and spices; cook 3 minutes while stirring. Add stock, cooked goose and reserved marinade, bring to boil. reduce heat to low and simmer for 1 hour. Add remaining ingredients and simmer for 5 minutes. Adjust seasonings, if necessary, and serve.

TEAL SCALOPPINE

It might take more than a few of these fast fliers to feed four adults, but the flavor and tenderness is beyond compare. Try this preparation method for all ducks.

4 servings

15	teal half breasts, skin removed
½	cup flour, seasoned with 1 teaspoon garlic powder, 1/4 teaspoon pepper, and 1/4 teaspoon salt
3	tablespoons olive oil
2	tablespoons butter
3	garlic cloves, minced
½	medium yellow onion, chopped
½	pound fresh mushrooms, thick sliced
½	cup dry white wine
½	cup game bird or chicken stock
	juice of 1 lemon
2	tablespoons fresh parsley, minced
1	teaspoon flour
½	cup sour cream
¾	cup fresh tomato, peeled, seeded and diced

Place duck breasts between waxed paper sheets and pound with a flat mallet to ¼ inch thick. Dredge each breast in seasoned flour. In a large skillet over medium-high heat, heat 2 tablespoons of the oil and 1 tablespoon of the butter. Place breasts in skillet and lightly brown on both sides, about 1 to 2 minutes per side. Remove breasts and set aside.

Add remaining butter and oil to pan and sauté garlic and onion for 2 minutes. Add wine, chicken stock and lemon juice. Bring to boil, reduce heat to medium and simmer, uncovered, for 6 to 8 minutes or until liquid is reduced by one-half. Add browned duck breasts, mushrooms and parsley, cover and cook for 3 more minutes. Remove breasts and keep warm. Blend remaining flour with sour cream, add to pan and cook, stirring occasionally, until sauce thickens. Place four breasts on each plate, pour equal amount of sauce over each and top with diced tomatoes.

SASKATCHEWAN SNOW GEESE

	Goose breasts
1	cup dry red wine
2	tablespoons balsamic vinegar
½	teaspoon cracked black pepper
½	teaspoon Kosher salt
2-3	garlic cloves, minced
¼	cup olive oil

Remove the skin and trim any visible gristle.

Combine all ingredients. Place breasts in marinade for 1 – 12 hours.. Pat dry and grill, broil or pan sear, but not past medium-rare.

SESAME
CRUSTED DUCK

The sesame crust helps to retain moisture and adds flavor, texture and eye appeal to large duck breasts.

4 servings

6-8 mallards, black or canvas back duck breast halves, skin intact
½ cup whole grain mustard
1 teaspoon freshly ground black pepper
½ teaspoon salt
1 cup sesame seeds
3 tablespoons peanut oil

In a medium bowl, combine pepper, salt and sesame seeds. Coat each breast with mustard. Press each breast evenly into seed mixture, coating both sides with seeds. In a large skillet over medium heat, heat oil and cook each breast on both sides until sesame seeds turn golden brown.

Turn each side gently only once to keep seed crust intact. Serve immediately.

THE TEN MINUTE DUCK

When you're in the mood for duck dinner, but really don't feel like cooking. Grab a skillet, a handful of ingredients and whip up a masterpiece in just ten minutes!

4 servings

4 - 6 large boneless duck breasts, skin intact
½ teaspoon freshly ground pepper
½ teaspoon garlic powder
½ teaspoon dried rosemary
¼ teaspoon salt
3 tablespoons olive oil
⅓ cup dry red wine
2 cups mushrooms, sliced
⅓ cup raspberry preserves

Rinse breasts with cold water and pat dry with paper towels. Season with next four ingredients. Heat oil in a large skillet over medium-high heat. Place breasts, skin side down, in skillet and cook until skin is medium brown, about 3 minutes. Flip breasts over and cook 3 minutes more. Add wine and mushrooms and cook 2 minutes. Remove duck from skillet and whisk in preserves for 1 minute. Slice duck breasts, arrange on plate and top with mushrooms and sauce.

LAST CHANCE DUCK BREASTS

A few birds like some of the divers and mergansers may require a little more time and effort for transformation into great duck dinners. This recipe also works well with ducks stuck to the back corner of your freezer, just under the muskrat salami given to you by Uncle Stinky a few years back.

4 servings

   6-8   boneless duck breasts. skin removed and cut into thin strips

Marinade
   10   whole garlic cloves, minced
   ½   cup white wine vinegar
   ½   cup dry white wine
   ½   cup game stock or beef broth
   3   tablespoons Worcestershire sauce
   2   tablespoons pickling spices

Preparation
   2   tablespoons olive oil
   ½   medium yellow onion, diced
   6   whole garlic cloves, roasted in a 350° F oven until softened
           and lightly browned
   1   tablespoon fresh rosemary, minced
   ¼   cup dry white wine
   1   tablespoon Worcestershire sauce
   4   ounces butter, chilled and cut into 4 pieces
        salt and freshly ground black pepper to taste

Combine marinade ingredients in a glass or plastic bowl, whisk to blend, add duck and toss to coat thoroughly. Cover and refrigerate for 48 hours.

Remove duck from marinade, drain well. Discard marinade. Heat oil in a large skillet over medium-high heat, add onion and saute for 3 minutes. Add duck and sauté for 3 minutes, stirring to sear all sides. Add next four ingredients. Sauté for 3 minutes more. Move contents to one side of pan. Remove pan from heat and whisk butter into liquid, one piece at a time until melted. Season with salt and pepper.

BARBECUED GOOSE
WITH HERBS AND WINE

The flavor improves dramatically when goose breasts are barbecued over smoky wood, charcoal or wood chips rather than propane. If fresh herbs simply are not available, substitute greatly reduced quantities of dried herbs.

4 servings

2-3	goose breasts *skin intact*
1	teaspoon white pepper
1	tablespoon garlic powder
1	teaspoon salt
1	cup dry white wine
1 ½	cups olive or peanut oil
½	cup white wine vinegar
½	cup fresh basil, chopped
2	tablespoons fresh rosemary, minced
2	tablespoons fresh sage, minced
2	tablespoons fresh oregano, minced
3	garlic cloves minced
1	teaspoon freshly ground black pepper

Season goose breasts with first 3 ingredients. In a non-metallic bowl, combine wine, oil and vinegar. Add goose breasts, cover and refrigerate for 4 to 6 hours. Drain and reserve marinade. Cook goose breasts on a medium barbecue until rare. Meanwhile, heat reserved marinade in a small pan until hot. Place cooked goose breasts in a plastic container with a tight-fitting lid. Add remaining ingredients and heated marinade. Place lid on container securely, shake up container to mix ingredients and allow to stand for 10 minutes without removing lid. Return goose to barbecue for additional heat, if needed. Slice goose breasts across the "grain," arrange on a platter and spoon herbs over sliced

THAI-SPICED
PINTAIL BREASTS

Increase amount of red curry paste for a fiery version of this dish.

6 servings

8-10   pintail breast halves
2   tablespoons honey
1   tablespoon red curry paste
½   teaspoon turmeric
¼   teaspoon ground cinnamon
1   tablespoon fresh ginger, peeled and minced
½   cup soy sauce
2   tablespoons peanut oil
1   tablespoon sugar
2   tablespoons rice vinegar
1   garlic clove, minced
½   cup water
    salt and pepper to taste

In a small bowl, combine honey, curry paste, turmeric, cinnamon, ginger and half of the soy sauce. Brush mixture over duck breasts, place into a container with any leftover marinade, cover and refrigerate for 15 to 24 hours.

Remove duck breasts, save marinade. In a heavy, large skillet over medium-high heat, heat oil and brown breasts on both sides, about 3 minutes each side. Add sugar, rice vinegar, garlic, water, remainder of soy sauce and reserved marinade. Cook for 2 to 3 minutes, remove duck breasts and bring to boil. Season with salt and pepper, as desired. Cut the duck into thin slices, arrange on each plate and spoon sauce evenly over each.

DUCK WELLINGTON

People often ask me where I get my inspiration for various recipes. Like most of us who cook a great deal, I often steal good ideas from others and tweak them a bit to make them my own. Occasionally, I even impress myself when a recipe I created in my mind work out even better than expected on the plate. Other times, I hit on what I think is a cute name and make a recipe to fit. I started out making Deer Wellington, thinking it would be a neat twist on a classic beef dish. Then it struck me that Duck Wellington sounds a bit like "Duke Ellington". Get it? The problem with inventing recipes that sound cute is that they don't always taste good. This one does work, but you may want to play around the size of the duck breasts and cooking times. I used a widgeon breast for the first attempt. It overcooked and was a tad dry. If your puff pastry bakes beyond light brown, the duck is probably going to be overcooked.

4 servings

4	large duck breast half fillets, skinless
	salt and pepper
1	tablespoon olive oil
3	tablespoons butter
$^1/_2$	small onion, finely chopped
3	cups mushrooms, finely chopped
2	garlic cloves, minced
1	lemon, juice only
$^1/_2$	teaspoon Worcestershire sauce
2	10 X 10 inch prepared puff pastry sheets, thawed for 20 minutes
1	egg, lightly beaten

Season duck breasts with salt and pepper. Heat oil and 1 tablespoon of the butter in a skillet over medium-high heat. Brown duck breasts on both sides, about 1 minute per side. Transfer to paper towels to cool. Add remaining butter, onion, mushrooms and garlic to pan and sauté until onions are translucent. Stir in lemon juice and Worcestershire sauce. Allow to cool. Cut each puff pastry sheet in half. When cooled, place some of the mushroom mixture on the center of the pastry. Set a duck breast on the mushrooms and top with additional mushrooms. Moisten the edges of the pastry, then fold it over the duck and mushrooms to make a neat package. Place each package, seam side down, on a lightly greased baking sheet. Brush tops with egg. Bake in a preheated 400 degree oven for 12 minutes.

DUCK BREAST
WITH SPICED APPLE AND DRIED CHERRIES

What's wrong with a recipe that is both easy and delicious? Nothing! If you can't find dried cherries in your market, substitute any dried berries (most stores carry "Craisins" – a sweetened cranberry) or even raisins. This preparation also works wonderfully with pork, upland game or antlered game.

4 servings

2	Granny Smith apples, peeled, cored and sliced into thin wedges
1	tablespoon brown sugar
1	tablespoon fresh lemon juice
$^2/_3$	cup dried cherries
$^1/_4$	teaspoon cinnamon
$^1/_2$	teaspoon ground coriander
	pinch cayenne pepper
2	tablespoons butter, chilled
6-8	duck breast half fillets, skin removed
	salt and freshly ground black pepper to taste
2	tablespoons olive oil

Place the apples into a medium saucepan with 3/4 cup water, brown sugar and lemon juice. Bring to a boil and then reduce heat and simmer until apples are just tender, about 10 minutes. Add cherries and simmer another 5 minutes. Drain liquid and stir in cinnamon, coriander, cayenne pepper and butter. Keep warm, but just warm. If sauce becomes too cool and congeals, heat over very low heat while stirring until warm, but not hot.

Season duck breasts with salt and pepper. Heat oil in a large skillet over medium-high heat and brown ducks breasts evenly on both sides until medium-rare. Spoon apple mixture onto each plate and top with duck breasts.

DUCK BREASTS
WITH ORANGE AND MINT SAUCE

I love the combination of orange and mint, especially when paired with a couple of juicy and delicious duck breasts. Served over rice with a glass of crisp California Sauvignon Blanc, this is livin'.

4 servings

6-10	duck breast half fillets, skin removed
	salt and pepper
1	tablespoon olive oil
3	tablespoons butter
1	medium red onion, diced
1	cup freshly squeezed orange juice
1/2	cup chicken broth
3	tablespoons Grand Marnier or triple sec
1	tablespoon cornstarch mixed with equal part cold water
2	oranges, peeled and sliced into rings or wedges
2	tablespoons fresh mint, minced
4	cups warm cooked rice

Heat 2 tablespoons of the butter in a sauce pan over medium-high heat. Add onion and sauté until translucent. Add orange juice and chicken broth and reduce liquid to about 3/4 cup. Stir in cornstarch mixture, a little at a time, until thickened. Just before serving, gently stir in orange segments and mint. Season with salt and pepper.

Season duck breasts with salt and pepper. Heat oil and remaining butter in a large skillet over medium-high heat. Brown on both sides until medium-rare. Mound rice on each plate. Slice duck and arrange around rice. Spoon sauce over duck.

PAN-SEARED SNOW GOOSE BREASTS

WITH PEPPERS AND ONIONS

4 servings

4	boneless snow goose breast halves, skin removed
$^{1}/_{4}$	cup olive oil
2	teaspoons Worcestershire sauce
$^{1}/_{2}$	teaspoon garlic salt
1	teaspoon hot pepper sauce (Tabasco)
1	medium yellow onion, thinly sliced
1	green bell pepper, coarsely chopped
1	red bell pepper, coarsely chopped
2	jalapeno peppers, seeded and minced
2	garlic cloves, thinly sliced
1	cup tomatoes, seeded and chopped
	salt and pepper to taste

Slice goose breasts thinly across the "grain" of the meat. Combine half of the olive oil, Worcestershire sauce, garlic salt, and hot pepper sauce in a glass bowl. Add sliced goose, cover and refrigerate for 1 to 2 hours. Heat remaining oil in a large skillet over medium heat. Add onion, peppers and garlic. Cook until onions are medium brown. Remove goose from marinade. Drain well and discard marinade. Add goose and stir-fry for 1 to 2 minutes or until just cooked, but not past medium-rare. Stir in tomato and season to taste with salt, pepper and additional hot sauce. Serve over a bed of Cajun rice.

GOOSE BREAST SUPREME

A simplified version of one of my favorite stuffed waterfowl breast recipes. I save this one for those special occasions when I really want to show off.

4 servings

- 4   skinless goose breast half fillets
- 6   garlic cloves, minced
- 1   tablespoon onion powder
- 1   teaspoon ground sage
- 2   tablespoons freshly ground black pepper
-   pinch salt
- 4   cups dry red wine
- 1/4   cup balsamic vinegar
- 1/2   cup brown sugar
- 1/2   cup blackberry preserves
- 8   thin slices prosciutto
- 1   bunch fresh basil
- 1   cup grated peppered jack cheese
- 1/4   cup seasoned breadcrumbs

Place goose breasts on a firm, flat surface. With a sharp knife, slice each breast half along the thinnest edge, stopping the cut 1/2 inch before the outer edge. This will "butterfly" the breasts and you can open them like a book. Rub on all sides with the garlic and season with the dry seasonings. Place on a plate, cover and refrigerate for 2 hours. Combine wine, vinegar and sugar in a sauce pan, bring to a boil and reduce liquid to 1 cup. Add preserves, bring to a boil, simmer on low heat for 5 minutes more. For each breast, open and place on a flat surface. Lay one slice of prosciutto across each breast half. That's 2 slices for each butterflied breast. Top with 3 to 4 basil leaves. Combine cheese and breadcrumbs and press over basil. Fold edges in over mixture and roll breasts like a burrito. Place in an 8 by 8-inch pan, seam side down. Place rolled breasts side by side and bake at 425 degrees for 8 to 10 minutes or until meat is rare to medium-rare (about 125 degrees internal temperature). Allow breasts to cool for five minutes, and then slice each into three medallions. Arrange medallions on plates and spoon sauce over.

CURRIED DUCK STIR-FRY

To most folks, curry is a pale yellow, or "yeller" as my Southern buddies say, spice which is used about once a year. Curry is actually a blend of spices and usually contain cinnamon, coriander, cumin, tumeric...as few as 5 to over 50 different ingredients. Unless you really want to store a bunch of spices you'll rarely use, buy the prepared stuff. Experiment with different varieties – some are hot, some are not. My favorite types of curry come from Thailand. They can be found in the Asian sections of most major markets throughout the U.S. Trust me, I've looked. They are curry pastes, not powders and are packaged in jars. I think the flavor is superior, but keep in mind that a little goes a long way. The following recipe calls for 1 tablespoon of yellow curry paste. You may wish to start with a little less. You can always add more.

4 servings

6-8	duck breast half fillets, skinless and thinly sliced into strips
2	tablespoons peanut or olive oil
½	red onion, roughly chopped
2	garlic cloves, minced
1	tablespoon yellow curry paste
1	cup coconut milk
1	cup chicken broth
2	tablespoons granulated sugar
1	cup carrots, thinly sliced
1	cup celery, sliced diagonally
1	cup snow peas, stems and strings removed
	salt to taste
6	cups warm cooked white rice
8	tomato wedges

Heat 1 tablespoon of the oil in a wok or large skillet over high heat. Sear duck while stir-frying for a minute or two, but make sure meat is still rare. Remove meat from pan and reserve. Add remaining oil to pan. Add onion and garlic and stir-fry 1 minute. Stir in curry paste and 3 tablespoons of the coconut milk. Cook for 1 minute and then add remaining milk, chicken broth and sugar. Cook for 3 minutes. Add carrots, celery, snow peas and salt to taste. Cook for 3 minutes. Return duck to pan to warm. Spoon duck, vegetables and sauce over warm rice. Garnish with tomato wedges.

DUCK
WITH BOURBON CREAM SAUCE

Don't worry about getting a little goofy (or goofier) from eating this delicious duck. The alcohol burns off during the cooking process. This recipe is also delicious with venison, goose, pork, beef and pheasant.

CAUTION: When you add bourbon to the pan, it may ignite! Slowly pour the bourbon into the pan without sticking your big head over the pan. Wait a few minutes for the alcohol to burn off.

4 servings

6 - 8	duck breast halves, skin intact or removed
	salt and freshly ground black pepper
1	tablespoon olive oil
2	tablespoons butter
3	cloves garlic, minced
¼	cup red onion, diced
1	tablespoon brown sugar
½	cup beef or chicken broth
¼	cup bourbon
⅓	cup heavy (whipping) cream

Liberally season duck breasts with salt and pepper. Heat oil and butter in a large skillet over medium-high heat. Add breasts, skin side down and cook until seared to medium brown, about 3 minutes. Flip breasts over and cook other side for 2 minutes more. Remove breasts and transfer to a plate lined with paper towels. Add garlic, onion and brown sugar to the pan. Stir to blend and cook while stirring for 3 to 4 minutes. Stir in beef broth and reduce liquid by one-half. Add bourbon very carefully (see CAUTION above) and cook for 2 minutes more. Add cream and cook until sauce is thickened. Return duck breasts to the pan to warm, but do not cook past medium-rare. Remove breasts, slice diagonally into 1/4-inch slices and spoon sauce over.

CRANBERRY DUCK

This is a simplified version of a great holiday favorite. The flavor is both sweet and sour and the texture is tender and juicy as long as you don't overcook it.

4 servings

2	cups dry red wine
½	cup orange juice
¼	cup balsamic vinegar
½	cup sugar
2	cups fresh cranberries
6-8	large duck breast half fillets
	salt and pepper
2	tablespoons olive oil

Add first 4 ingredients to a saucepan and bring to a boil over medium-high heat. Reduce heat to medium-low and simmer for 10 minutes. Add cranberries and simmer until cranberries soften. Season sauce with salt and pepper to taste. Adjust flavor to suit your own taste. If the sauce is too tart, stir in a little sugar. Too sweet, a little more vinegar. You get the idea. Season the duck breasts liberally with salt and pepper. Heat olive oil over medium-high heat in a large skillet. Add duck breasts and sear on one side, about 3 to 4 minutes. Flip over brown other side until breasts are rare to medium-rare. Remove breasts from skillet and let stand for 2 to 3 minutes. Slice thinly across the grain of the meat. Spoon a little sauce on each plate and shingle breast slices over sauce.

DUCK BREASTS
With BALSAMIC BERRY SAUCE

It's fast, hot, easy and delicious!

4 servings

- 4   large duck breast fillets, skin on or off
       salt and pepper
- 1   tablespoon olive oil
- ¼   cup balsamic vinegar
- ½   cup cheap red wine
- 2   garlic cloves, minced
- 1   tablespoon plum preserves (or brown sugar)
- 1   tablespoon fresh rosemary leaves, minced (optional)
- 3   tablespoons chilled butter, cut into 3 pieces
- 1 ½ cups fresh berries (frozen will do also)

Season duck breasts with salt and pepper. Heat oil in a large skillet over medium high heat. Add duck breasts and brown on one side. Flip over and cook for 1 minute. Add balsamic vinegar and next 3 ingredients. Remove duck breasts when just medium-rare and keep warm. Add rosemary and reduce liquid in pan to about 1/4 cup. Taste liquid and add more vinegar or plum preserves to suit your taste. Too sour? Add more preserves. Too sweet? Add more vinegar.

Whisk in butter until melted. Stir in berries. Slice duck and arrange on plates. Spoon sauce over.

UPLAND GAME

Since growing up in Virginia with an abundance of bobwhite quail, wild turkey, mourning doves, ruffed grouse, squirrels and cottontail rabbits, I have always thoroughly enjoyed hunting all types of upland game. Few experiences can compare to the exhilaration of hunting behind a brace of well-trained pointing dogs on a crisp fall morning. From Gambel's quail found in Arizona, to western Idaho's Hungarian partridge and northern California's riceland pheasants, chasing upland birds is the impetus for my fondest hunting memories.

Reaping the rewards of a game bird hunt requires attention during preparation. Upland bird flavors are typically subtle and hardly "gamy." Very little, if any, marinating is called for. Cooking times are minimal. Of course, you can prepare a quail or grouse dish that "falls right off the bone" by stewing for several hours, but the finished product will taste more like the other ingredients than the bird itself. Tender, juicy game birds that taste like game birds should be cooked quickly with relatively high heat after judicious seasoning.

Light-fleshed game birds such as quail, chukar and pheasant should be just pink when cooked. Darker meat birds like doves and Hungarian partridge should be cooked in a similar fashion until firm, but juicy. With few exceptions, the skin should not be removed from the birds to protect the lean meat from drying out. If you do not like the taste of game bird skin, remove the skin after cooking. If desired cover the breasts with bacon, julienned vegetables or fresh herbs for additional protection and flavoring, especially if the skin has been removed or torn during cleaning. When cooked, the juice in the fattiest part of the thigh will run clear when pricked.

Practically any dish that calls for chicken can be substituted with rabbit or hare. I recommend that you experiment with your favorite chicken recipe. Don't tell your guests about the substitution until the meal is well under way. The tender beige flesh when cooked, is tougher and stringier in older animals than younger ones. Unless you are a collector of mounted large rabbits, avoid taking them if you have a chance of finding smaller rabbits.

It is universally recommended that you wear rubber gloves when cleaning rabbits to avoid exposure to the bacteria, tularemia, which causes flu-like symptoms in exposed humans. The disease can be transmitted by exposure to the skin and through eating an infected rabbit. It is also wise to cook rabbits thoroughly as the disease cannot be killed by freezing.

The following recipes can be adapted for use with all fowl, wild and domestic. Trim excess fat from commercially-raised chickens and game hens to more closely approximate the finished game dish.

BRAISED COTTONTAIL RABBIT
IN RED WINE WITH MUSHROOMS

Rabbit hunters love this tender small game animal when prepared properly.

6 servings

3	rabbits, cleaned and cut into 6 pieces (2 legs, 2 shoulders with front legs and 2 trimmed rib cages with fillets)
1	cup onions, coarsely chopped
⅔	cup carrots, diced into 1/4" cubes
½	cup red bell pepper, coarsely chopped
2	cups fresh mushrooms, halved
1	cup tomatoes, coarsely chopped
2	tablespoons garlic, minced
4	cups game bird stock or chicken broth
2	cups dry red wine
¼	cup olive oil
2	teaspoons fresh oregano, finely chopped
2	tablespoons fresh rosemary, finely chopped
2	tablespoons fresh basil, coarsely chopped
1	cup flour seasoned with salt and pepper
	salt and freshly ground pepper to taste

Pre-heat oven to 325° F. Place rabbit pieces in a sturdy paper or plastic bag. Add seasoned flour and shake to coat evenly. In a large sauce pan or stock pot, heat olive oil over medium high heat and brown rabbit pieces on all sides. Remove rabbit and set aside.

Add onions, carrots and peppers in pan and sauté until onions turn light brown. Add garlic, tomatoes, oregano and 1 T fresh rosemary. Add wine and stir to deglaze pan.

Reduce by one-half of original volume of liquid. Add chicken stock and rabbit. Place in pre-heated oven for 1 hour. Add mushrooms and remaining rosemary. Cook for 5 minutes more. Remove rabbit and mushrooms, arrange on serving dish and place in oven (turned off) to keep warm. Place sauce pan on stove over high heat and reduce liquid by three fourths or until liquid thickens. (Note: You can save some cooking time, if desired, by thickening sauce with a equal mixture of cornstarch and cold water, adding a little at a time until thickened) Season with salt and pepper. Once sauce is thickened, add basil and reduce heat. Remove warmed rabbit pieces and mushrooms from oven and pour sauce over each.

GAME BIRD PIE

A great dish for a busy week. Prepare a day or two ahead and heat to serve at dinner

4 - 6 servings

12	ounces basic pastry dough
1	pound cooked game bird meat, cut into small pieces
¼	cup butter
1	cup fresh mushrooms, sliced
¼	cup flour
¼	teaspoon freshly ground black pepper
2	tablespoons fresh parsley, minced
	pinch salt
⅔	cup milk
⅓	cup game bird stock or chicken broth
⅓	cup gruyére or Swiss cheese, grated
1	egg

On a floured surface, divide pastry dough into 2 pieces and roll each into 2 — 11 inch circles. Cover with a damp towel and set aside. In a large sauce pan over medium heat, add 1/2 of the butter and sauté mushrooms for 3 minutes. Remove mushrooms. Add remaining butter, heat to melt, stir in flour and cook for 2 to 3 minutes. Add pepper, parsley, salt, milk and stock. Bring to boil and cook until thickened. Remove from heat and stir in mushrooms and meat. Allow mixture to cool and stir in cheese.

Place one of the pastry circles into the bottom of a lightly greased pie plate, allowing a rim of pastry to fall over edges of pie plate. Spread filling evenly over pastry. Place remaining pastry over mixture and crimp edges together with bottom pastry. Beat egg lightly and brush top layer of pastry. Bake in a pre- heated 400° F oven for 30 minutes or until pastry is golden brown. Allow to cool for 5 minutes before serving.

HERB ROASTED WILD TURKEY
WITH CHERRY CHUTNEY

If fresh herbs are not available, substitute with half-quantities of dry herbs even though the finished dish will have a less aromatic flavor. The turkey must be cleaned and plucked carefully so that the skin is intact.

4 - 6 servings

1	large tom turkey, skin intact
½	cup fresh basil, chopped
1	tablespoon fresh rosemary, minced
2	tablespoons fresh tarragon, finely chopped
4	garlic cloves, minced
	salt and pepper
10	strips thick-sliced smoked bacon

Cherry Chutney (see page 164)

Preheat oven to 350° F. Starting at the neck opening and working towards the small part of the breast, carefully maneuver fingers between the skin and breast of the turkey. Chop 4 of the bacon strips into small pieces. Combine fresh herbs, garlic and chopped bacon and spread evenly between the skin and breast. Sprinkle with salt and pepper and place remaining bacon strips over the breast. Place in oven and roast 10 minutes for each pound of turkey. Remove turkey from oven when internal temperature reaches 145° F. Let turkey set for 10 minutes. Carve and serve with chutney.

ROASTED GARLIC
VINAIGRETTE

2	tablespoons shallot, finely chopped (or substitute the white part of green onions)
⅓	cup white wine vinegar
1	tablespoon dijon mustard
½	teaspoon salt
1	pinch white pepper
1	egg, white only
4	garlic cloves, roasted in a 350° F oven until softened and lightly browned
1	cup olive oil

In a food processor or blender, process first 7 ingredients until blended. While machine is running, add oil in a thin stream until emulsified.

Note: If you do not have a processor or blender, mash the garlic in a medium bowl, add other ingredients except oil and whisk in oil, a little at a time until emulsified.

PHEASANT
WITH CASHEWS AND SNOW PEAS

Incredible flavor and texture combines with moist pheasant breast pieces. Keep an eye on the clock. Cooking time shouldn't exceed six minutes.

4 servings

4	pheasant breast halves, skin removed and cut into 1 inch pieces
3	garlic cloves, minced
1	tablespoon dry cooking sherry
1	tablespoon soy sauce
3	tablespoons cornstarch
1	tablespoon hoisin sauce
2	tablespoons peanut oil
½	cup game bird stock or chicken broth
1 ½	cups snow peas, fresh or frozen, strings and ends removed
½	cup sliced water chestnuts
⅓	cup salted cashews

In a medium bowl thoroughly mix garlic, sherry, soy sauce, cornstarch and hoisin sauce. Add pheasant pieces. Cover and refrigerate for 30 minutes. Heat oil in a wok or large skillet over high heat. Add pheasant and marinade and stir-fry for 2 to 3 minutes or until meat is just firm. Stir in stock and cook for 2 minutes. Add snow peas and water chestnuts and cook for 1 minute. Stir in cashews and serve immediately.

PAN-FRIED PHEASANT BREASTS
WITH TARRAGON MUSTARD SAUCE

A crispy coating protects against drying out lean pheasant breasts.

4 servings

4 - 6	boneless pheasant breast halves, cut in half, with skin intact
2	large eggs
2	tablespoons dry cooking sherry
¼	cup green onions, diced fine
½	cup flour, seasoned with garlic salt and pepper
¾	cup seasoned bread crumbs
2	tablespoons butter
2	tablespoons vegetable oil
¼	cup dry white wine
¼	cup dijon mustard
2	tablespoons fresh tarragon, chopped fine
1	teaspoon sugar
½	cup heavy cream
	salt and white pepper to taste

Pound pheasant breast pieces between waxed paper sheets until 1/4 inch thick. In a small bowl, beat eggs with sherry. Add green onions to egg mixture. Dredge pheasant thoroughly in seasoned flour and dip in egg mixture. Coat with bread crumbs, pressing crumbs into breast. Place on waxed paper and refrigerate for 2 to 3 hours.

In a large skillet, heat oil and butter over medium-high heat and pan-fry breast pieces until lightly browned, about 3 minutes per side. Remove, place on paper towels and keep warm. Deglaze skillet with wine for 2 minutes while loosening solids from pan with a wooden spoon or spatula. Add mustard, tarragon, sugar and cream. Cook until sauce thickens. Adjust seasoning with salt and pepper. Place two breast pieces per person on plate and spoon sauce over each.

JAMAICAN
BARBECUED PHEASANT

This toned-down version of Jamaican "jerk" marinade will not overpower the delicate meat of the pheasant, but will certainly add a touch of fire to the

4 servings

- 2 pheasants, skin intact and split into 4 halves
- ¾ cup soy sauce
- ½ cup red wine vinegar
- ¼ cup vegetable oil
- ¼ cup honey
- ½ cup green onions, including tops, diced
- 1 medium red onion, diced
- 1 jalapeño pepper, seeded and diced
- ½ teaspoon ground cloves
- ½ teaspoon ground nutmeg
- ½ teaspoon ground allspice
- ½ teaspoon chili flakes
- ¼ teaspoon freshly ground black pepper

Make an incision at the inside of the thigh and leg joints of each pheasant half, cutting through the skin to the joint. Rinse pheasant halves under cold water and pat dry with paper towels. Place remaining ingredients in a food processor or blender and blend for 15 to 20 seconds. Pour mixture over pheasant, coating evenly. Cover and refrigerate for 12 hours, turning occasionally to marinate.

When barbecue coals are ash white, move coals to the sides of the barbecue. Place pheasant halves, breast side down, in the center of the well-greased barbecue. If using a gas barbecue, heat to medium before adding pheasants to grill. Cook for 4 to 5 minutes, turning a quarter turn during cooking to create "diamond" grill marks on breasts. Flip pheasant halves over, cover and cook for 3 to 4 more minutes. Cooked meat should be barely pink at the breast bone.

CRISPY BAKED PHEASANT

An alternative to deep-frying, crunchy pheasant pieces with plenty of character. Try it with sweet summer corn on the cob, coleslaw and a glass of freshly brewed iced tea.

4 servings

- 2   pheasants, skin intact, cut into
        6 pieces each (breast, leg, thigh)
- 1   cup flour seasoned with 1 tablespoon garlic powder, 1 tablespoon onion
        powder and 1 tablespoon dried basil flakes
- 3   eggs, lightly beaten with 3 table spoons dijon mustard
- 2   cups seasoned bread crumbs
- 1   tablespoon cracked black popper
- 3   tablespoons mustard seeds
- 3   tablespoons sesame seeds
- 2   tablespoons celery seeds
- ½   teaspoon salt

Dredge pheasant pieces in seasoned flour to coat evenly. Coat each floured piece with egg mixture. Combine remaining ingredients in a medium bowl and mix well. Roll each pheasant piece in coating mixture and refrigerate for 30 minutes. Pre-heat oven to 375° F. Bake pheasant pieces in a lightly greased baking dish, uncovered, until golden brown, about 35 to 40 minutes.

QUAIL
WITH ORANGE-HONEY GLAZE

A great quick and easy recipe

4 servings

- 8   quail, skin intact
- ½   teaspoon powdered coriander
- 5   tablespoons unsalted butter
- 1   tablespoon olive oil
- 2   tablespoons honey
- ¼   cup freshly squeezed orange juice
        salt and freshly ground pepper

Rinse quail and pat dry with paper towels. Season lightly with salt, pepper and coriander.

In a large skillet over medium-high heat, combine 2 tablespoons butter, olive oil and 1 tablespoon honey. Add the quail and sauté for about 5 to 6 minutes or until quail is lightly browned on all sides. Add remaining honey and orange juice and cook until liquid starts to thicken. Remove quail and arrange on plate. Remove skillet from heat and whisk in remaining butter. Season as desired with salt and pepper. Pour sauce over each quail.

STUFFED PHEASANT BREAST MEDALLIONS

For best results, you'll need a very sharp boning knife.

4 servings

4	pheasant breast halves, skin intact
4	slices Canadian bacon
1	large red bell pepper, roasted, peeled, seeded and cut into 4 sections
12	fresh basil leaves
4	garlic cloves, roasted and mashed into paste
2	tablespoons olive oil
¼	teaspoons salt
½	teaspoons freshly ground black pepper

Preheat oven to 425° F. Place the pheasant breast halves on a cutting surface and cut a "pocket" into each by inserting a sharp boning knife into the side of the breast and making a cut as wide as a slice of Canadian bacon. Work the knife throughout the breast carefully. Do not puncture the flesh other than at the entrance point.

On each slice of Canadian bacon, spread an equal amount of the roasted garlic paste, top with a section of red pepper and 3 basil leaves. Carefully, fold the Canadian bacon and insert into pheasant pocket. Fold the edges of the breast down to cover the pocket opening, working the skin down evenly to cover the top of the stuffed breast. Place each breast side-by-side in a small baking pan as snugly as possible. Brush breasts with olive oil and season with salt and pepper.

Place in oven and bake until browned, about 10 to 12 minutes. Remove from oven. Allow to cool slightly and slice each breast with the boning knife into 2 or 3 medallions. Arrange on plate.

RABBIT FLORENTINE

Subtle seasonings complement the delightful, moist rabbit pieces.

4 servings

- 1 ½ cups rabbit, boned and cut into 1 inch pieces
- ½ cup flour
- 1 teaspoon garlic salt
- 1 teaspoon onion powder
- ½ teaspoon freshly ground black pepper
- ½ teaspoon ground nutmeg
- 4 strips smoked bacon, diced
- 3 tablespoons olive oil
- 2 garlic cloves, minced
- ½ cup yellow onion, diced
- ⅔ cup game stock or beef broth
- 1 cup fresh mushrooms, sliced thin
- 8 ounces spinach leaves, washed and stalks removed
  salt and pepper to taste
- ⅓ cup goat cheese, crumbled (optional)
- 4 cups cooked white rice

In a paper bag, combine flour, garlic salt, onion powder, pepper and nutmeg. Place rabbit pieces in bag and coat evenly with flour mixture. In a large skillet over medium heat, cook bacon until browned. Remove bacon and set aside. Heat oil and brown rabbit pieces evenly on all sides. Add garlic and onion and cook for 3 minutes. Stir in game stock, bring to boil, cover and cook for 5 minutes. Remove cover, add mushrooms and cook for 2 minutes. Add spinach leaves and stir until spinach is just-cooked. Season with salt and pepper. Remove from heat. Place one cup of warm cooked rice on each plate. Ladle rabbit and sauce equally over each and top with goat cheese and cooked bacon.

RABBIT JAMBALAYA

If you don't have three rabbits lying around, substitute them with, or add ducks or game birds to this traditional Cajun dish to yield 6 cups of cubed meat.

6 - 8 servings

8	ounces andouille sausage, cut into 1/4 inch slices (you may substitute other spicy, smoked pure-pork sausage)
2	tablespoons butter
2	tablespoons vegetable oil
⅓	cup flour, seasoned with 1 teaspoon *each* salt, garlic powder, onion powder, black pepper and paprika
3	cottontail rabbits, boned and cut into 1/2 inch cubes
1	medium yellow onion, diced
1	green bell pepper, diced
2	celery stalks, diced
3	garlic cloves, minced
1	tablespoon brown sugar
2	teaspoons paprika
2	bay leaves
1	teaspoon dried basil leaves
¾	teaspoon dried thyme leaves
¾	teaspoon cayenne pepper
½	teaspoon black pepper
½	teaspoon garlic powder
	dash Tabasco
1	14 ½ oz can diced tomatoes, not drained
1	cup tomato sauce
3	cups game bird stock or chicken broth
2	cups uncooked white rice
1	cup green onions, tops included, diced
½	cup fresh parsley, minced

In a paper bag, add seasoned flour and rabbit pieces. Toss to coat meat lightly. In a large heavy stock pot over medium-high heat, add half of the oil and butter. Cook sausage for 2 to 3 minutes. Add rabbit and cook until lightly browned. Remove rabbit and sausage from pot and add remaining oil and butter, cooking over medium-high heat. Add onion, bell pepper, celery and garlic. Cook for 3 minutes. Stir in brown sugar and cook for 2 more minutes. Add remaining ingredients except rice, green onions and parsley. Bring to a boil, reduce heat to low and simmer for 25 minutes. Add rabbit and sausage and cook for 10 to 15 minutes. Stir in rice, bring back to boil. Reduce heat to low, cover and simmer for 25 minutes. Stir in green onions and parsley and remove from heat. Adjust seasoning with salt and pepper. Serve in large bowls.

RABBIT
WITH PENNE PASTA AND ANCHOVY SAUCE

When it comes to anchovies, most people either like them or they don't. If you fall into the first group, you'll love this simple rabbit dish.

4 servings

1	rabbit, boned and cut into small pieces
2	tablespoons olive oil
8	anchovy fillets
¼	teaspoon freshly ground black pepper
2	garlic, minced
½	cup parma ham, diced (or substitute just-cooked diced smoked bacon)
¼	cup dry red wine
2	cups tomato sauce
1	cup fresh tomato, diced
3	tablespoons fresh parsley, chopped
¼	cup black olives, sliced
4	cups cooked penne pasta
2	tablespoons butter
¼	cup Parmesan cheese, grated

Heat oil and brown rabbit pieces lightly in a large skillet over medium-high heat. Add anchovies, garlic and pepper. Cook for 3 to 4 minutes, stirring 2 or 3 times. Add ham or bacon and cook for 3 minutes. Add wine and cook for 2 minutes. Add tomato sauce, bring to boil, reduce heat to low, cover and cook for 6 to 8 minutes. Add diced tomato, parsley and black olives. Cook for 3 minutes more. Toss warm pasta with butter. Top with sauce and sprinkle Parmesan cheese over sauce.

SAUTEED QUAIL
WITH APPLE CREAM SAUCE

The delicate flavor of quail is enhanced by this flavorful sauce

4 servings

- 12   quail, skin intact
- ⅛   teaspoon white pepper
- ⅛   teaspoon salt
- ⅛   teaspoon ground coriander
- 2   tablespoons butter
- ¾   cup dry white wine juice of 1/2 lemon
- 1   tablespoon shallot, minced
- 1   firm Granny Smith apple, peeled and diced very fine
- 1   ablespoon honey
- ½   cup heavy cream
  salt and white pepper to taste

Season quail lightly with pepper, salt and coriander. In a large skillet over medium heat, melt butter and lightly brown quail on all sides about 2 to 3 minutes per side. Remove quail, increase heat to medium-high and de-glaze pan with 2 tablespoons of the wine, scraping pan to remove solids. Add remaining wine, lemon juice and shallots and reduce liquid by one-half. Add apple, honey and cream and return quail to pan. Reduce until liquid thickens. Season with salt and pepper to taste. Place 3 quail per person on plate and spoon sauce evenly over each.

ROASTED QUAIL
WITH RED BELL PEPPER SAUCE

Fortunately, quail season coincides with late-season red bell peppers which can be a bit pricey in the winter and spring Serve with Two-Color Polenta (see page 156).

4 servings

- 8   quail with skin intact
- 3   garlic cloves, minced
- 1   tablespoon lemon pepper
- 4   slices smoked bacon, cut in half
- 1   cup Grilled Red Bell Pepper Sauce
  (see page167)

Rub quail with garlic, season with lemon pepper and place 2 bacon halves over each breast. Place breast side up in a roasting pan and roast in a pre-heated 475° F oven for 8 to 10 minutes. Since oven temperatures vary greatly, be careful not to overcook birds. Check occasionally to make certain that quail is still tender and not overcooked. Cooked breast meat should be barely pink when done. Remove quail from oven, place 2 on each plate and drizzle sauce over each.

PHEASANT BREAST NAPOLEON
WITH ROASTED GARLIC VINAIGRETTE

This colorful dish can be served as an entrée or in a scaled-down version as an appetizer. Save this one for special occasions when you really want to impress your guests. Napoleons can be assembled during the day, refrigerated and heated for service later in the evening.

4 servings

4	pheasant breast halves, skin removed
½	cup flour, seasoned with 1 teaspoon garlic salt and ½ teaspoon black pepper
2	eggs, lightly beaten with 1 tablespoon cold water
1½	cups seasoned bread crumbs
½	cup peanut or corn oil
8	slices eggplant, approximately ¼ inch thick and 4 inches in diameter
2	tablespoons butter
1	cup pitted black olives, finely chopped
1	garlic clove, minced
1	teaspoon capers, mashed
2	teaspoons olive oil
2	anchovy fillets, or 1 tablespoon anchovy paste
1	bunch fresh basil
4	ounces goat cheese, softened (or substitute cream cheese)
½	cup sundried tomato pesto (see page 171)
1	cup tomatoes, seeded and diced
	freshly ground black pepper

Prepare vinaigrette (Page 66) and let stand at room temperature for 1 hour before serving. If vinaigrette separates, briefly return to processor or blender before serving. Cut each pheasant breast in half widthwise. Place each piece between wax paper sheets and pound lightly with the flat side of a mallet until meat is 1/8 to 1/4 inch thick. Dredge each piece in seasoned flour, dip in beaten eggs and coat with bread crumbs. In a large skillet over medium-high heat, heat oil until hot and fry each piece until lightly browned. Remove breast pieces and drain on paper towels. Discard oil, wipe skillet and melt butter over medium- high heat. Sauté eggplant slices in butter for 1 minute each side. Remove and drain on paper towels. In a small bowl, combine olives, capers, olive oil and anchovies. Mix well, breaking up anchovy fillets. Prepare sundried tomato pesto.

In a baking pan or casserole dish, lay out 4 eggplant slices, about 1 inch apart. Spread a thin layer of goat cheese over eggplant. Spread 1 1/2 tablespoon of the olive mixture (*tapenade*) over goat cheese. Pick basil leaves and place 3 to 5 leaves, depending on size of leaves, over olive mixture. Place pheasant over basil leaves. Spread pesto thinly over pheasant. Repeat steps for second layer. Place pan or dish in a 300° F oven for 6 to 8 minutes or until warmed throughout. Remove Napoleons with a spatula and place one on each plate. Chop remaining basil leaves and combine with tomatoes and vinaigrette. In a small saucepan, warm vinaigrette. Do not boil or sauce may separate. Drizzle a little vinaigrette over each and spoon remaining vinaigrette on plate around Napoleon. Grind pepper over each.

WILD TURKEY BREAST STIR-FRY
WITH DRIED CHERRIES

The reason I included dried cherries in the title of this recipe is because one doesn't normally associate dried berries with an Asian stir-fry. I was torn between creating a stuffed turkey breast, specifically a turkey breast with a dried cherry stuffing or a stir-fry. Not wanting to do without either, I combined the flavors of the East and, well...dried cherries. While feasting on the finished product, I found myself hoping that the next bite would have a dried cherry. If you can't easily get your hands on dried cherries, try "Craisins" –a sweetened cranberry, raisins or just about any dried fruit.

4 servings

2	wild turkey breasts, boneless and skinless; cut into thin strips
2	tablespoons sesame oil
2	tablespoons soy sauce
1	tablespoon cornstarch mixed with equal part cold water
1	lemon, juice only
3	garlic cloves, minced
2	tablespoons fresh ginger, peeled and minced
1	tablespoon brown sugar
2	tablespoons peanut oil
1/2	cup dry-roasted peanuts
2	green onions, roughly chopped
1	cup snow peas, trimmed
1/2	cup dried cherries
8	8-ounce can sliced water chestnuts
4	cups warm steamed rice

Combine sesame oil, soy sauce, lemon juice, garlic, ginger and brown sugar in a non-reactive bowl (glass, wood, plastic). Add turkey, toss to coat and refrigerate for 2 – 3 hours. Heat oil in a wok or large skillet over medium-high heat. Remove turkey from marinade. Reserve marinade. Add turkey and stir-fry for 2 – 3 minutes. Add peanuts and stir-fry 1 minute. Add reserved marinade and green onions and heat liquid to boiling. Add snow peas, dried cherries and water chestnuts and heat to warm. Serve immediately over rice.

AN UNUSUAL QUAIL RECIPE

There are those to whom hunting dogs are a means to locate and retrieve game. During the off-season, their dogs sit in kennels – going through the daily routine and waiting for the kennel door to open. On a good day, he gets a pat on the head, a friendly whistle or perhaps some table scraps. They are ready to take to the field in a second, giving their owners every bit of energy they can muster; running, swimming, climbing, jumping or holding rock-solid at the intoxicating scent of a game bird.

My own bird dogs are as much a part of the family as, well as I am. While attending college, my English setter Winston slept at my feet in the classroom. I had a Gordon setter, Hank (the Tank) that was arguably the best ditch dog in the universe. When the ditch stopped moving, you could almost guarantee that a pheasant was about to explode from the tulles. There have been others and then there was Jack.

Jack was neither the best bird dog I have owned nor the most poised. The classic English setter is lean and mean with a tail held high like a flag on a windy day. Jack's tail never rose above half-mast. His coat was coarse, yet his head was soft as a baby chick. He was thick, not slick, but he found birds when there were birds; often after others had tried and failed. Jack followed me wherever he could, sleeping under my desk any hour or curled up on his personal bed next to my own. He was a social buddy, always eager to greet the next visitor. I never had to worry about Jack mixing it up with other dogs or running off at night. He was devoted to me and my family.

Jack had to be put to rest following a brief battle with what probably was a brain tumor. Most people who follow these recipes either have or had great dogs during some part of their lives. Jack's memory will live on for as long I do. There will be other dogs, but not another Jack. This recipe is for him. We sure loved to hunt quail together.

1 serving

4 quail
salt and pepper

Season quail with a little salt and pepper. Grill, sauté, bake or broil until done. When cooled, remove meat from bones. Feed meat to dog. Scratch dog liberally around the head, neck, ears and bellies. Take him for a ride in the pickup and then a long run. He may not be here tomorrow.

DOVE RAVIOLI
WITH TOMATO-BASIL VINAIGRETTE

Don't let the name of this recipe scare you off. It's much easier than it may sound and a great way to stretch your doves if you're a few birds shy of a limit. Hey, is that like "a few bricks short of a load" or " a few sandwiches short of a picnic?"

4 servings

10-12	dove breast halves, skin and rib cages removed, seasoned with salt and pepper, broiled until rare and then cooled
½	cup Monterey Jack cheese, grated
⅓	cup ricotta cheese
2	garlic cloves, minced
¼	cup yellow onion, chopped
1	tablespoon dried Italian seasoning
¼	cup seasoned breadcrumbs
40	round wonton wrappers
¼	cup cornstarch mixed with equal part cold water
	Vinaigrette
¼	cup white wine vinegar
1	teaspoon Dijon mustard
1	teaspoon granulated sugar
½	cup olive oil
1	cup ripe tomato, chopped
¼	cup fresh basil, chopped
	salt and pepper

Add cooked and cooled dove breasts to a food processor and pulse until cut into pea-sized pieces. Add next 6 ingredients and pulse until ingredients are finely minced, but not obliterated.

To make ravioli, place 1 wonton wrapper on a flat surface and spread a thin layer of the cornstarch mixture around the outside edges. Place a small blob of filling in the center of the disc, about the diameter of a 50-cent piece and about 1/4-inch high. Place a second wonton wrapper on top of the filling and gently press the edges of the top wrapper onto the moistened edges of the bottom wrapper. Place the finished raviolis into a gently boiling pot of boiling lightly salted water. Use plenty of water and don't crowd the pot with too many ravioli at a time. Cook for 3 – 4 minute or until ravioli are tender and translucent.

To prepare vinaigrette, whisk the first 3 ingredients together in a medium bowl. Slowly add oil while whisking. Whisk in tomato and basil and season with salt and pepper.

To serve, place 8 – 10 ravioli on a plate and spoon room temperature sauce over.

DOVE STROGANOFF

For those who insist on cooking your doves for a fairly long time, here's one variation of a classic dish. As dove breasts cook beyond medium-rare, they toughen up like inexpensive stew meat and then must be cooked for an hour or more in liquid to render tender. The breasts should be simmered in the beef broth, etc. until they start to pull apart easily with moderate pressure. If you cook them too long, they will shred completely and look bad.

4 servings

1	large yellow onion, diced
2	tablespoons butter
1	tablespoon olive oil
3	cloves garlic, minced
24	dove breast halves, seasoned with salt and pepper
1	cup dry red wine
1	cup beef broth
1	teaspoon Worcestershire sauce
4	cups mushrooms, sliced (I use crimini and shiitake mushrooms)
$2/3$	cup sour cream
$1/4$	cup fresh basil, thinly sliced
4-5	cups cooked warm fettuccine noodles

   In a large skillet over medium heat, sauté onion in butter and olive oil until onion is translucent. Add garlic and sauté 1 minute more. Add dove breast halves and sauté for 5 – 7 minutes, browning each evenly. Add half of the wine and beef broth and stir to loosen any bits from the bottom. Add Worcestershire. Cover and simmer for 1 1/2 to 2 hours or until breasts become tender again. Save remaining wine and broth to add to pan if necessary. When breasts begin to get tender, add mushrooms and make sure there's enough wine and broth to just cover the bottom of the pan about 1/4 inch. Cook for 5 minutes to soften mushrooms. Stir in sour cream and basil. Simmer to warm. Serve over pasta.

GRILLED DOVES
WITH A BALSAMIC-CHERRY GLAZE

With a recipe like this, you know this has to be from California. All we need is some sundried tomatoes, roasted garlic and fresh goat cheese, although I can never seem to find a really fresh goat. Luckily, this dish isn't nearly as complicated as it might sound. Amaze your friends and splash some of this glaze on your ducks sometime. If you don't have any balsamic vinegar, dust the cobwebs off your wallet and go get some. It's available anywhere and the grocery store variety costs about the same as a good red wine vinegar.

4 servings

16   dove breasts, whole, on the bone; preferably with skin intact olive oil
     salt and pepper to taste
1 1/2   cups balsamic vinegar
1/2   cup brown sugar
2/3   cups cherry preserves

Rub the doves with olive oil and season with salt and pepper. Heat the vinegar and sugar in a sauce pan to boil. Reduce heat to medium and simmer, uncovered until the liquid reduces by one-half. Stir in the cherry preserves. Place the dove breasts over medium-hot coals and baste with glaze while cooking. Remove breasts when medium-rare and drizzle a little glaze over each.

JALAPENO DOVE BROCHETTE

Fire up the barbecue and grill up some fresh dove breasts with a Southwestern flair. Not a bad way to spend the afternoon or evening with a few hunting buddies after a successful dove shoot. Get all of the ingredients ready the day before the shoot so you can get right down to the business of cooking after the hunt. Don't forget the ice cold beer to take the edge off the jalapenos!

5 – 6 servings

60	doves breast halves; skin on or off
½	cup firmly packed brown sugar
2	tablespoons fresh ginger; peeled and minced
½	cup soy sauce
1	teaspoon sesame oil
½	cup rice vinegar (or substitute 1/3 cup white wine vinegar)
¼	cup tomato paste
½	teaspoon coarsely ground black pepper
15	jalapeño peppers; seeded and cut into 4 strips each
30	strips bacon; partially cooked
20	wooden skewers; soaked in water for 30 minutes

Combine sugar with next 7 ingredients in a bowl and mix well. Add dove breasts and marinate for 1 hour. For each skewer, place a strip of bacon on a flat surface. Lay a strip of jalapeño , then dove breast, then another jalapeño strip and dove breast. Wrap with bacon place 3 bacon-wrapped breast "bundles" side by side. Place 2 skewers through each set of three bundles, putting the skewers about 3/4-inch apart from one another. Grill over medium-hot coals until medium-rare.

WILD TURKEY BREAST STIR-FRY
with Dried Cherries

The reason I included dried cherries in the title of this recipe is because one doesn't normally associate dried berries with an Asian stir-fry. I was torn between creating a stuffed turkey breast, specifically a turkey breast with a dried cherry stuffing or a stir-fry. Not wanting to do without either, I combined the flavors of the East and, well...dried cherries. While feasting on the finished product, I found myself hoping that the next bite would have a dried cherry. If you can't easily get your hands on dried cherries, try "Craisins" –a sweetened cranberry, raisins or just about any dried fruit.

4 servings

2	wild turkey breasts, boneless and skinless; cut into thin strips
2	tablespoons sesame oil
2	tablespoons soy sauce
1	tablespoon cornstarch mixed with equal part cold water
1	lemon, juice only
3	garlic cloves, minced
2	tablespoons fresh ginger, peeled and minced
1	tablespoon brown sugar
2	tablespoons peanut oil
$1/2$	cup dry-roasted peanuts
2	green onions, roughly chopped
1	cup snow peas, trimmed
$1/2$	cup dried cherries
8	8-ounce can sliced water chestnuts
4	cups warm steamed rice

Combine sesame oil, soy sauce, lemon juice, garlic, ginger and brown sugar in a non-reactive bowl (glass, wood, plastic). Add turkey, toss to coat and refrigerate for 2 – 3 hours. Heat oil in a wok or large skillet over medium-high heat. Remove turkey from marinade. Reserve marinade. Add turkey and stir-fry for 2 – 3 minutes. Add peanuts and stir-fry 1 minute. Add reserved marinade and green onions and heat liquid to boiling. Add snow peas, dried cherries and water chestnuts and heat to warm. Serve immediately over rice.

DOVE AND APPLE PATÈ

Here's a great recipe to impress people who don't like wild game, just don't tell them what it is until they've taken a bite or two. A little later, you should start a conversation about the flavors of wild game and let them express their disdain for all things bagged and tagged. Then ask them how they liked the pate...too much apple? Not enough pepper? Or was the dove a little too gamy?

Makes approximately 1 cup

- 3 green onions, white part only; finely minced
- 1 garlic clove, minced
- 2 tablespoons unsalted butter
- ½ Granny Smith (who is this woman?) apple; peeled, cored and finely diced
- 1 cup dove breast halves; skinned and deboned (about 16 – 20 halves)
  pinch salt
  pinch freshly ground pepper
- 2 tablespoons brandy
- 3 tablespoons heavy cream
- ½ teaspoon fresh tarragon (or substitute pinch dried tarragon)

In a medium skillet over medium heat, melt half of the butter. Add onion and garlic and sauté for 2 – 3 minutes. Add apple and cook for 3 minutes more.

Transfer contents of pan to a food processor. Add the rest of the butter to the pan and lightly brown dove breasts until medium-rare, about 3 minutes. Season with salt and pepper. Remove pan from heat and slowly stir in brandy, a little at a time. *Caution: Brandy May Ignite!* Return pan to heat and cook over medium heat until brandy evaporates.

Add cooked doves to food processor and add cream and tarragon. Process until mixture is smooth. Add a little more cream if mixture is too thick. If mixture is too thin, add a small piece of bread.

PHEASANT
with Parmesan Mushroom Cream Sauce

Reminiscent of a creamy Alfredo sauce paired with whole earthy mushrooms, this versatile dish works great for just about any upland game.

4 servings

2	tablespoons kosher salt
1	tablespoon black pepper
1½	cups all-purpose flour
2	pheasants, preferably with skin intact; each bird quartered
3	tablespoons olive oil
2	tablespoons butter
½	cup yellow onion, finely diced
3	garlic cloves, minced
¾	cup chicken broth
¼	cup dry white wine
½	cup heavy (whipping) cream
3	cups fresh whole small button mushrooms, stems removed
½	cup shredded parmesan cheese

Combine kosher salt, pepper and flour in a large plastic resealable bag. Add pheasant pieces and shake to coat evenly. Heat olive oil and butter in a large skillet over medium-high heat. Add pheasant pieces and brown evenly on all sides. Transfer browned pheasant to a plate and carefully discard oil from skillet.

Reheat skillet (less oil) over medium-high heat. Add onion, garlic, chicken broth and wine. Cook until onions are translucent, about five minutes. Add browned pheasant, cover and cook for 10 minutes. Remove cover and stir in heavy cream and add mushrooms. Reduce heat to medium and cook for 10 minutes more. Cook until pheasant pieces are done and sauce is thickened. Season sauce with additional kosher salt and pepper.

Remove pheasant pieces and arrange on plates. Stir cheese into pan until melted. Spoon mushrooms and sauce over pheasant pieces.

BRAISED SQUIRREL
In Canterbury Sauce

4 servings

3	squirrels, quartered
1	cup flour
1	teaspoon each salt and pepper
2	tablespoons butter
2	tablespoons bacon grease
1	tablespoon olive or vegetable oil
1	large yellow onion, coarsely chopped
2	garlic cloves, minced
3	cups whole mushrooms (smaller is better)
2	medium carrots, peeled and cut into 2-inch pieces
3	celery stalks, trimmed and cut into 2-inch pieces
¼	pound cooked bacon (pre-cooked weight)
¼	cup chicken stock
1¼	cups dry red wine
2	tablespoons fresh parsley, chopped
1	teaspoon Italian seasoning
3	tablespoons tomato paste
	salt and pepper

Combine flour salt and pepper in a bowl. Dust squirrel pieces with the seasoned flour. Heat a large frying pan and melt the butter and bacon grease. Lightly brown the squirrel pieces evenly on all sides and transfer to a lightly greased casserole or baking dish. In another skillet (or clean the first one!), heat oil over medium heat and add onion, garlic, mushrooms, celery, carrots and cooked bacon. Cook until onions are translucent and not browned. Add chicken stock, wine, parsley, Italian seasoning and tomato paste, stirring over heat until the tomato paste dissolves. Pour over squirrel in the casserole dish. Cover and place in a preheated 325 degree oven for 2 – 3 hours or until meat begins to pull away easily from the bone. Turn squirrel pieces every 45 minutes or so. Season with salt and pepper when done.

DOVE RAVIOLI
with Tomato-Basil Vinaigrette

Don't let the name of this recipe scare you off. It's much easier than it may sound and a great way to stretch your doves if you're a few birds shy of a limit.

4 servings

10-12	dove breast halves, skin and rib cages removed, seasoned with salt and pepper, broiled until rare and then cooled
½	cup Monterey Jack cheese, grated
⅓	cup ricotta cheese
2	garlic cloves, minced
¼	cup yellow onion, chopped
1	tablespoon dried Italian seasoning
¼	cup seasoned breadcrumbs
40	round won ton wrappers
¼	cup cornstarch mixed with equal part cold water

Vinaigrette

¼	cup white wine vinegar
1	teaspoon Dijon mustard
1	teaspoon granulated sugar
½	cup olive oil
1	cup ripe tomato, chopped
¼	cup fresh basil, chopped
	salt and pepper to taste

Add cooked and cooled dove breasts to a food processor and pulse until cut into pea-sized pieces. Add next 6 ingredients and pulse until ingredients are finely minced, but not obliterated. To make ravioli, place 1 won ton wrapper on a flat surface and spread a thin layer of the cornstarch mixture around the outside edges. Place a small blob of filling in the center of the disc, about the diameter of a 50-cent piece and about 1/4-inch high. Place a second won ton wrapper on top of the filling and gently press the edges of the top wrapper onto the moistened edges of the bottom wrapper. Place the finished raviolis into a gently boiling pot of lightly salted water. Use plenty of water and don't crowd the pot with too many ravioli at a time. Cook for 3 to 4 minutes or until raviolis are tender and translucent.

To prepare vinaigrette, whisk the first 3 ingredients together in a medium bowl. Slowly add oil while whisking. Whisk in tomato and basil and season with salt and pepper. To serve, place 8 to 10 raviolis on a plate and spoon room temperature sauce over.

APPLE ROASTED WILD TURKEY

Overcooking a wild turkey will result in a dry and tasteless bird. A farm-raised domestic turkey derives more than thirty percent of its calories from fat. The wild bird has only 1 percent total fat...quite a difference. The best way to avoid overcooking any turkey – wild or domestic – is to use a meat thermometer and roast it with the breast down. While most game cookbooks recommend removing wild turkey from the oven when the thermometer reaches 180 degrees or more, in my opinion this will ruin it. Take it out at 145 to 150 degrees, let it stand for 10 to 15 minutes and enjoy a tender and juicy treat.

Makes 1 Turkey

1	wild turkey, wiped dry with paper towels and liberally seasoned with salt and pepper
½	cup butter
2	medium red onions, roughly chopped
8 -10	garlic cloves, smashed
6	tart apples such as Granny Smith, cored and cut into wedges
1	cup unfiltered apple juice
1	cup dry white wine
1	cup chicken broth
3	tablespoons flour

In a large skillet, sauté onions and garlic in half of the butter until onions are translucent. Pour contents of skillet into a large roasting pan. Mix in apples. Set turkey, breast side down in pan, using apples and onions to prop up bird so that it does not fall over. Add apple juice, wine and chicken broth. Cover well with foil and roast in a 325 degree oven for approximately 10 minutes per pound. When the meat thermometer reaches about 135 degrees, flip the bird over and remove the foil. Remove the bird from the oven when the meat thermometer reads 145 to 150 degrees. Set the bird on a carving platter. Strain the liquid from the roasting pan through a strainer into a large bowl. Heat remaining butter in a medium saucepan and whisk in flour to make a roux. Cook for 4 to 5 minutes while stirring. Gradually whisk in about 3 to 3 1/2 cups of the strained liquid (you may need to add additional chicken broth) until gravy is of desired consistency. Season with salt and pepper. Slice turkey and serve with gravy on the side.

BACON-FRIED SQUIRREL

Anything fried, squirrel included, tastes pretty good. The squirrels are first fried and then simmered in liquid until tender. Young squirrels taste much better than old ones. If you are worried about fat and cholesterol, eat a carrot.

4 servings

4	young squirrels, each cut into 6 to 8 pieces
1/2	teaspoon salt
1/2	teaspoon freshly ground black pepper
1/2	teaspoon garlic powder
1/4	cup all-purpose flour
8	slices bacon, chopped
1/4	cup onion, sliced
2	celery stalks, sliced
1	tablespoon fresh rosemary leaves, minced
2	teaspoon lemon juice
2	cups chicken broth
4	cups warm cooked rice

Combine salt, pepper, garlic powder and flour. Dredge squirrels in flour mixture. Cook bacon in a heavy skillet over medium heat until browned. Fry squirrel pieces in bacon grease until medium brown. Add remaining ingredients except rice and reduce heat to simmer. Cover and cook for about 1 1/2 hours or until squirrel pieces are tender. Serve with warm rice.

ROASTED WILD TURKEY

The traditional way of roasting a turkey is to set it on its back and lay strips of bacon over the top, to keep it moist. I used to do it myself the same way. But now, I've found a better way. When you put bacon over the top, it'll help keep it from drying out, but if the skin's on, not much is going to get past the skin. If you like the taste of bacon, why not add some bacon flavor to the meat and get it right up there next to it? And another thing... who decided that turkeys should be cooked breast side up? All the juiciness goes to the back of the bird. So you baste it and baste it, hoping that the basting will somehow make the breast moist. Doesn't work. What does work is roasting the bird, and that's any large bird, breast side down. Here's a better way to roast a wild turkey.

1	wild turkey, skin intact
	salt and freshly ground black pepper
4	strips smoked bacon, diced
1	lemon, sliced and diced
½	cup finely diced onion
3	cloves garlic, minced
½	cup fresh herbs, your choice – minced
	(or substitute 2 tablespoons dried Italian seasoning)
3	carrots, whole
3	celery stalks, whole
2	medium potatoes, cut into 4 wedges
1	medium onion, cut into 4 wedges
2	cups dry white wine or chicken broth
	large piece heavy-duty aluminum foil

1. First, you have to carefully separate the skin from the body without tearing the skin. If you do poke through the skin once or twice, you're still fine. Start at the neck and put a hand inside, working towards the top of the breast. Feel where the skin connects to the breast and begin working your fingers in between, separating skin from breast. Continue working your hands down the breast towards the back of the bird. Season the turkey inside and out with salt and pepper.

2. Combine 1/2 teaspoon salt and 1/4 teaspoon pepper with the bacon, lemon, onion, garlic and herbs. Spread mixture in the area you've created between the skin and the breast.

3. Place turkey, breast side down, in a roasting pan. Arrange carrots, celery, potato and onion under each side of the breast to keep it from falling over. If it still won't stay up, it's no big deal. Just flip it over to the other side after about 45 minutes of cooking time.

4. Pour wine or broth into pan and cover pan with foil. Place into a 350 degree preheated oven

5. Depending on the size of your turkey, cooking time will average between 1 and 1 1/2 hours. Remove when breasts are 155 degrees. Allow to rest for 5 – 10 minutes before carving. Legs will not be tender! Remove them and use for soups and stocks.

WILD TURKEY BREAST
with Peach and Pecan Chutney

Please stop overcooking your wild turkey! When overdone, the meat is dry, tough and chewy. Then you have to throw it into the Crock Pot and cook it for several weeks. Just because this recipe is about cooking wild turkey breasts, it doesn't mean you should discard the rest of the bird. The bodies and thighs are great for making stocks, soups and stews and the legs make great Billy clubs. Fresh peaches and wild turkeys are not usually "harvested" at the same time. Feel free to substitute other fresh or frozen fruits such as nectarines, pears, plums or apricots. In a pinch, dried fruits will work as well.

6 servings

2	wild turkey breasts, skin removed
1	cup dry sherry
¼	cup soy sauce
½	cup orange juice
⅓	cup peanut or soy oil
4	garlic cloves, minced
½	teaspoon freshly ground black pepper
6	cups warm cooked rice

Chutney

6	medium firm peaches; peeled, seeded, diced and chopped into 1 to 2 inch pieces
	pinch or two of salt
1 - 2	jalapeno peppers (you decide how hot you want it), seeded and finely minced
¾	cup granulated sugar
½	cup white vinegar
2	teaspoon fresh ginger, minced
½	cup roasted pecans, chopped

Combine sherry with next 5 ingredients. Add to turkey in a plastic, ceramic or glass bowl. Cover and refrigerate for 2 to 4 hours.

Prepare chutney. Combine all ingredients and simmer for 1 hour or until peaches are soft. Remove turkey from marinade and discard marinade. Breasts can be baked or grilled, but do not cook beyond 150 degrees. Allow the cooked breasts to rest for 5 minutes before slicing. To serve, mound some rice on each plate. Slice turkey and arrange slices over rice. Spoon chutney onto turkey.

PHEASANT COBB SALAD
with Green Goddess Dressing

Whatever became of Green Goddess Dressing? You can't find it at the grocery store. Something's fishy and it's not the anchovy in the Green Goddess Dressing. Since you can't buy the stuff, here's a simple way to make it and serve with a delicious pheasant breast salad.

4 servings

4	pheasant breast half fillets, skinned
2	tablespoons olive oil
1	tablespoon Italian seasoning
	salt and pepper
4	hard boiled eggs, shelled and roughly chopped
1½	cups cheddar cheese, cut into small cubes
1½	cups Swiss cheese, cut into small cubes
8	strips crispy bacon, chopped
2	cups tomato, seeded and diced
½	cup red onion, diced
2	cups cucumber, peeled, seeded and diced
1	large head iceberg lettuce, chopped
1	head Romaine lettuce (outer leaves removed), chopped

Rub pheasant breasts with olive oil, Italian seasoning and salt and pepper. Grill or cook in a lightly oiled pan until just cooked. Allow to cool and chop into 1/2 inch cubes. Combine iceberg and Romaine lettuces and arrange on 4 plates. Arrange remaining ingredients in mounds or rows on top of the lettuce. Serve with dressing on the side.

Green Goddess Dressing

2	cups mayonnaise
4	anchovy fillets, minced
2	green onions, chopped
⅓	cup chopped fresh parsley
1	tablespoon tarragon vinegar
1	teaspoon chopped fresh tarragon

Ingredients can be mixed together in a bowl or, for a greener color, blended in a blender or food processor.

MARINATED PHEASANT
with Pecan Pesto Vinaigrette

Let's say you found a pheasant in the back of your freezer and it's a year old or more. The thing about meat is, it just doesn't get better with prolonged freezing. This is true with beef, more so with poultry and fish...forget about it. When it comes to fish, fresh is always best. But this recipe is about pheasant. If your bird has been frozen for awhile, it just might need a little help. Freezing tends to dry out meats, especially if you have not caught on to the vacuum-packaging thing. If you don't have a vacuum-packaging machine, go get one now. One of the best ways to help out a tired old frozen bird is with a good marinade. Marinades will add flavor to meats that are long past fresh. Don't use marinades to cover up foods that either look bad or smell bad. There's a reason they got that way and they should be disposed of. I like to serve this with rice.

4 servings

2   pheasants, quartered

Marinade

½   cup olive oil
1   cup chicken broth
2   lemons, juice only
½   cup onion, sliced
4   garlic cloves, minced
1   teaspoon Dijon mustard
1   tablespoon Italian seasoning

Combine marinade ingredients. Place pheasant pieces in a ceramic, plastic or glass dish and pour marinade over. Cover and refrigerate, turning occasionally. Marinate for 6 – 12 hours. To cook, remove leg/thigh sections and place in a well-oiled baking dish. Pour marinade over. Cover with foil and bake in a 375 degree oven for 1 hour. Add breast pieces, cover and bake for 20 minutes more or until pheasant breast pieces are just cooked. To serve, arrange pheasant pieces on plates and drizzle vinaigrette over.

Pecan Pesto Vinaigrette

½   cup pecan pieces, roasted in a 325 degree oven until slightly browned
2   garlic cloves, chopped
1   cup fresh basil leaves
1   lemon, juice only
¼   cup Parmesan cheese
½   cup olive oil
⅓   cup white wine vinegar
     salt and pepper

In a food processor or blender, process pecan pieces, garlic, basil, lemon and a few tablespoons of the olive oil until it forms a paste. Add parmesan cheese and vinegar. Pulse to blend. While motor is running, add remaining oil in a thin stream until emulsified. Season with salt and pepper.

BAKED QUAIL
with Crab-Stuffed Tomatoes

4 servings

Baked Quail

- 8 dressed quail
  - olive oil
  - salt and pepper
- 8 thick onion slices
- 3 tablespoons brown sugar
- ½ cup dry white wine

Rub quail evenly with olive oil. Season with salt and pepper. Coat onion slices with olive oil and season with salt and pepper. Place onion slices in a baking dish. Sprinkle brown sugar over onion and place 1 quail on each onion. Pour wine into dish, cover and bake in a preheated 375 degree oven for 12 – 15 minutes or until quail are just cooked and still just a tad pink at the thigh joint.

Crab-Stuffed Tomatoes

If crab meat isn't in your budget, try it with bay shrimp or fresh fish.

- 4 large tomatoes, cored at the stem end and hollowed out with a spoon
- 2 cups crab meat
- ½ cup shredded parmesan cheese
- ¼ cup Japanese breadcrumbs (panko) or substitute any other breadcrumbs
- ½ teaspoon lemon zest
- ¼ cup fresh basil leaves, chopped
- 2 tablespoons mayonnaise
  - salt and pepper
  - olive oil

In a bowl, combine crab meat with next 5 ingredients. Season with salt and pepper. Place crab stuffing inside tomato. Drizzle olive oil over tomato. Place tomatoes in a baking dish and bake at 375 degrees for 6 to 7 minutes.

For each serving, place two quail (with onion underneath) and one stuffed tomato on plate.

BRAISED RABBIT
with Pears

In most parts of the country, rabbit dishes are not as popular as other game animals. Big game, upland birds and waterfowl seem to be to quarry of choice for most American hunters. I suppose that doesn't upset the rabbits all that much. I suspect they would rather hang out with their buddies than in your oven.

Cooked properly, rabbits are moist, delicate and meaty. You can substitute rabbit for just about any recipe that calls for chicken. As a rule, younger rabbits are better table fare than older ones. I've had the best luck braising cut-up rabbits, usually with some kind of wine. The following recipe is a good example.

4 servings

2	young rabbits, each cut into 6 to 8 pieces
	salt and freshly ground pepper
½	cup all-purpose flour
3	tablespoons olive oil
1	medium onion, finely diced
3	cups dry red wine
1	cup chicken broth
2	tablespoons balsamic vinegar
1	tablespoon brown sugar
2	bay leaves
2	sprigs fresh rosemary
½	teaspoon salt
2	firm, slightly not-quite-ripe pears; skin removed, cored and halved
3	tablespoons chilled butter

Season rabbit pieces and dust lightly with flour. Heat oil in a large skillet over medium-high heat. Add onion and sauté for 3 to 4 minutes. Add rabbit pieces and brown each evenly. Add wine, broth, vinegar, sugar, bay leaves, rosemary and salt. Bring to a boil, then reduce heat to medium-low. Cover and simmer for 30 minutes. Add pears to the pan, cover and simmer for 30 minutes more. Remove rabbit and pears and arrange on plates. Remove bay leaves and rosemary from pan. Whisk in butter until melted and spoon sauce over rabbit.

BIG GAME

Among game-shy individuals, big game animals frequently receive the unwarranted distinction of being unpleasant tasting. While mature males taken during rutting season may be a bit tougher and more pronounced in flavor than a young animal, the most important influences on the quality of the finished dish are the handling of the animal immediately after the hunt and the method of transportation and storage. To guarantee the most flavorful finished product, all large game animals should be carefully field-dressed, butchered, labeled and refrigerated or frozen as soon as possible.

You may choose to marinate antlered game prior to cooking. My favorite marinade consists of a hearty dry red wine, garlic, pickling spices and a touch of a good vinegar. Be careful not to marinade more than 24 hours since the meat may actually get tougher with prolonged marinating. Some meats, like bear, will benefit from marinating, particularly if your guests include neophyte wild game diners. Vacuum packaging is a good way to marinate quickly. The process opens the pores of the meats and vegetables, allowing better and faster penetration of the marinade. Normal marinating times of two to eight hours can be reduced to 15 to 30 minutes when vacuum packaged with FoodSaver.

It is wise to invest in a good meat thermometer to determine the doneness of large game. Experience will allow you to rely on finger pressure to test for the temperature of the cooked meat. The less the meat gives to pressure, the more it is cooked. Periodically place a firm finger or two on the meat during cooking. You'll discover that the period of time required for the meat to turn from medium-rare to beyond redemption is remarkably brief. Avoid making test cuts into the meat while it cooks, unless that is part of an anticipated ritual among you and your guests. Searing the outside of game meats will help to seal in flavor and moisture. Sampling during cooking with an occasional cut, will not.

Beyond medium-rare, antlered game will quickly toughen. If your guests usually cringe at the sight of rare meat, carve the meat out of sight and cover it with a rich, ruby red wine sauce. Temperatures should range from 130°F (rare) to 145°F (medium-rare). All bear and wild pigs should be cooked to at least 150°F as a precaution against trichinosis.

While the recipes within this section specify a particular type of big game animal, all are interchangeable. Deer, elk and caribou can be used for any dish specifying one of these animals. Wild boar recipes work equally well with trimmed pork. All antlered game recipes can be used with similar cuts of beef.

BAKED BOAR RIBS
WITH SWEET-HOT BARBECUE SAUCE

It takes a few of these lean ribs to make a meal. Prolonged baking in sauce will make the meat fall right off the bone

4 servings

- 6-8 pounds boar ribs, sawed in half, if possible
  - *black pepper*
  - *garlic powder*
- 3 cups Sweet-Hot Barbecue Sauce (see page 169)

Baking Sauce

- 12 ounces flat beer
- 2 lemons, sliced into fourths
- 1 large yellow onion, sliced into rings
- ½ cup cider vinegar
- 3 garlic cloves, minced
- ½ cup brown sugar
- 2 cups tomato sauce
- 2 tablespoons tomato paste
- ¼ cup soy sauce
- ¼ cup Worcestershire sauce
- ½ teaspoon black pepper
- ½ teaspoon cayenne pepper

Combine above ingredients in a large sauce pan or stock pot and bring to a boil. Reduce heat and cook for 5 minutes.

Liberally season ribs with black pepper and garlic powder. Arrange in a large roasting pan and place in a 450° F oven until well browned on both sides, about 6 to 8 minutes per side. Pour baking sauce over ribs, cover, lower heat to 375° F and bake for 1 1/2 to 2 hours, turning frequently to bake ribs evenly. Remove ribs from oven when meat can be pulled free from the bone. Pour off baking sauce and discard. Brush ribs with barbecue sauce and return to oven for 10 minutes more. Serve with additional sauce on the side.

BOAR
WITH BLACK BEAN SAUCE

My favorite wild boar recipe. Prepare ahead and warm before serving

6 servings

¾	cup cooked black beans, rinsed and smashed into paste
⅔	cup dry sherry
⅓	cup soy sauce
4	garlic cloves, minced
2	teaspoons fresh ginger, minced
1	tablespoon brown sugar
3	tablespoons rice vinegar
½	teaspoon sesame oil
2 ½	pounds boar stew meat, sinew removed and cut into 1 inch cubes
3	tablespoons peanut oil
1	cup game stock or beef broth
1	medium yellow onion, coarse chopped
1	large red bell pepper, coarse chopped
2	tablespoons cornstarch mixed with
2	tablespoons cold water
	freshly ground black pepper to taste

Combine black beans, sherry, soy sauce, garlic, ginger, sugar, vinegar and sesame oil. Add boar meat, toss, cover and refrigerate for 1 hour. In a wok or large heavy-duty skillet over medium-high heat, heat oil. Remove meat from sauce, reserve sauce and brown meat evenly in oil. Add sauce and game stock and bring to boil. Reduce heat to low, cover and simmer, stirring occasionally, for 45 minutes to 1 hour or until boar meat softens and pieces can be broken apart easily with your fingers. Add onion and bell pepper, increase heat to medium and cook 3 to 4 minutes or until onions become translucent. Stir in cornstarch mixture, a little at a time, until sauce thickens. Season with pepper.

WILD BOAR CHILE VERDE

Serve with warm flour tortillas and cold Mexican beer

6 - 8 servings

3 pounds boar shoulder, cut into 1 inch pieces
3 tablespoons olive oil
2 cups yellow onion, chopped
8 garlic cloves, chopped
1 cup green bell pepper, chopped
1 cup red bell pepper, chopped
1 cup Anaheim pepper, chopped
3 jalapeño peppers, seeds removed and diced fine
1 tablespoon dried oregano flakes
2 tablespoons chili powder
2 tablespoons cumin
1 teaspoon cayenne pepper
2 cups fresh tomatillos, quartered (or canned, juice removed)
4-5 cups chicken broth
1 cup fresh cilantro
salt and pepper to taste

In a large stock pot, heat oil over medium-high flame. Add boar and lightly brown on all sides. Add onion, garlic and peppers and sauté until onion is translucent. Add oregano, chili powder, cumin, cayenne pepper, tomatillos and enough chicken broth to a level just below the top of the other ingredients. Lower heat and simmer 1 hour, adding more chicken broth as needed to keep mixture moist. Check meat to see if it has softened and begun to shred. If not, simmer for additional time. Add cilantro and simmer for 10 more minutes.

Caution: When preparing hot peppers such as jalapeños, make sure to wear rubber gloves and wash hands thoroughly afterwards. If you cut a jalapeño and then touch your eyes, you will appreciate this word of caution.

STUFFED BOAR CHOPS
WITH PORT WINE SAUCE

Great with garlic mashed potatoes and a glass of peppery zinfandel.

4 servings

Port Wine Sauce (see page 170)

4	1 ½ to 2 inch-thick chops
2	tablespoons vegetable oil
4	ounces cream cheese, softened
⅓	cup walnut pieces
½	cup dried apricots, diced
1	tablespoon shallot or green onion, minced
1	tablespoon fresh rosemary, minced
1	tablespoon fresh thyme
	salt and freshly ground black pepper

With a sharp boning knife, cut a 2 inch slit into the side of each chop. Work the knife into the chop, forming a "pocket" for the stuffing. Season each chop with salt and pepper. Combine the remaining ingredients and stuff equal amounts into each pocket.

In an oven-safe skillet over medium heat, brown chops lightly. Place in pre-heated 375° F oven until meat is firm and stuffing begins to run out, about 20 to 25 minutes. Top each chop with port wine sauce.

WILD BOAR ROAST
WITH A FRUITY CRUST

The aroma of this savory roast is surpassed only by its magnificent flavor.

6 - 8 servings

1	3 to 4 pound boneless wild boar loin, trimmed
2	eggs
1	cup flour
¾	cup seasoned bread crumbs
2	tablespoons fresh rosemary, minced
3	garlic cloves, minced
1	teaspoon freshly ground black pepper
½	teaspoon salt
¼	teaspoon ground nutmeg
2	tablespoons honey
2	tablespoons grated orange peel
1	tablespoon grated lemon peel
½	cup fresh (preferably) or canned pineapple, mashed into paste
1	Granny Smith apple, peeled and grated

Completely dust roast with 1/4 cup of the flour. *Fruity Crust:* In a bowl, combine remaining ingredients and mix well into paste. Spread paste evenly over bottom of roast and place in a roasting pan. Spread remaining paste over top and sides of roast. Place in a 450° F oven for 10 minutes to lightly brown the crust. Reduce heat to 350° F, cover and roast for 25 to 30 minutes more or until internal temperature reaches 155° F. Remove from oven, let stand for 5 minutes and slice with a sharp, thin knife into 1/4 to 1/2 inch thick slices. Try to keep crust as intact as possible while slicing.

BRAISED ELK ROAST
WITH VEGETABLES AND HERBS

Sensational cold weather dish for hearty appetites

6 servings

2-3 pounds elk shoulder roast, trimmed of fat and silver skin, cut into six equal portions
6 smoked bacon slices, diced
3 tablespoons peanut oil
12 pearl onions
3 celery stalks, cut into 2 inch pieces
4 med. carrots, peeled and cut into 1-inch pieces
10 new red potatoes, halved
4 garlic cloves, sliced
1½ cups red wine
¼ cup game stock or beef broth
3 bay leaves
2 tablespoons fresh rosemary, diced fine
1 tablespoon fresh thyme, chopped
2 tablespoons fresh sage, chopped
½ teaspoon salt
½ teaspoon freshly ground pepper

In a heavy stock pot, heat oil over medium-high heat and brown bacon. Add elk and brown evenly on all sides. Add onion, celery, carrots, potatoes and carrots. Stir in and cook for 3-4 minutes. Add wine, stock and bay leaves. Cover, reduce heat to low and simmer for 2 hours. Add fresh herbs, salt and pepper and cook, covered, for 30 more minutes. Serve in large bowls with a fresh herb garnish and warm bread.2-3

BLACKENED ELK STEAK

You'll need a cast iron skillet, an oxygen tank and a taste for Cajun spice

4 servings

4	10 ounce elk sirloin or top round steaks, cut as thick as possible
2	tablespoons peanut oil
1	teaspoon garlic powder
1	teaspoon onion powder
½	teaspoon dried thyme
½	teaspoon cayenne pepper
½	teaspoon black pepper
½	teaspoon white pepper
1	tablespoon paprika
½	cup sour cream

Rub or brush steaks with oil. Combine remaining ingredients and coat steaks evenly with spice mixture. Heat a large cast iron skillet over high heat in a well-ventilated area. The skillet must be "white hot."

Note: Restaurants featuring blackened meats and fish will leave the skillet on over high heat throughout meal periods. The blackening process can be a smoky one. Blackening without substantial heat will result in a more oily steak and the time required to blacken the meat will cause the meat to be overcooked and dry. Open the windows and let your neighbors know that there's no need to call the fire department. Also, try not to breathe in the fumes since they can irritate your respiratory system. Are you sure you want to try this? You bet!

Place steaks in the skillet for about 3 minutes per side until blackened, but not cooked beyond medium-rare. Carefully remove steaks from skillet and place 2 tablespoons of sour cream over each.

BBQ'D CARIBOU STEAK
WITH BLEU CHEESE AND GRILLED ONIONS

Easy preparation of my favorite big game animal

4 servings

4	6 - 8 ounce caribou sirloin steaks
½	teaspoon garlic powder
½	teaspoon onion powder
½	teaspoon freshly ground black pepper
1	pinch salt
¼	cup Worcestershire sauce
2	tablespoons sugar
4	large whole onion slices, intact
⅓	cup bleu cheese crumbles

Combine garlic powder, onion powder, black pepper and salt and sprinkle over steaks. Cover and refrigerate for 1 hour. In a small bowl, mix Worcestershire sauce and sugar and immerse onion slices to coat thoroughly.

Place steaks and onion slices on a well-greased medium-hot charbroiler or barbecue kettle. Cook steaks approximately 3 minutes per side or until meat is rare to medium-rare. Cook onion slices until just soft and lightly browned on both sides, turning carefully with a spatula.

Place onion slice on each steak and top with equal portion of crumbled bleu cheese.

CHARLES SPINETTA'S
VENISON ROAST

The Charles Spinetta Winery and Gallery in Plymouth, California, has done a great deal to support sportsmen's groups including Ducks Unlimited, Quail Unlimited and California Waterfowl Association. If you are in the area, stop by and have a glass of wine with Charlie and browse through the winery's spectacular wildlife art gallery. Each of Spinetta's varietal wines features a beautiful label featuring renowned wildlife artists Joe Garcia and Sherrie Russell Meline. Charlie is a devoted outdoorsman and a great wild game chef as evidenced by the following recipe.

4 - 6 servings

2 - 3	pounds venison roast, fat and sinew removed and butterflied. (See Page 91)
1	cup Charles Spinetta Zinfandel
⅓	cup red wine vinegar
½	cup olive oil
1	red onion, diced
6	garlic cloves, minced
1	tablespoon juniper berries, crushed
1	tablespoon freshly ground black pepper
½	teaspoon salt
3	bay leaves

Prepare venison roast as specified. Combine remaining ingredients and whisk to blend well. Lay butterflied roast out flat in a shallow container. Pour marinade over meat, cover and refrigerate for 6 to 8 hours, turning meat over every 2 hours. Remove meat from marinade. Starting from the shortest edge, roll roast tightly and tie securely. Roast in a pre-heated 450° F degree oven for 5 minutes. Reduce heat to 375° F and roast for an additional 15 minutes or until internal temperature reaches 135° F to 140° F. Remove roast from oven, let stand for 2 to 3 minutes. Remove string and slice into equal portions. Serve with a glass of Charles Spinetta Zinfandel.

KOREAN BARBECUED
VENISON STEAK

This recipe is inspired by an innovative home chef, Jeanne Bernardi, and was intended to be used with beef flank steak. I think it works equally well with all antlered game, particularly those cuts which can be a bit tough.

4 servings

2	pounds venison, sinew removed and cut into 4 equal portions and then each portion cut into 3 equal pieces
⅓	cup soy sauce
3	tablespoons sesame oil
3	garlic cloves, minced
3	tablespoons sesame seeds
⅓	teaspoon black pepper
2	teaspoons fresh ginger, minced or ½ teaspoon ground ginger
⅔	cup green onions, diced fine
⅓	cup brown sugar
12	bamboo skewers, soaked for 30 minutes in water

On a firm surface or cutting board, pound venison pieces with the flat side of a mallet into ½ inch thick strips. Combine remaining ingredients in a bowl, add meat and toss. Cover and refrigerate for 24 hours. (For faster turnaround use your FoodSaver vacuum packaging system). Skewer marinated meat on bamboo skewers and grill over white-hot coals or medium-hot gas barbecue for 2 to 3 minutes per side or until medium-rare.

BRANDY-PEPPERCORN
VENISON STEAK

For a low-fat version of this dish, omit the heavy cream

4 servings

4	7-ounce venison steaks, trimmed
1	tablespoon soft green peppercorns
1	tablespoon pink peppercorns
1	tablespoon black pepper, coarse ground
2	tablespoons whole grain mustard
2	tablespoons olive or peanut oil
2	garlic cloves, minced
½	cup game stock or beef broth
¼	cup brandy
½	cup heavy cream
	salt to taste

Combine peppercorns and black pepper in a bowl and mash together with a spoon. Coat venison steaks with mustard and rub peppercorn mixture over steaks. Heat oil in a large skillet over medium-high. Add garlic and sauté for 2 minutes. Add steaks and brown on both sides, about 3 to 4 minutes each side. Pour all but 1 teaspoon of the brandy over steaks and cook for 2 minutes. *Caution: Brandy may ignite! Keep away from any flame until alcohol burns off.*

Remove steaks from pan and keep warm. Add stock or broth, scraping pan with a spoon or spatula to loosen peppercorns, garlic and venison scraps and cook until liquid is reduced by one-half. Add cream and cook until sauce thickens. Place steaks on a plate and spoon equal quantities of sauce over each.

HERB - CRUSTED
ELK LEG ROAST

The herb crust adds remarkable flavor and seals in moisture

4 - 6 servings

1	2 ½ to 3 pound elk leg roast, boned, gristle and silver skin removed
1	cup dry red wine
2	tablespoons Worcestershire sauce
1	teaspoon coarse grind black pepper
¼	cup flour seasoned with salt and pepper
8	ounces butter, softened
2	tablespoons fresh rosemary, minced
2	tablespoons fresh sage, minced
1	tablespoon fresh thyme, minced
1	tablespoon fresh tarragon, minced
3	garlic cloves, minced
2	shallots, minced
¾	cup seasoned bread crumbs
1	teaspoon coarse ground black pepper

Combine wine, Worcestershire sauce and 1 teaspoon pepper for marinade. Marinate roast for 24 hours in refrigerator.

Pre-heat oven to 450° F. Remove roast from marinade and pat dry. *Herb Crust:* Sift seasoned flour over roast. Combine remaining ingredients to make a paste. Place the roast in a roasting pan and spread the paste evenly over top and sides of roast, applying hand pressure to help paste adhere to roast. Place in oven for 10 minutes, reduce oven temperature to 375° F and cook until center of roast is 135° F to 140° F, about 25 more minutes. Remove from oven and let stand for 10 minutes before carving into equal portions.

ELK TENDERLOIN
WITH CRISPY CORNMEAL CREPES AND FRESH PAPAYA

A combination of flavors, textures and presentation does justice to the choicest cut of antlered game

4 servings

2	pounds elk tenderloin, trimmed of fat and sinew
12	cornmeal crepes (see below)
1	cup sour cream
1	teaspoon freshly squeezed lemon juice
¼	teaspoon ground coriander
1	cup red bell pepper, finely diced
2	cups fresh papaya, peeled, seeded and diced into 1/4 inch cubes
1	cup red bell pepper, finely diced
¼	cup fresh cilantro leaves, diced
1	tablespoon freshly squeezed lime juice
¼	teaspoon ground cumin
	salt and freshly ground black pepper

Prepare cornmeal crepes as directed. Season tenderloin with salt and black pepper. Combine sour cream, lemon juice and coriander. Mix well to blend. In a separate bowl, toss papaya with remaining ingredients. Roast tenderloin in a 425° F oven until internal temperature is 135°F, about 8 to 12 minutes, depending on the thickness of the meat. Remove from oven and let stand for 3 to 4 minutes. Cut meat into 4 equal portions and slice each portion into 5 slices. Return to oven for a minute or two, if necessary, to warm meat. Fan 3 crepes across two-thirds of each plate, placing towards one side of the plates and leaving one-third of the plate uncovered. Place one-fourth of the sour cream mixture on the center of the plate, on the inside edges of the fanned crepes. Mound one-fourth of the papaya mixture on the center of the sour cream. Fan the tenderloin slices, overlapping the edges of each slice, against the papaya and towards the uncovered portion of the plates.

CORNMEAL CREPES

¾	cup flour	2	tablespoons butter, melted
¼	cup yellow cornmeal	1	cup water
1	medium egg	2	tablespoons beer
1	pinch salt		

In a medium bowl, combine flour and cornmeal. Add egg and salt and mix in. Mix in 1 tablespoon of the butter, a little at a time. Slowly mix in water and beat batter until creamy. Cover and refrigerate for 3 hours. Remove from refrigerator and stir in beer. Heat a crepe pan or small non-stick pan over medium- high heat and add remaining 1 tablespoon of butter. Wipe pan with towel. Ladle a small amount of batter onto center of pan, moving pan quickly to coat bottom with a very thin layer of batter. Cook until lightly browned, flip crepe and cook other side. If crepes do not crisp, place side by side on a baking sheet in a 400° F oven for 4 to 5 minutes.

STUFFED ELK ROAST
WITH SWEET AND SOUR ZINFANDEL SAUCE

Don't let the directions scare you. This preparation is easier than you may think and you'll get better with practice.

6 servings

1	2 ½ to 3 pound boneless elk shoulder roast
12	ounces peppered Monterey Jack cheese, grated
1	bunch fresh basil
6	ounces prosciutto, deli-shaved (have your butcher slice as thin as possible without shredding the prosciutto)
1	tablespoon fresh ground black pepper
3	garlic cloves, mashed into paste
	butcher string for tying roast
2	tablespoons olive oil

Butterflying Your Roast

Trim any excess fat, gristle and silver skin from the roast. Be careful not to make any deep knife cuts into the roast while trimming so that the butterflied roast will remain intact. Lay the roast on a cutting surface and begin butterflying by making a knife cut through the bottom third of the roast along the side, stopping about 3/4 of an inch before slicing through the roast. Open the roast at the "hinge" and make a second cut through the larger section, starting at the hinge, stopping the cut again 3/4 inch before slicing through the roast, following the path of the first cut. Flatten the roast with the palm of your hand.

Note: For especially thick roasts, butterfly the meat into four or five "hinged" sections.
Meat should be no more than 1/2 to 3/4 inches thick before stuffing.

Pick whole basil leaves and lay flat on the butterflied roast, covering the entire inside surface. Distribute the grated cheese evenly over the basil. Lay the prosciutto in strips over the cheese. Cut a piece of string 3 feet long. Begin rolling roast by folding, grasping an edge parallel to the hinges and folding the first inch of the edge over tightly. Continue rolling the roast carefully, tucking in the stuffing as the roast is rolled. Use both hands to insure that the roast is rolled as snugly as possible. Loop the string over one end and make a knot. Continue looping the string around the roast and pull the long end of the string through each loop, pulling tightly each time, until you reach the end of the roast. Tie off the string and cut off any excess. Rub garlic over the roast and coat with pepper.

In an oven-safe skillet over medium-high flame, heat olive oil. Place the roast in the skillet and sear until it is browned on all sides. Place skillet in a 375°F oven for 12 to 15 minutes or until meat is cooked to medium-rare. Remove roast from oven and let it sit for 5 minutes. Remove string and slice into 6 sections. Spoon sauce on each plate and place roast section on sauce.

EAST/WEST
VENISON MEDALLIONS

Asian and Western flavors team up to create this quick and delicious venison dish. Prepare ingredients ahead and stir-fry just before serving while your guests take in the magnificent aroma.

4 servings

1 ½   pounds boneless venison leg or shoulder roast, trimmed of silver skin and sinew
¼   cup low-sodium soy sauce
½   teaspoon sesame oil
½   cup dry red wine
3   tablespoons rice vinegar
1   teaspoon dried oregano
½   teaspoon dried thyme
¼   teaspoon chili powder
2   tablespoons molasses
1   tablespoon peanut oil
2   garlic cloves, minced
¼   medium red onion, coarsely chopped
½   medium red bell pepper coarsely chopped
¼   cup fresh basil, chopped
1   cup Chinese pea pods, ends and strings removed
¼   cup sliced water chestnuts
1   tablespoon cornstarch mixed with equal part cold water
       freshly ground black pepper to taste

Cut venison into 12 equal pieces. With the flat side of a mallet, lightly pound each piece into round medallions of approximately equal thickness. Combine next 8 ingredients and marinate medallions, covered, for 2 hours in refrigerator. Heat oil in a medium-high wok or large skillet and add garlic. Cook for 1 minute. Remove medallions from marinade and stir-fry for 2 minutes. Add onions and peppers and stir-fry for 2 minutes more. Add marinade and bring to boil. Add remaining ingredients and stir-fry until sauce thickens, about 2 to 3 minutes. Season with pepper and serve.

VENISON MEDALLIONS
WITH MUSHROOM SAUCE

The sauce is a velvety blend of fresh mushrooms, wine, cream and vegetables. Once you see just how easy it is to make the real deal, you'll think twice about using the canned goo in the future.

4 servings

Mushroom Sauce

2	tablespoons butter
2	tablespoons flour
½	cup chicken broth, cool
¼	cup dry white wine
¼	cup whipping cream
1	teaspoon Worcestershire sauce
	dash Tabasco
½	cup red and green bell pepper, diced
2	green onions, white and green part, diced
2	garlic cloves, minced
2	cups fresh mushrooms, thinly-sliced
	salt and pepper to taste
12	2 – 3 ounce venison medallions cut from the loin or eye of round
	salt and pepper
2	tablespoons olive oil
4	sprigs Italian parsley

Melt butter in a medium saucepan over medium heat. Stir in butter and cook while stirring until butter/flour mixture is smooth and beige in color, about 3 – 5 minutes. Stir in cool chicken broth, a little at a time, until incorporated. Stir in wine and cream until incorporated. Add remaining sauce ingredients and simmer for 10 – 12 minutes, stirring often.

Season medallions with salt and pepper. Heat oil in a large skillet over medium-high heat, add medallions and sear on both sides until medium-rare. To serve, spoon sauce on to plate, arrange medallions over sauce and garnish with parsley.

VENISON, MUSHROOM & BLUE CHEESE BURGER

Complaints are common regarding the lack of flavor from ground venison. The meat is very lean and can suffer miserably from overcooking. I often add some ground fatty meat to my ground venison to add flavor and moisture. In this instance, I have used a creamy cheese, onions and mushrooms for flavor. While most of us prefer to have our meat ground for us by a game processor shortly after harvest, you'll discover that freshly ground meat tastes better than previously ground and then frozen burger.

You can also trim up hunks of meat, freeze it and then thaw and grind into burger before cooking.

Makes 4 big burgers

1½	pounds ground venison
2	tablespoons butter
2	cloves garlic, minced
1	medium onion, finely diced
2	cups mushrooms, coarsely chopped
½	cup blue cheese crumbles
2	tablespoons breadcrumbs
	salt and pepper to taste
4	burger buns
4	lettuce leaves
4	slices tomato

Melt butter in a medium skillet over medium heat. Add onion and garlic until onions are translucent. Stir in mushrooms and sauté until soft. Transfer to a medium bowl and allow to cool. Add ground venison, blue cheese, breadcrumbs, salt and pepper and mix well with your hands to blend. Form into 4 large patties. Grill, pan-fry or broil patties until browned. Add to bun with lettuce, tomato and your choice of other condiments.

VENISON
WITH TOMATOES AND GREEN PEPPERS

This popular Chinese beef dish tastes even better with venison.

4 servings

1	pound venison round steak, sliced into ¼ inch thick strips
½	teaspoon freshly ground black pepper
2	tablespoons peanut oil
2	garlic cloves, minced
½	teaspoon fresh ginger, minced
¼	cup soy sauce
½	teaspoon sugar
1	large green bell pepper, cut into 1 inch squares
2	medium tomatoes, cored and cut into eighths
3	tablespoons cornstarch
¼	cup cold water

Season venison strips with pepper. Heat oil in a wok or large skillet over medium-high heat. Add garlic and ginger. Stir-fry 30 seconds. Add venison, and stir-fry for 2 minutes. Add soy sauce, sugar, peppers, cover and cook for 3 minutes. Add tomatoes, cover and cook for 2 minutes. Mix cornstarch with water and stir in a small amount at a time until sauce begins to thicken. Remove from heat and serve with steamed rice.

GRILLED VENISON CHOPS
WITH APRICOT-GINGER SAUCE

When you are short on time, try this easy dish.

6 servings

12 venison chops
¼ cup olive oil
2 teaspoons fresh garlic, minced
1 teaspoon fresh ginger, minced or ⅓ teaspoon powdered ginger
1 ounce unsalted butter
2 cups beef or game stock
¼ cup orange juice
⅓ cup apricot preserves
2 teaspoons cornstarch mixed with 2 teaspoons cold water

Sauce

In saucepan over medium heat, melt butter and sauté garlic and ginger for 3 to 4 minutes. Add stock, orange juice and apricot preserves and cook over medium-high heat until sauce is reduced to about 1 1/2 cups. Add cornstarch mixture as needed to thicken. Reduce heat to simmer or remove from heat and warm prior to serving.

Brush each venison chop with olive oil and grill on a barbecue or charbroiler until rare to medium rare. Place two chops on each plate and spoon sauce over each.

NEW MEXICO VENISON CHILI

The perfect cure for a winter chill. This version is a bit spicy, so reduce chipotle and/ or jalapeño chilies if you prefer a milder version.

6 - 8 servings

1	2 1/2 to 3 pound venison shoulder, sirloin or rump roast, cut into 1 inch cubes
¼	teaspoon salt
½	teaspoon cumin
½	teaspoon chili powder
4	tablespoons olive oil
4	strips smoked bacon, diced
1	large yellow onion, diced
2	Anaheim peppers, seeded and diced
1	medium red bell pepper, seeded and chopped
2	jalapeño peppers, seeded and diced very fine
	(see Caution, page 102 - Wild Boar Chile Verde)
5	garlic cloves, minced
1	4 ounce can chipotle chiles in adobo sauce
¼	teaspoon dried oregano flakes
1	tablespoon ground cumin
¼	teaspoon dried pepper flakes
3	tablespoons chili powder
4	cups canned pinto beans, drained
3	cups canned diced tomatoes, drained
¼	cup fresh cilantro, chopped
	salt to taste

In a paper bag or large bowl, toss venison with first 3 ingredients. Heat oil in large skillet over medium heat and brown seasoned meat evenly. Add bacon, cook 3 minutes. Add onion, peppers and garlic. Cook 3 to 4 more minutes or until onions become translucent, but not browned. Transfer contents of skillet to a large stock pot over medium heat and add remaining ingredients except cilantro and salt. Cover and cook until chili begins to bubble, stirring occasionally. Reduce heat to simmer, cover and cook until meat is tender, about 1 1/2 hours. Stir in cilantro, season with salt and serve.

ELK LOIN
With Asian Barbecue Sauce

Marinate your elk loin for just about 30 minutes in this spirited Asian marinade and sauce. You don't want to mask the flavors of the elk, just enhance them. If you don't have an elk loin handy, try this sauce with waterfowl, wild pig and any antlered game.

4 servings

2   pounds elk loin, all fat, gristle and silver skin carefully removed

Asian Barbecue Sauce

$^1/_4$	cup dry red wine
1	tablespoon olive oil
$^1/_2$	cup hoisin sauce
2	tablespoons grainy or Dijon mustard
4	garlic cloves, minced
$1^1/_2$	tablespoons soy sauce
1	teaspoon dark molasses
2	tablespoons ketchup
$^1/_4$	teaspoon red chili flakes

Combine all barbecue sauce ingredients and mix well. Place elk loin in a zipper-lock bag and our all but 1/2 cup of sauce into bag with elk. Squeeze out air and close securely. Let meat stand at room temperature for 30 minutes.

Place marinated elk on a medium-hot grill and cook evenly until medium-rare. To serve, slice across the grain into medallions and serve with sauce on the side.

STUFFED ELK
with Port Wine Sauce

This recipe calls for elk tenderloin, but you can use just about any of the large sections excised from the hindquarter or ham. The key is to remove all visible gristle, silver skin, etc. You'll find that you have beautiful hunks of meat, the texture and taste of which is comparable to the tenderloin.

4 servings

1 1/2	pounds elk tenderloin, silver skin removed
	salt and freshly ground pepper to taste
1/2	cup Gruyere or Swiss cheese, grated
1/4	cup breadcrumbs
2	cloves garlic, minced
2	green onions, minced
1	tablespoon fresh rosemary, minced

Port Wine Sauce

3	cups port wine
2	shallots, minced (or substitute the white part of 3 green onions)
2-3	fresh rosemary sprigs
1	tablespoon sugar
1/2	cup heavy cream
	salt and freshly ground pepper to taste

To prepare sauce, combine first 3 ingredients in a medium sauce pan and bring to a boil. Reduce heat to medium and reduce liquid, uncovered, to 1 cup. Strain out rosemary and shallots. Add sugar and cream and continue to reduce liquid to about 1 cup. Season with salt and pepper.

Cut elk into 4 relatively equal-sized pieces. With a sharp boning knife, cut a slit into each piece to form a pocket. Season inside and out with salt and pepper. In a bowl, combine cheese, breadcrumbs, garlic, onions and rosemary and stuff inside each piece of tenderloin. Place enough stuffing in each so that it is evenly distributed, but not overstuffed. You should be able to close the seam where you made the pocket. Place each seam side down in a baking pan. Roast in a preheated 400 degree oven for 7 – 8 minutes or until meat is evenly browned. Remove from oven and let stand for 3 – 4 minutes.

To serve, slice each stuffed tenderloin into 3 pieces. Arrange on plates. Spoon sauce over part of meat and spoon extra sauce onto plate.

HORSERADISH DEER BURGER

Serve with a dollop of South Carolina Barbecue Sauce.

4 servings

1	pound ground venison
¼	cup minced onion
1	teaspoon salt
½	teaspoon black pepper
1	dash Worcestershire sauce
½	tablespoon ketchup
½	cup seasoned breadcrumbs
1 - 2	tablespoons prepared horseradish
½	teaspoon ground sage
4	slices bacon
4	slices cheese, your choice
4	buns, lettuce and tomato

Mix venison well with next 8 ingredients. Shape into four patties. Wrap a piece of bacon around each patty and secure with toothpick or skewer. Broil, grill or pan sear each side until done. Melt cheese over top and serve in a bun with your choice of condiments.

VENISON ELIZABETH

Deer and strawberries? I know it sounds a bit odd, but you'll enjoy the balance of the sweet flavors of ripe berries and just enough balsamic vinegar to give it an acidic edge.

4 servings

2	pounds venison loin; all fat, gristle and silver skin removed
1/4	teaspoon coarse salt
1	teaspoon cracked black peppercorns
2	tablespoons olive oil
1/4	cup beef broth or game stock
1/2	cup dry red wine
1/4	cup balsamic vinegar
2	garlic cloves, minced
1	tablespoon fresh rosemary, minced
2	cups fresh ripe strawberries, quartered

Season venison with salt and pepper. Heat oil in a large skillet over medium-high heat and sear venison evenly until browned, but not cooked beyond rare. Add beef broth to the pan and stir to loosen bits. Add red wine and cook for 30 seconds. Remove venison from pan. Add vinegar, garlic and rosemary and reduce liquid by about two-thirds. Return venison to pan to warm. Add strawberries and cook about 1 minute. To serve, slice venison into medallions and top with strawberries and sauce.

GRILLED VENISON
with Balsamic Syrup

Whether you're a propane, charcoal or real wood cooker, make sure that the grill is lubricated and hot before putting game to flame.

4 servings

4	6 to 8 ounce venison round or loin steaks, trimmed of all fat, gristle and silver skin
$^1/_4$	cup olive oil
4	cloves fresh garlic, minced
2	teaspoons freshly-squeezed lemon juice
$^1/_2$	teaspoon garlic powder
$^1/_2$	teaspoon onion powder
$^1/_4$	teaspoon freshly ground black pepper
$^1/_4$	teaspoon kosher salt (or pinch of table salt)
1	red bell pepper, quartered
1	orange bell pepper, quartered
1	green bell pepper, quartered
8	jalapeño peppers, whole
8	green onions, white part and about 6 inches of the green tops
1 $^1/_2$	cups balsamic vinegar
$^1/_3$	cup brown sugar or honey

In a large bowl or plastic bag, combine all ingredients except vinegar and brown sugar. Toss to coat and let stand at room temperature for 1 hour. To make syrup, place balsamic vinegar and sugar in a small saucepan and reduce liquid to about 1/2 cup. Test syrup for sweetness. Add a little sugar or vinegar to your liking. Fire up the grill and grill vegetables and venison until just done. Venison should be juicy and not cooked beyond medium-rare. Veggies should be charred but still crisp, not burnt and limp.

To serve, arrange vegetables on plate. Top with venison and drizzle syrup over.

VENISON JERKY

A great way to use up a whole bunch of deer, this jerky recipe is particularly good with older, tough animals. If you don't have any deer meat, try it with trimmed skinless duck or goose breasts or any antlered game. Make sure that you remove any fat, gristle, silver skin, etc. before marinating the meat. This jerky is not brined or cured so it should be either refrigerated or frozen, if you plan on keeping it around for over 1 week.

2 - 3	pounds trimmed deer meat, sliced thinly into strips
1	teaspoon hoisin sauce
1	cup soy sauce
1	cup pineapple juice
1	tablespoon brown sugar
$^1/_3$	cup rice vinegar
1	teaspoon fresh ginger, minced
2	garlic cloves, minced
1	tablespoon (or more) Tabasco or Asian chili-garlic sauce

Combine marinade ingredients in a large bowl. Add meat and toss to coat evenly. Cover and refrigerate for 12 – 24 hours. Place meat strips on a cookie rack over a sheet pan and place pan in a 160 degree oven or dehydrator. Make sure oven door is cracked open about 1/2 inch so that moisture will escape. Meat should be dried in 4 – 5 hours.

SILVER SAGE VENISON CHILI

Silver Sage Caterers, founded by Greg Cornell and me, receives more requests for the chili recipe than any other item we prepare. Leftovers have been auctioned off at dinners we've catered for sporting groups such as California Waterfowl Association. For our signature beans, we use chunks of sirloin and linguica sausage. We substitute cubed venison shoulder for beef for this version. If you can't find linguica, use andouille or any good-quality smoked medium-hot sausage. If your sausage does not release a good bit of oil when cooked, you should add some vegetable oil to help brown the venison. I like to serve this with warm flour tortillas. It is important to stew the venison until tender. To do so, you may need to add some more diced tomato or salsa so that there is sufficient liquid to keep the meat moist while cooking.

8 to 10 servings

1	pound linguica sausage, diced
2	pound venison shoulder roast, trimmed of excess fat and gristle and then cut into 1/2-inch cubes
1	medium onion, diced
8	garlic cloves, minced
2	green bell peppers, seeded and diced
2	jalapeno peppers, seeded and finely diced
1	quart canned diced tomato, with juice
1	cup canned diced roasted green chiles
1	quart green chile salsa (or substitute tomato salsa)
2	tablespoons chile powder
2	teaspoons cumin
2	tablespoons dried oregano flakes
3	cups cooked pinto beans, drained
3-4	tablespoons tomato paste
¼	cup fresh cilantro, chopped
	salt, pepper and Tabasco to taste

In a large stockpot over medium heat, add linguica and cook until lightly browned. Add venison and brown evenly. Add next 4 ingredients and cook for a few minutes. Add diced tomato and next 5 ingredients and simmer until venison is tender. It will take 2 to 3 hours. Add additional salsa or tomato if necessary to keep meat moist while cooking. When meat is just tender, add beans, 2 tablespoons of the tomato paste and cilantro. Heat to warm beans. If you want to thicken the chili, add additional tomato paste as necessary. Season with salt, pepper and Tabasco.

ELK TOSTADA

Here's a way to make good use of antlered game neck and shoulder roasts. I like to season the meat liberally with salt, pepper, garlic powder and maybe some hickory or mesquite powder and then slow-roast them either in a conventional oven or, even better, a smoky barbecue. Once the meat is evenly browned and thoroughly cooked, it begins to pull away from the bone and gristle with ease. Your cooking time will vary according to the temperature and type of roasting apparatus used. As a general rule, an average elk shoulder roast will take about 3 to 4 hours at 350 degrees. Keep checking on the roast by pulling the meat from the roast. When it comes off easily, remove the roast from the oven and let stand for 15 to 20 minutes before pulling the meat.

4 servings

4	cups cooked pulled elk roast meat, warm (see above)
4	large corn tortillas, deep-fried until crispy
2	cups cooked black beans
6	cups romaine or iceberg lettuce, thinly chopped
8	thin slices red onion
2	cups peppered jack cheese, grated
$^1/_2$	cup chopped black olives
$1^1/_2$	cups red or green salsa
$^1/_4$	cup sour cream

For each serving, place a tortilla on a plate. Top with 1/2 cup black beans, 1 1/2 cups lettuce, 1 cup shredded elk, 2 slices red onion, 1/2 cup cheese, 2 tablespoons olives, some salsa and a dollop of sour cream.

ELK
With Barley Soup

I look forward to cold weather here in northern California so that I can enjoy a steaming bowl of soup. Any antlered game animal will do. Also, try this recipe with ducks or geese, but save it for less than premium species like divers and snow geese. I cannot overemphasize how much better the soup will taste if you make your own broth or stock from the carcasses and trim of your animals. Roast 'em with some vegetables and throw everything into a pot. Cover it with water, bring to a boil and simmer, uncovered, for 5 to 6 hours or, better yet, overnight. Save the liquid and discard the rest.

This recipe calls for onions, carrots and celery, but you can use whatever vegetables you have lying around. If you can't find barley, use rice, pasta or potatoes. I like to serve it with homemade croutons topped with some melted bleu cheese.

6 to 8 servings

	pounds elk meat, trimmed and cut into 1 inch cubes
2	salt and pepper
	tablespoons vegetable oil
2	large onion, diced
1	stalks celery, diced
4	carrots, diced
3	garlic cloves, minced
4	quarts game broth or beef broth
2	sprigs fresh rosemary (optional)
2	cups cooked barley (prepare as per package)
3	

Season meat liberally with salt and pepper. Heat oil in a large stock pot over medium-high heat, add meat and brown evenly. Add onion, celery, carrots and garlic. Cook 5 minutes or until onions are translucent. Add broth and rosemary and cook over medium heat until meat is soft. Depending on the cut of meat, it may take an hour or two. Remove rosemary and stir in barley. Serve with warm bread or croutons.

WILD PIG ENCHILADAS

In my opinion, the best way to cook wild pig or boar is by slow roasting or slow smoking over natural wood coals. Something about the flavor of seasoned smoky fall-off-the-bone pig just makes my mouth water. The smoking/roasting method takes a little time, but it's well worth it. If you don't have a smoker, use any non-propane barbecue and drop a few moist wood chunks onto the coals before adding meat. There will be more than enough cooked meat for the enchiladas. Use the leftovers for a great sandwich!

4 servings

2	pounds boneless wild pig loins
8-10	garlic cloves, minced
2	tablespoons ground cumin
2	tablespoons chili powder
⅓	cup tequila
3	tablespoons lemon juice
3	tablespoons lime juice
¼	cup honey
2	tablespoons freshly ground black pepper
1	teaspoon salt
	Tabasco sauce, as desired
1	medium yellow onion, chopped
3	cups homemade or canned enchilada sauce
8	corn tortillas
2	cups peppered jack cheese
1	cup fresh tomato, diced

Poke holes throughout the loins. Combine the next 10 ingredients in a non-reactive bowl. Place loins in bowl and toss to coat. Cover and refrigerate for 12 to 24 hours, turning occasionally.

Place loins in a medium-low heat smoker or barbecue and slow-cook until internal temperature is about 150 degrees, about 1 1/2 hours.

Remove and place in a baking dish, cover with onions and enchilada sauce and bake in a 375 degree oven for 1 hour or until meat starts to fall apart. Dip tortillas in pan sauce. Place pulled meat and a little cheese in each tortilla. Roll up and place seam side down in a baking dish. Top with remaining sauce and cheese and bake in a 375 degree oven until cheese is melted and lightly browned.

SOUPS AND STEWS

Upon returning from a cold, wet day in pursuit of wild game, nothing warms the body better than a heaping bowl of a hearty game stew. If I anticipate spending a long day in the field, I will prepare my soup or stew a day ahead and reheat it upon my return from the hunt. A simmering pot of game stew, a mixed greens salad, and a loaf of warm bread makes a casual and comfortable repast.

Soups and stews are relatively forgiving, and an excellent way for the inexperienced game cook to begin his or her pursuit of wild game cooking superiority. They typically simmer over low temperatures while the meat becomes tender and the flavors blend into an aromatic masterpiece.

While you develop your own signature stock pot creations, there are a few simple rules to follow. Always add the more delicate leafy fresh herbs such as basil, cilantro and parsley about 30 minutes or less before removing the dish from heat. Fresh herbs will lose the majority of their flavors if cooked for extended periods. Hardier herbs such as rosemary, sage and thyme may be added earlier without losing much flavor. With a few exceptions, I prefer to add fresh vegetables about 1 hour or less before the stew or soup is finished. Those who prefer their vegetables less crisp can add fresh vegetables earlier. Stock pots used for cooking stews and soups should be of heavier gauge, rather than thin-walled. Heavy-duty stock pots cook more evenly and are far less likely to burn the ingredients within.

Stews are a good way to make use of odds and ends and tougher cuts of meat; however, make certain that the fat and sinew is carefully trimmed from flesh to avoid the unpleasant taste of gristle and fat. Tip: Many of the following recipes make six or more servings. To prevent waste and spoilage, and have a delicious meal several days (or weeks) later, use your vacuum packaging system and store the pieces in your freezer until needed.

Make use of small quantities of assorted game meats for a unique dish. Keep in mind that large game meats will require more cooking time than upland game and ducks. When cooking with a combination of game animals, it is wise to add delicate game birds after big game cuts have been cooking for awhile. When cooking, do not allow the meat to cook so long that it disintegrates.

HEARTY BOAR SOUP

This soup, inspired by French Master Chef Paul Bocuse, makes good use of boar bones and frequently discarded scraps. If you can hot-smoke the bones and meat rather than roasting them, so much the better!

6 - 8 servings

3-4	pounds wild boar bones and joints with some meat attached
½	pound dried pinto beans, soaked overnight
½	pound dried white or navy beans, soaked overnight
3	quarts water
½	teaspoon salt
¼	teaspoon freshly ground black pepper
1	cup leeks, white part only, washed and diced
1 ½	cups carrot, diced into ¼ inch cubes
1 ½	cups zucchini, diced into ¼ inch cubes
1	cup green beans, strings removed and cut into ½ inch pieces
2	cup potatoes, diced into ½ inch cubes
3 ½	ounces dry small elbow macaroni pasta
6	garlic cloves, minced
1	cup fresh basil leaves
¾	cup olive oil
2	cups ripe tomatoes, peeled, seeded, chopped and drained
	salt and pepper
1	cup Parmesan cheese, freshly grated

Pre-heat oven to 375° F. Place boar pieces in roasting pan and roast in oven until well browned. Place soaked beans, browned boar and water in a large stock pot and bring to a boil. Reduce heat to low, add salt and pepper and simmer for 1 hour while skimming any foam or fat that rises to the surface. Add leeks, carrots, zucchini, green beans and potatoes, and continue simmering for an additional hour. Meanwhile, place 1/2 cup of the liquid from the stock pot, garlic and basil in a food processor or blender. Blend for 10 seconds. While processing at low speed, add the oil in a thin stream until emulsified. Add tomatoes and process for 2 to 3 seconds. Add pasta and cook until tender, about 15 minutes. Remove boar bones. Remove stock pot from heat and stir in mixture from processor. Let stand for 10 minutes. Serve in bowls and top with Parmesan cheese.

PORTUGUESE
VENISON STEW

The linguica sausage makes it "Portuguese." If linguica is unavailable, you can substitute one of your favorite spicy pork sausages. Top with garlic croutons.

6 to 8 servings

½ pound linguica sausage, sliced 1/4 inch
1   pound venison stew meat, cubed into 1 inch pieces
½ cup green bell pepper, coarsely chopped
½ cup red bell pepper, coarsely chopped
½ cup red onion, finely chopped
1   cup russet potato, peeled and cubed into1 inch pieces
3   garlic cloves, minced
4   cups game stock or beef broth
2   cups tomato, diced
1   teaspoon oregano flakes
1   tablespoon fresh rosemary, diced fine
2   bay leaves
½ teaspoon freshly ground black pepper
    salt to taste

In a large stockpot over medium-high heat, cook linguica slices until browned. Add onions and peppers and cook for an additional 3 minutes. Add venison and brown evenly. Stir in potatoes, stock, and garlic. Bring to a boil and reduce heat to simmer. Add oregano, rosemary, bay leaves and pepper. Cover and simmer until venison is tender, about 1 hour, depending on the quality of the meat. Remove bay leaves, add tomato and season with salt as desired.

RABBIT MULLIGATAWNY SOUP

Always one of my favorite year 'round soups. Try it with light-fleshed game birds as well.

2   cups cottontail rabbit or hare, cut into 1/2 inch cubes
¼   cup flour
1   teaspoon garlic powder
1   teaspoon salt
½   teaspoon freshly ground black pepper
3   tablespoons vegetable oil
¼   cup dry white wine
2   tablespoons butter
½   cup carrots, diced
½   cup celery, diced
⅓   cup red onion, diced
2   teaspoons Madras curry powder
1   quart game bird stock or chicken broth
2   garlic cloves, minced
1   pinch coriander
1   teaspoon freshly grated ginger
⅔   cup Granny Smith apple, diced into 1/4 inch cubes
1   cup cooked rice
½   cup diced tomato
   salt and white pepper

Combine flour, garlic powder, salt and ground black pepper. Place in a bag, add rabbit pieces and toss to coat thoroughly. In a medium size stock pot over medium-high flame, heat oil and sauté rabbit until browned. De-glaze pot with wine, scraping any bits from pan. Add butter and sauté carrots, celery and onion for 3 minutes. Sprinkle curry powder over contents of pan and stir to blend. Add stock, garlic, coriander and ginger. Bring to boil, stir and reduce heat to low. Cover and simmer for 20 minutes. Add apple cubes and rice. Cook 6 to 7 minutes more. Add diced tomato and season

UPLAND GAME BIRD
CHOWDER

Reminiscent of New England clam chowder, this dish is exceptional with a mixed bag of light-fleshed game birds such as quail, grouse, turkey or pheasant. Serve with warm sourdough bread.

8 servings

3	cups upland game birds, boned and cut into bite-sized pieces
16	slices lean bacon, coarsely chopped
1	cup yellow onion, finely chopped
½	cup green bell pepper, coarsely chopped
1	cup celery, coarsely chopped
1 ½	pounds new red potatoes, skin on and quartered
1	cup game bird stock or chicken broth
1	quart whole milk
1 ½	cups heavy cream
1	tablespoon Worcestershire sauce
1	teaspoon Tabasco sauce or similar hot sauce
	salt and white pepper to taste

In a large saucepan over medium heat, cook the bacon until crisp. Place on paper towels to drain. Discard all but 2 tablespoons of the bacon drippings, and sauté the onion, bell pepper, celery and potatoes for 3 to 4 minutes. Add the game bird pieces and continue to cook until the onions are translucent and the meat is lightly browned. Add the chicken stock, milk, cream and Worcestershire sauce and bring to a boil. Reduce heat to a simmer, add hot sauce. Stir occasionally and cook until the potatoes are tender. Add bacon and season with salt and pepper.

RESOLUTION STEW

Guaranteed to bring good luck for the New Year and a great way to utilize a variety of game meats. Stew can be prepared a day or two ahead.

8 - 10 servings

2-3 pounds varietal game meat, waterfowl and/or game birds, boned and cut into bite-sized pieces.
1 cup flour, seasoned with salt and pepper
¼ cup vegetable oil
½ pound bacon slices
2 celery stalks, chopped
1 medium onion, chopped
1 green bell pepper, chopped
2 carrots, diced
1 jalapeño pepper, seeded and finely diced
2 tablespoons garlic cloves, minced
1 16 ounce canned diced tomatoes, not drained
2 10 ounce packages frozen black-eyed peas
3 cups game stock or beef broth
1 tablespoon Worcestershire sauce
½ teaspoon chili flakes
2 bay leaves
salt and black pepper to taste

Coat game meat with seasoned flour. Heat oil in a large, heavy stock pot and add meat. Cook until evenly browned. Remove meat, add bacon and cook until crispy. Add celery, onions, peppers and carrots until onions become translucent. Add remaining ingredients, cover, and cook over low heat until meat is tender, about 2 to 3 hours.

SOUTHWESTERN SMOKED PHEASANTSOUP

A light and flavorful soup, best when fresh sweet corn is in season.

6 servings

2	Honey Mustard Smoked Pheasants (see page 149), meat pulled from the carcass in thin strips
½	cup peanut or corn oil
3	corn tortillas, cut into 1/4 inch strips
½	cup Monterey Jack cheese
1	quart game bird stock or chicken broth
1	tablespoon freshly squeezed lemon juice
¼	teaspoon ground cumin
⅛	teaspoon cayenne pepper
⅓	cup red bell pepper, diced
1	cup raw fresh sweet corn kernels
1	jalapeño pepper, seeded and diced fine
¼	cup fresh cilantro, chopped
	salt and freshly ground black pepper

In a medium sized skillet over medium-high flame, heat oil and fry tortilla strips until crispy. Lay fried tortillas on a sheet pan, sprinkle cheese over and bake in a 350° F oven until cheese is just melted. Remove from oven and cool. In a medium stock pot, heat stock, lemon juice, cumin and cayenne pepper to boil. Add pheasant, bell pepper, corn and jalapeño and cook for 5 minutes. Stir in cilantro, season with salt and pepper. Ladle soup into bowls and garnish with tortilla strips.

WILD TURKEY TORTILLA SOUP

Adapted from The No Salt, Lowest Sodium Light Meals Book by Donald A. & Maureen A. Gazzaniga, This delicious recipe will show all you hunters who are in need of a no salt lifestyle that you can still hunt, cook, and fish and enjoy life without added salt. You can freeze some of this soup either in Mason jars or in plastic containers for up to 3 months. Note: Make broth the day before you make the soup so you can chill the broth and skim the fat off. (The broth for this soup is on the next page.) Sodium levels are listed with each ingredient.

Makes 12 cups

Sodium Per Recipe: 751.4 mg sodium
Sodium Per Cup: 62.6 mg sodium

⅓	cup chopped onion (1.584. mg)
3	cloves garlic, peeled & chopped (1.53 mg)
¾	teaspoons ground cumin (2.646 mg)
¾	teaspoon dried oregano (.169 mg)
¼	teaspoon no-salt chili powder* (trace)
¼	teaspoon pepper (.704 mg)
8	cups homemade turkey broth (77.6 mg)
1	14-ounce can diced no-salt-added tomatoes (75 mg)
1	4-ounce can diced green chilies (80 mg)
1	14-ounce can no salt corn or 1 10-ounce package of frozen, unsalted corn (14.2 mg)
10	corn tortillas (no salt in ingredient list of tortillas) (6" wide) (trace)
1 ½	pounds cooked wild turkey meat** (432 mg)
2	Tablespoon chopped fresh cilantro (5.184 mg)
8	ounces (approximately) Low Sodium Cheddar*** (80 mg)
	Optional garnish: 1 firm ripe avocado (20.8 mg)

In a 5-6 quart nonstick pan or other pan sprayed with olive oil, over medium heat, sauté onion for 5 minutes or until translucent, then add garlic, cumin, oregano, chili powder and pepper until spices are fragrant, about 1 minute. Add 8 cups of the turkey broth, tomatoes (including juice) and green chilies. Cover and bring to a boil over high heat.

Meanwhile, stack tortillas and cut into 1/8-inch wide strips. Add to boiling broth. Reduce heat, cover; simmer for 15 minutes, stirring occasionally.

Cut cooked turkey meat into ½ inch pieces. Peel the avocado if using, pit and thinly slice.

Add turkey and corn to broth. Make sure the turkey gets heated through. Stir in cilantro. Ladle into soup bowls, garnish with avocado, and add cheese to taste. May freeze leftover for future use.

*Grandma's Chili Powder is a national brand that does not add salt to chili powder.
**Or cooked domestic white turkey meat.
***Brands include Heluvagood and Rumiano.

WILD TURKEY BROTH

Adapted with permission from The No Salt, Lowest Sodium Light Meals Book by Donald A. & Maureen A. Gazzaniga

Use carcass from any of your wild turkey recipes including the Roasted Wild Turkey on page 92 for this wonderful soup broth. You can also use the carcass of a domestic turkey to make this broth. Broth will freeze well for up to 3-months. Sodium levels per ingredient in parenthesis after each ingredient.

Makes: 12 cups

Sodium Per Recipe: 394.1 mg
Sodium Per Cup: 32.8 mg

1	large cooked wild turkey carcass* (217.9 mg)
12	ounces turkey meat, no salt, cooked, attached to bones** (135.2 mg)
1	large onion, quartered (4.5 mg)
3	celery tops (34.8 mg)
2	teaspoons Don's Flavor Enhancer*** (1.721 mg)

Cover turkey carcass with water in large stovetop pan. (Usually a 12-quart or larger pan needed). Bring to boil, then simmer, covered for about 2 to 3 hours. When done, cool and strip meat from bones. Throw bones away. Cool in refrigerator overnight. Separate fat from broth. (Make sure all bones are removed so that very small bones don't show up later in your soups. Store in quart sized Mason jars in refrigerator for up to 2 weeks. Use immediately to make terrific "turkey broth" soups. See our Low Sodium Vegetable Soup for your first effort.

*Based on one-pound turkey frame, wild or domestic, stripped.
**Estimated amount of turkey meat left on handpicked frame after serving meat from whole turkey.
***Replaces salt. Borrowed from *The No Salt, Lowest Sodium Light Meals Book.* To make, mix together 1/2 teaspoon onion powder, 1/3 teaspoon unsalted garlic powder, 1/4 teaspoon paprika, 1/3 teaspoon dry mustard powder, 1/4 teaspoon ground thyme, 1/4 teaspoon white pepper, 1/3 teaspoon celery seed and a pinch of ground cloves.

COOKING WITH SMOKE

Choice of wood for smoking is a matter of personal preference. I like fruit wood, which is found in abundance in many areas of the United States. I've had good luck with pear wood. You can purchase chips or chunks of wood, or gather green wood and chop them into small pieces yourself.

If you do not have a conventional smoker, you can utilize your gas grill or barbecue kettle with surprisingly good results. Put a handful or two of wood chips which have been soaked in water for 30 minutes in a disposable foil pan and place the pan directly on the lava rock on one side of the gas grill. Set the meat to be smoked over the pan as the wood chips begin to smoke. Since removing a hot barbecue grate can be an unnerving experience, you may not be able to finish the meat with smoke, but the flavor of smoke will permeate the flesh. In a barbecue kettle, spread ash-white hot coals around the sides of the bottom grate and sprinkle soaked wood chips over the coals. Place the meat in the center of the grill, away from direct heat and place the lid over the kettle.

I have enjoyed some outstanding meats cooked in makeshift smokers made from 50 gallon metal drums. A fire box is constructed out of metal around the outside of the opening. The heat is controlled by partially opening or closing the lid. The fire box is stoked with a mixture of green and seasoned pear wood. The smoke and fire is drawn into the drum by the draft created by the top opening. A group of close friends host an annual free duck feed where 200 ducks are slow-cooked in such contraptions with excellent results. Everyone contributes a duck or two and a raffle is held to raise money for the next year's side dishes and beverages. The birds are seasoned only with salt and pepper, yet the flavor and tenderness is sensational.

Experience and personal preference will tell you when to remove meat from smoke. Keep in mind that you can always finish an underdone game dish in an oven or by placing it back in the smoker. Over-smoked game will dry out much as it does with other cooking methods. The resulting meat will be tough and chewy and may taste more like charcoal than wild game.

Experiment with smoking any game for 15 minutes with a heavy smoke prior to preparing as specified in other recipes. Game stews and roasts will greatly benefit from the smoky flavor, recalling the aroma of camp cooking after a long day afield. Smoke seasoned game birds make an excellent salad tossed with crisp mixed greens, sunflower seeds and a fresh raspberry vinaigrette. The many uses of smoked game is limited only by your imagination.

If you find that smoking fish and game is your thing, take a serious look at Cookshack Smokers. Their smoker ovens are built to last for decades and the quality of the meat produced by a Cookshack smoker is the absolute best. My favorite go-to smoker is Cookshack's AmeriQue. Check them out at www.Cookshack.com.

GARLIC SMOKED
WILD TURKEY

I have a weakness for garlic. Lots of garlic. If you are not quite so inclined, reduce the portion of garlic in this recipe accordingly. The vegetables will add a little moisture during prolonged smoking and can be served as a side dish. Carve the meat from the smoked bird and serve with Grilled Red Bell Pepper Sauce (see page 167).

4 servings

⅓	garlic cloves
⅓	yellow onion, quartered
2	celery stalks, cut into 2 inch pieces
	carrot, cut into 1 inch pieces
1	tablespoons fresh parsley, minced
½	bay leaves
½	teaspoon salt
½	teaspoon freshly ground black pepper
1	cup olive oil
2	large tom turkey, skin intact
	strips smoked bacon

Stuff turkey with onion, celery, carrot, parsley, bay leaves and 2 cloves of garlic. Cut in half. Truss legs. Mince 6 garlic cloves and combine with salt, pepper and olive oil. Rub mixture over turkey and refrigerate for 2 to 3 hours. Mince remaining 2 garlic cloves and add to water pan in water smoker or to a water pan added to a dry smoker, close to the heat source. Place bacon over turkey breast and smoke at approximately 150°F for 4 to 5 hours or until breast meat close to the rib cage reaches 145°F. Remove bacon and let stand for 15 minutes before carving.

SMOKED BOAR TENDERLOIN
WITH BALSAMIC CHERRY SAUCE

This preparation works best with a barbecue kettle with hot coals seasoned with soaked fruit wood chips. Skewer large earthy mushrooms and add to the barbecue about half way through the cooking process for a great side dish.

4 servings

3	garlic cloves
1	teaspoon freshly ground black pepper
½	teaspoon ground allspice
¼	cup brown sugar
2	pounds, boar tenderloins, trimmed of fat and sinew
1	cup Balsamic Cherry Sauce (see page 172)

Combine first 4 ingredients and rub over tenderloins. Cover and refrigerate for 3 to 4 hours. Soak 3 cups fruit wood chips in water for 30 minutes. Prepare sauce and keep warm. Place briquettes or wood chunks to one side of barbecue and burn until coals are ash-white. Drain wood chips and sprinkle over coals. Wait until wood chips begin to smoke. Place lightly greased grill over coals, leave vents open just a bit and place tenderloins on grill, away from coals. Smoke for 10 minutes and then move tenderloins over coals. Cook until medium or until internal temperature reaches 140°F. For each serving, slice tenderloin into 1/4 inch slices, arrange on plate and spoon sauce over half of slices.

SMOKED DUCK
WITH A CITRUS GLAZE

Try this preparation with a trio of plump drake mallard, canvasback or black ducks. There is actually enough marinade for a few more ducks if you have a surplus or a big appetite. Perhaps you could smoke a couple of extra birds for a sandwich or salad during the week.

6 servings

4-6	large ducks, skin intact
1	cup orange juice
1	cup grapefruit juice
¼	cup freshly squeezed lemon juice
¼	cup freshly squeezed lime juice
1	cup dry white wine
½	cup soy sauce
2	dashes Tabasco
½	cup brown sugar
2	teaspoons fresh ginger, minced
½	teaspoon ground coriander
¼	teaspoon white pepper
½	teaspoon freshly ground black pepper
¼	cup maple syrup
½	cup orange marmalade
2	large navel oranges, peeled and cut into wedges
3-4	sprigs fresh cilantro

Rinse ducks inside and out with cold water and pat dry with paper towels. Combine next 11 ingredients, stir to mix well and pour over ducks. Cover and refrigerate 12 to 24 hours. Remove ducks from marinade and air dry for 1 hour. Transfer marinade to a large sauce pan over medium-high heat and reduce liquid to 1 cup. Add black pepper, maple syrup and marmalade and heat to blend ingredients. Smoke ducks with low heat (125° F or less) for 2 hours. Transfer to a baking dish.

Baste with a little sauce, reserving about 1 cup, and bake in a 425° F oven for 6 to 8 minutes until skin is crisp and internal temperature is 135° F to 140°F. Remove ducks from oven and let stand for 5 minutes. Carve breasts from breastbone and remove legs and thighs. Slice breasts diagonally into 1/2 inch slices. Arrange sliced breasts around the outside edges of a large serving platter. Place legs in the center of the platter, garnish platter with oranges and cilantro and serve with warmed reserved sauce.

ANGEL HAIR PASTA
WITH SMOKED DUCK AND MUSHROOMS

Thin-sliced smoked duck team up with delicate angel hair pasta and fresh mushrooms. Although the recipe does not specify a particular type of mushroom, use the more earthy and flavorful varieties such as portabella, porcini, chanterelle or morel.

4 servings

4 - 6	large smoked boneless duck breasts, skin intact and sliced diagonally into ¼ inch thick strips
1	tablespoon olive oil
4	tablespoons butter
1	shallot, finely diced
2	garlic cloves, minced
2	cups fresh mushrooms, hard part of stems removed and stems and caps sliced thick
1	cup game bird stock or chicken broth
¼	cup fresh parsley, minced
½	cup tomatoes, seeded and diced
	salt and freshly ground black pepper to taste
5	cups hot, cooked angel hair pasta freshly grated Parmesan cheese

Heat olive oil and 2 tablespoons of butter in a large skillet over medium heat. Add shallot and garlic, sauté 2 to 3 minutes. Add mushrooms and sauté until they release juices. Add game bird stock, increase heat to medium-high and cook, uncovered for 5 minutes. Add duck, parsley and tomatoes. Stir to warm. Remove from heat and stir in remaining 2 tablespoons butter. Serve over pasta and garnish with cheese.

GOOSE JERKY

Comparing the taste of a delicious plump Speckled Goose to a lean Snow Goose is like comparing filet mignon to hamburger. I would usually choose hamburger over the Snow Goose. To make them edible however, I turn Snow Geese into jerky. This recipe works very well with other species, too.

    4   goose breast halves, skin, silver skin
        and all gristle removed and sliced across
        the "grain" into 1/4 inch thick strips
    1   cup Worcestershire sauce
    ½   cup low-salt soy sauce
    6   garlic cloves, minced
    2   teaspoons fresh ginger, grated (optional)
    ¼   cup Balsamic vinegar
    ½   cup honey or 2/3 cup brown sugar
    ¼   cup cracked black pepper
    2   tablespoons chili flakes

Thoroughly rinse sliced goose strips with cold water and drain well. Combine remaining ingredients in a sauce pan and heat to blend flavors and dissolve honey or sugar. Cool marinade and toss in a large bowl with goose strips. Cover and refrigerate for 12 hours, tossing occasionally to marinate evenly. Remove meat from marinade. Lay on a rack or screen in a smoker with low heat (below 125° F) and smoke for 8 to 10 hours or until jerky is thoroughly dried. Cool and store in a jar with a tight-fitting lid or a FoodSaver vacuum sealed bag. Jerky may also be frozen indefinitely and thawed as needed.

Note: Jerky can be prepared without a smoker by laying the marinated strips on a sheet pan and baking at very low temperature in a conventional oven for about 4 to 5 hours..

SMOKED PHEASANT
WITH PISTACHIO PESTO CREAM SAUCE

The birds are flavored, not fully cooked in the smoker and then sautéed to retain moisture. Great with angel hair pasta.

6 - 8 servings

Pistachio Pesto Cream Sauce (see page 169)

4	pheasants, halved with skin intact

Prior to smoking, marinate the pheasants in the following:

2	cups water
2	cups dry white wine
1	cup soy sauce
6	garlic cloves, minced
½	teaspoon sesame oil
½	cup green onions, diced fine
1	cup brown sugar
2	lemons, juiced

Mix in a very large bowl or tub and add pheasant halves, coating all surfaces with marinade. Cover and refrigerate for 10 to 12 hours, turning pheasants every 3 hours. Remove from marinade and air dry in a cool place for 2 to 3 hours prior to smoking. Smoke for 2 hours with low heat and your favorite fruit wood. Remove from smoker and carefully remove meat from bones, keeping meat pieces and skin intact.

Prepare Pistachio Pesto Cream Sauce found in the Game Sauces section of this book.

Sauté smoked meat in a large skillet with 2 tablespoons olive oil, 1/4 cup white wine and 1 teaspoon minced fresh garlic until just cooked. Meat should be a little pink. Slice breasts and thighs and arrange around pasta. Spoon sauce over pheasant slices.

HONEY MUSTARD
SMOKED PHEASANT

This sweet smoked pheasant is great as an appetizer, cubed in a salad or sliced and sauced as an entrée. Smoked pheasants can be wrapped tightly or vacuum-sealed and frozen for up to 6 months.

Requires 4 pheasants

2	cups dry white wine
1	cup honey
½	cup whole grain or dijon mustard
3	tablespoons freshly squeezed lemon juice
4	garlic cloves, minced
¼	cup soy sauce
1	tablespoon fresh thyme, minced
2	tablespoons freshly ground black pepper
¼	cup olive oil
4	pheasants, skin intact and cut in half along breastbone and backbone

Combine first 4 ingredients in a medium sauce pan over medium heat, bring to boil and stir to blend ingredients. Remove from heat, cool, add garlic, soy sauce, thyme and pepper and whisk in olive oil, a little at a time. Rinse pheasants in cold water and pat dry with paper towels. Place in a container and pour marinade over pheasants. Cover and refrigerate for 12 hours, turning occasionally to marinate evenly. Remove from marinade and allow to air-dry for one hour before smoking. Place in a water smoker or a dry smoker with a pan of water placed close to the heat source. Smoke for 3 to 4 hours over low heat (approximately 150° F) or until pheasant breast reaches internal temperature of 145° F.

SIDE DISHES

A handful of my favorite accompaniments for wild game dishes may be found in this section.

Your choice of side dishes should be dictated by what is available at your local market. I usually visit the produce section *before* choosing a side dish, so that I can determine which seasonal fruits, vegetables and herbs look good at the time. Although much of the produce appearing in our markets is available year around, the flavor of those items which have been imported are usually not as pronounced as ripe local varieties.

Choose side dishes that complement your main course in both color and flavor. If your game dish is dark in color, prepare a colorful side dish such as an assortment of mixed vegetables. Monochromatic plates are less pleasing to the eye than those that have been assembled with more thought and planning. If my choice of entrée is based on a selected ethnicity such as Thai or Asian, I select side dishes that are indigenous to the region, but do not contain the same ingredients as the entrée. Thusly, you won't bring together two similar dishes that compete with each other.

CORN CAKES

4 servings

2 cups fresh sweet corn kernels
⅓ cup red bell pepper, diced fine
¼ cup green onion, diced
¼ cup fresh cilantro leaves, minced
½ cup seasoned bread crumbs
1 teaspoon baking powder
¼ teaspoon salt
⅛ teaspoon freshly ground black pepper
2 eggs
¼ cup peanut or vegetable oil

Combine all ingredients except oil. Mix thoroughly. Divide mixture into 4 equal portions. Divide each portion in half and form a small patty out of each piece, pressing down between your hands to firm up each cake. Heat oil in a large skillet over medium-high heat. Brown each cake lightly on both sides. Serve immediately or transfer to a baking dish, cover with foil and keep warm in a 200° F oven for up to 30 minutes.

GARLIC MASHED POTATOES

4 -6 Servings

3 pounds baking potatoes, peeled and quartered
⅓ cup sour cream
2 tablespoons butter
3 garlic cloves, roasted in a 350° F oven until softened and lightly browned, then   mashed into a c oarse paste
salt and pepper to taste

Place potatoes in a stock pot, cover with water and add 1 teaspoon salt. Boil, covered, for 20 minutes until potatoes are cooked. Remove stock pot from heat. Drain potatoes in a colander, return to stock and mash. Add remaining ingredients and mash until light and fluffy.

WILD RICE PILAF

6 - 8 servings

4 ounces butter
1 medium onion, chopped
2 celery stalks, diced
1 large carrot, diced
½ cup slivered almonds
1 cup wild rice
1 cup brown rice
2 cups fresh mushrooms, chopped
2 cups game stock, game bird stock or beef broth

In a large skillet, melt butter over medium-high heat and sauté next 4 ingredients for 2 to 3 minutes. Add rice and mushrooms and sauté for 4 minutes more. Transfer contents of skillet to a casserole dish, stir in broth, cover and bake in a pre-heated 350° F oven for 1 hour.

BOAR FRIED RICE

4 servings

¼ pound wild boar trim, fat removed and diced into ¼ inch cubes
2 tablespoons peanut oil
½ teaspoon salt
½ teaspoon sugar
1 garlic clove, minced
⅓ cup green onion, diced
½ cup celery, diced
2 cups chilled cooked white rice
1 cup bean sprouts
¼ cup soy sauce
3 eggs, lightly beaten

In a wok or large skillet over high heat, heat oil and add boar, salt and sugar. Cook for 3 - 4 minutes. Add onions, celery and garlic and stir-fry for 2 minutes. Add rice and bean sprouts and stir-fry for 1 minute. Stir in soy sauce, move rice to sides of wok or skillet and add eggs to center. Cook eggs until set, scramble and stir into rice.

GRILLED VEGETABLES
WITH COMPOUND BUTTER

4 servings

6 ounces butter, softened
¼ cup fresh basil, minced
2 tablespoons lemon rind, yellow part only, minced
2 zucchini, sliced lengthwise into 4 slices
1 small red onion, sliced into 4 slices lengthwise into 2 slices
1 red bell pepper, seeded and quartered

2 tablespoons red wine vinegar
2 garlic cloves, minced
½ teaspoon dried basil flakes
½ teaspoon dried oregano flakes
¼ teaspoon chili flakes
¼ cup olive oil

Divide butter in half. Blend one half with basil and the other half with lemon rind. On a piece of wax paper, spread basil mixture on the center to form a rectangle about 1 ½ inches wide by 3 inches long. Place in refrigerator for 10 minutes. Spread lemon mixture over cooled layer. Fold wax paper over, twist ends and form into a cylinder. Place in freezer for 1 hour. Remove from freezer 10 minutes before slicing.

Prepare vegetables as indicated. In a medium bowl, combine vinegar, garlic and dried seasonings. Whisk in oil, a little at a time. Add vegetables, toss and marinate for 1 hour, tossing occasionally. When barbecue coals are ash-white or gas grill is medium-hot, place carrot and onion pieces on grill. Cook until grill marks appear on down side. With tongs, turn carrot and onion over and arrange remaining vegetables on grill. Remove all vegetables when marked on both sides. Cooked vegetables should be a little crisp. Transfer to a serving dish and top with sliced compound butter.

MUSHROOM SAUTE

4 - 6 servings

2 tablespoons butter
¼ cup dry white wine
1 garlic clove, minced
1 pound fresh assorted mushrooms (porcini, crimini, portabella, etc.), hard part of stems removed and caps and stems sliced thinly
   salt and freshly ground black pepper to taste
⅓ cup pecan pieces, lightly toasted in a 350° F oven
2 tablespoons fresh parsley, chopped
1 teaspoon fresh rosemary, minced

In a large skillet over medium heat, melt butter, add wine and garlic and cook for 3 minutes. Add mushrooms, cook 4 to 5 minutes, stirring occasionally. Season with salt and pepper. Add remaining ingredients, stir and cook for 2 minutes more.

VEGETABLE WONTONS

Your guests will beg for more.

25 Won Tons

1	tablespoon soy sauce
2	tablespoons dry sherry
½	cup carrots, gratedcup celery, diced fine
½	teaspoons peanut oil
2	garlic cloves, minced
2	tablespoon fresh ginger, grated
1	green onions, chopped fine
2	egg yolks
2	cup mushrooms, minced
½	cup water chestnuts, chopped
⅓	won ton wrappers
25	peanut oil for trying

Dipping Sauce:

¼	cup soy sauce
¼	cup rice vinegar
2	tablespoons hot chili oil

In a non-reactive bowl, combine first four ingredients. Let stand for 15 minutes. In a hot wok or large skillet over high heat, heat 2 teaspoons peanut oil and carrot, celery, marinade and next 6 ingredients. Stir-fry for 4 minutes. Remove contents and cool.

Place about 1 tablespoon of mixture on the center of each won ton wrapper. Lightly moisten the edges of each wrapper and fold over, forming a half circle. Press down firmly along all edges. Heat peanut oil over medium-high heat in a small deep sauce pan or deep fryer. Fry won tons a few at a time, until golden brown. Transfer to paper towels to drain. Combine dipping sauce ingredients and serve with won tons.

POTATO AND APPLE PANCAKES

6 servings

1 ½   pounds baking potatoes, washed and peeled
2   Granny Smith apples, peeled and cored
2   large eggs
1   medium onion
1   dash nutmeg
¾   teaspoon salt
¼   teaspoon freshly ground
      black pepper
3   tablespoons flour
½   cup vegetable oil

Grate potatoes and apples with a hand grater or food processor fitted with a grating disk. Place grated potatoes and apples into a large bowl of ice water. Let stand for 20 minutes. Drain well and pat dry with paper towels or a clean dish towel. Wipe out bowl and combine remaining ingredients except oil, mixing well. Add potatoes and apples and mix thoroughly to coat evenly. Divide mixture in half and make 6 equal portions out of each. Form each portion into a ball. Add enough oil to just cover the bottom of a large skillet evenly. Heat to medium-high. Place a few portions at a time into the oil, flatten out with a spatula and brown on both sides. Remove cooked pancakes and place on paper towels to drain. Allow 2 pancakes per person.

JULY 4TH GREEN BEANS

Chilled colorful side dish for a warm summer lunch or dinner.

4-5 servings

¼   cup chopped fresh basil
2   garlic cloves, minced
1   tablespoon lemon juice
1   tablespoon dijon mustard
1   tablespoon honey
¼   teaspoon freshly ground black pepper
1   pinch salt
½   cup rice vinegar
¼   cup of olive oil
3   cups blanched fresh green beans
½   each: red, yellow and orange bell peppers, eeded and sliced into
          1/4 inch thick strips
⅓   cup slivered almonds, lightly coated with sugar and baked in a 325° F oven
          until golden brown
⅓   cup crumbled gorgonzola or bleu cheese

In a medium bowl, combine first 6 ingredients. Add olive oil while whisking vigorously. Add remaining ingredients, toss to coat well. Cover and refrigerate for 1 hour.

TWO-COLOR POLENTA

Colorful side dish is a wonderful substitute for standard starch dishes such as rice or potatoes. Great with marinara or grilled red bell pepper sauces.

6 - 8 servings

3 ½	cups chicken broth
½	teaspoon salt
1	cup dry polenta
2	tablespoons butter
1	cup fresh basil, minced
½	cup pine nuts, roasted in 325° F oven until lightly browned
½	cup Parmesan cheese.
1	cup gorgonzola cheese, crumbled

In a medium sauce pan, bring chicken broth and salt to a boil. Gradually stir in polenta, reduce heat to simmer and cook, stirring constantly, for 20 to 25 minutes. Blend in butter.

In a blender or processor, add basil, pine nuts and parmesan cheese. Process to mix ingredients and grind nuts. Lightly grease a 9" pie pan. In a bowl, add 1/2 of polenta and mix well with basil mixture. Place contents of bowl into bottom of pie pan and spread smooth with spatula. Rinse bowl and place remaining polenta in bowl. Mix in cheese and carefully spread mixture over first layer. Place in 350° F oven for 45 minutes. Remove from oven and let stand for 1 hour to set. Slice into wedges and warm in a 250° F oven to serving temperature.

FISH RUB

Rubs are usually associated with something you put on meat. Mix up a bunch of dry or fresh herbs, salt and pepper and plaster the mixture onto a big steak or roast. The flavor of the rub penetrates the meat after several hours and adds remarkable flavors. Rubs are also great on fish, but I tend to use less pronounced flavors in the mix since there's virtually no fat to dilute the taste of a spicy rub. This is great on dorado, yellowtail, striped bass and salmon.

4 servings

2	teaspoons garlic powder
2	teaspoons Kosher salt
1	tablespoon freshly ground black pepper
¼	teaspoon cayenne pepper
2	teaspoons ground cumin
2	teaspoons dried oregano leaves (or 3/4 teaspoon ground oregano)
1	teaspoon paprika
¾	teaspoon brown sugar
2	tablespoons olive oil
1	2 lb. striper fillet (or 4 6 – 8 ounce fillets)
⅓	cup mayonnaise
1	tablespoon lime juice
	pinch granulated sugar

Combine first 8 ingredients in a small bowl. Rub fish with olive oil and then rub dry ingredients into fish. Wrap in plastic wrap for 8 – 12 hours. Remove plastic wrap and grill or broil fish until just cooked, but not overcooked. Combine mayo, lime juice and granulated sugar and put a dollop of the mixture on top of the fish.

BASIC DRY RUB FOR JERKY

A good way to start your batch of jerky. A little sweet, a little spicy.

For 2 lbs of meat

- 2 teaspoons Kosher salt
- 1 teaspoon freshly ground black pepper
- 1 teaspoon garlic powder
- ½ teaspoon cayenne pepper
- 1 tablespoon brown sugar

Combine ingredients. Coat meat slices on both sides, cover. Refrigerate for 12 - 24 hours before drying.

REALLY GOOD GARLIC BREAD

Originally called, "World's Greatest Garlic Bread", but it may be a bit of a stretch. Food is subjective and who's to say they've got the greatest? How about "Really Good Bread"?

- 1 pound loaf crusty sourdough bread, split lengthwise
- ½ cup melted butter
- ½ cup mayonnaise (yes, mayonnaise)
- ⅓ cup sweet yellow onion, finely diced
- 3 tablespoons (or more) garlic cloves, minced
- 2 tablespoons fresh basil leaves, chopped
- 1 tablespoon fresh oregano leaves, chopped
- ⅔ cup shredded Parmesan cheese
- ½ cup jack cheese
- ½ cup cheddar cheese

Combine all stuff and spread on inside halves of bread. Place on a baking sheet and bake in a preheated 400 degree oven until lightly browned.

DUCK SAUSAGE

By request from Jeff Smalley of Auburn, Alabama. Jeff wants to know what to do with all of the coots, spoonbills and mergansers he shoots. I use the recipe for widgeon, gadwall, etc. This makes a great breakfast sausage.

4 to 6 servings

    2 cups duck breasts
    1 cup boneless pork shoulder
    2 tablespoons butter
    ⅓ cup yellow onion, finely diced
    1 celery stalk, finely diced
    1 jalapeno pepper, seeded and finely diced
    3 garlic cloves, minced
    ¼ cup orange juice
    ½ teaspoon cracked black pepper
       salt to taste
    1 egg
       vegetable oil for sautéing

Place duck and pork shoulder in a food processor and grind thoroughly. Place ground mixture in a large bowl.

Heat butter in a skillet and sauté onion, celery, jalapeno and garlic until onion is translucent. Add orange juice and cook until liquid reduced by one-half. Add pepper and salt to taste. Remove from heat and allow to cool. Add mixture to bowl with ground duck, etc. Add egg and mix thoroughly with your hands.

Form meat into egg-sized balls and then press into patties. Add enough oil to just coat the bottom of a skillet over medium heat. When oil is hot, add patties and sauté on each side until well-browned and cooked throughout.

MONSTER DUCK RAVIOLI

Ravioli are little round or square pillows of noodle dough filled with an assortment of cheeses, meats and/or vegetables. This recipe pretty much fits the definition with the exception of the word "little". Little ravioli prepared the traditional way take hours to prepare. This big monster ravioli is quick, easy and it'll make your friends stand up and shout, "What the heck is this thing?"

4 servings (one ravioli per person)

6	duck breast halves, skin removed
3	tablespoons olive oil
1	medium onion, diced
2	garlic cloves, minced
2	cup fresh mushrooms, chopped
1½	cups tomato sauce
	pinch or two red pepper flakes
1	tablespoon Italian seasoning
	salt and pepper
½	cup Parmesan cheese
⅔	cup mozzarella cheese, shredded
8	wonton skins (available in the produce section of your market)

Thinly slice duck breast and then roughly chop. Heat 1/2 of the oil in a large skillet and brown duck pieces for 1 – 2 minutes. Remove duck. Add remaining oil, onion, garlic and mushrooms and sauté for 5 minutes. Add 1 cup tomato sauce, pepper flakes and Italian seasoning. Simmer for 5 minutes. Return duck to pan and season with salt and pepper. Heat water to a low boil in a large pot. Add won ton skins and boil for 2 minutes. Remove skins and drain. For each ravioli, place one skin on a plate, top with one-fourth of the duck mixture and both cheeses. Place another skin on top, drizzle remaining tomato sauce over the top and serve.

CAJUN DUCK LEGS

All too often, duck hunters are irresponsible with the ducks they harvest. They'll cut out the breasts and throw the rest of the duck away. Cajun cooks know how to make the most of all parts of the duck, including the legs. Here's my own version of a Cajun-inspired dish using a mess of duck legs and thighs. I prefer to cook them with the skin on, but skinless legs work fine, too.

6 – 8 appetizer servings

2	cups andouille sausage (or any smoked sausage), sliced into 1/2-inch thick pieces
25 - 35	duck legs
1	cup yellow onion, roughly chopped
1	red bell pepper, roughly chopped
1	green bell pepper, roughly chopped
2	celery stalks, diced
1	14.5 ounce can diced tomato, with juice
4 - 5	garlic cloves, minced
2 - 3	bay leaves
	dash or two Tabasco
2	tablespoons Worcestershire sauce
2	tablespoons prepared Cajun seasoning
2	cups chicken broth
	cooked warm rice

In a large heavy-duty deep baking dish or Dutch oven, brown sausage over medium heat. Add duck legs and cook until all legs are evenly browned, about 20 minutes. Add onion and next 9 ingredients. Stir to combine ingredients and add enough chicken broth to cover contents of dish. Cover and place in a 400 degree oven for 1 1/2 hours. Remove from oven and check for doneness. Legs are done when the meat can be pulled off of the bone with minimal effort. Remove any legs that are done. Add additional chicken broth as needed to just cover legs. Return covered dish to the oven for 30 minutes. Check for doneness every 30 minutes until all legs are tender. Serve over warm rice.

GAME SAUCES

A flavorful sauce is almost as important as proper game preparation. Unfortunately a common practice among game cooks is to match wild game with a can of prepared soup or a dry soup mix and stew for several hours until the meat is moist and tender. While one cannot argue that the dish is indeed edible, it hardly does justice to that animal which we worked so hard for and dreamed about during the off-season. Pairing a magnificent pheasant with a can of cream of chicken soup and a slow-cooker should, at minimum, be a misdemeanor punishable by disposal of the can of soup at the target range.

I suppose that many people choose the soup/sauce route to take the "gamy" out of game. By following the aforementioned handling and cooking techniques, virtually all offensive flavors are eliminated. Combine a deftly handled game animal with a rich and flavorful sauce and you may even convince staunch non-game diners that they have been missing out on some extraordinary meals.

Several recipes specify utilizing certain parts of an animal, most notably, the breasts of game birds and waterfowl. Small game carcasses are also seldom used in preparation. The best way to make use of the carcasses, bones, trim, legs and thighs is to wrap, label and freeze them until there is sufficient inventory to make a large quantity of game stock. The advantage of homemade stock is a more pronounced and less salty flavor than commercially prepared broths and bouillon. Once a rich stock has been prepared, pour the stock through a strainer, cool and skim off and discard any fat that forms on the top. Stocks can then be placed in small units and frozen. I prefer to freeze my stocks in ice cube trays. Once frozen, I package the cubes in Food Saver VacLoc bags and thaw them out when needed. The Food Saver is also great for storing the above items and preventing freezer burn until you have enough to make your stock.

I prefer not to "drown" game dishes in sauce. If you find that a particular sauce is especially pleasing or popular, offer additional sauce in a serving bowl. When serving, place a small quantity of sauce on the plate, arrange the game artistically over the sauce and drizzle a little sauce over the meat. Garnish with a sprig of fresh herbs or a celery leaf and you are on your way to a well-earned reputation for remarkable game cooking.

GAME STOCK

Make good use of frequently discarded bones to create a marvelous game stock.

Approximately 1 quart

1 ½ to 2	pounds big game neck, back and/or rib bones and bird carcasses
2	tablespoons vegetable oil
1	medium onion, quartered, not peeled
1	large carrot, sliced into 1 inch pieces, not peeled
2	celery stalks, cut in half
2	quarts cold water
1	bay leaf
½	teaspoon coarse ground black pepper

Pre-heat oven to 350° F. Rub oil over bones and/or carcasses and place in roasting pan with vegetables. Place pan in oven and roast until bones and vegetables are browned, but not burnt. Transfer contents, including drippings, to a large stock pot over medium-high heat and add remaining ingredients. Bring to boil, reduce heat to simmer and cook, uncovered, for 6 to 8 hours. During cooking, keep enough liquid in pot to cover bones. Add additional water, if necessary. Strain, cool and refrigerate or freeze until needed.

CHERRY CHUTNEY

Game Birds, Waterfowl, Big Game

Approximately 4 cups

2 ½	pounds pitted cherries, fresh or frozen
1	cup diced yellow onion
2	tablespoons fresh ginger
2	garlic cloves, minced
1 ½	cups sugar
2	teaspoons mustard seeds
⅛	teaspoon ground cinnamon
¼	teaspoon celery seed
¼	teaspoon dried red pepper flakes
2	teaspoons salt
⅛	teaspoon ground allspice
½	teaspoon ground coriander
1 ½	cups white wine vinegar
¼	cup light corn syrup

Place all of the ingredients except vinegar and corn syrup into a heavy saucepan. Bring mixture to a boil. Cook until reduced to a thick consistency, stirring often.

Mix together vinegar and corn syrup and add to chutney. Boil down to a syrupy consistency. Remove from heat and cool. Chutney will slightly thicken as it cools.

GAME BIRD STOCK

Homemade game bird stock offers more intense, rich flavors than canned broth. Don't be afraid to add your own personal touches such as the addition of fresh herbs and seasonings. Freeze usable bird parts until you have enough for stock preparation.

Approximately 1 quart

- 2½   pounds upland game bird carcasses, wings and thighs
  all-vegetable pan coating spray
- 1   large onion, not peeled and quartered
- 2   medium carrots, not peeled and sliced into 1 inch pieces
- 2   celery stalks, cut in half
- 4   garlic cloves, cut in half
- 2   quarts cold water
- 3   black peppercorns (or 1/4 teaspoon coarse grind black pepper)
- 2   sprigs of fresh thyme
- 2   4 inch sprigs of fresh rosemary
- 1   bay leaf

Pre-heat oven to 350° F. Spray bottom of roasting pan with pan coating. Place bird parts, onions, carrots, celery and garlic in pan, and spray again to coat lightly. Roast in oven until bones and meat are browned, but not burnt. Transfer contents, including drippings and scraps to large stock pot. Add remaining ingredients and bring to boil. Reduce heat to low and simmer for 6 to 8 hours. If necessary, add water to just cover bones during cooking. Strain, cool and refrigerate or freeze until needed.

CALIFORNIA HORSERADISH CREAM SAUCE

for California Ducks and/or Geese

Makes 1 cup sauce

- 1   cup heavy (whipping) cream
- 1   tablespoon Worcestershire sauce
- 2-3   cloves garlic, minced
- 2   teaspoons fresh rosemary, minced (or substitute 1/2 teaspoon dried)
- 3   tablespoons prepared horseradish
  pinch freshly ground black pepper

Prepare sauce in saucepan.

Combine all ingredients in a saucepan over medium-high heat, bring to a boil then reduce heat to medium-low and simmer until thickened, about 5 – 6 minutes.

BROWN SAUCE

A rich, full-flavored sauce which can either stand alone as a game sauce for venison and waterfowl or be used as a base for a multitude of game sauces.

Approximately 1 quart

1 ½ - 2   pounds big game neck, back and/or rib bones
2   tablespoons vegetable oil 1 medium onion, not peeled and cut into quarters
2   celery stalks, cut in half
1   large carrot, cut into 3 pieces
2   quarts beef broth
⅓   cup flour
⅓   cup vegetable oil
2   garlic cloves, sliced
1   teaspoon coarse grind black pepper
1   bay leaf
½   cup tomato purée
½   cup fresh tomatoes, diced

Coat bones with oil and place in a roasting pan with onion, carrots and celery. Place in a 350° F oven and roast until well browned, but not burned. Transfer contents, including drippings, to a large stock pot over medium-high heat and add beef broth. In a small skillet, heat oil until very hot. Carefully add flour, whisking constantly, until *roux* mixture is browned, but not burnt. If roux burns, discard and repeat process. Add finished roux to stock pot and stir to mix. Add remaining ingredients, bring to boil, reduce heat to low and simmer, uncovered for 3 to 4 hours. Strain and refrigerate or freeze until needed.

RASPBERRY SAUCE

Waterfowl, Upland Game, Antlered Big Game

Approximately 1 cup

1   cup dry red wine
1   cup game stock or beef broth
1   shallot, diced
3   fresh rosemary sprigs
½   cup frozen raspberries, sweetened
¼   cup raspberry preserves
1   tablespoon cornstarch mixed with 1 tablespoon cold water
    salt & ground black pepper to taste

In a medium sauce pan over medium-high heat, bring first 4 ingredients to a boil. Reduce heat to medium and cook until liquid is reduced to about 1 cup. Stir in raspberries and preserves and simmer for 12 to 15 minutes. Pour through strainer and return to pan. When there is approximately 1 cup of sauce, increase heat to medium-high. Add cornstarch mixture, a little at a time while stirring, until sauce thickens. Season with salt and pepper.

GRILLED RED BELL PEPPER SAUCE

For use with Upland Game

Approximately 1 cup

1	large or 2 small red bell pepper
½	red onion, sliced into 2 rings
1	tomato, cut in half
2	tablespoons olive oil
¼	garlic cloves, minced
⅓	teaspoon dried red pepper flakes
1	tablespoon red wine vinegar
⅓	cup heavy cream
2	tablespoons fresh basil, minced
	(or 1/2 teaspoon dried basil flakes)

salt and freshly ground black pepper

Brush onion, garlic and tomato with 1 tablespoon olive oil. On a greased barbecue grill over white-hot coals, place bell pepper over hottest part of grill. Place onion and tomato on grill and cook until grill marks appear on both sides. Remove and set aside. Place garlic on foil or small pan and cook until lightly browned. Cook bell pepper until blackened on all sides. Remove bell pepper from grill and place in a small paper bag. Close top of bag and allow to steam for 10 minutes. Remove bell pepper, pull out stem, tear along one side to open up pepper. Remove seeds. Place blackened side out on a flat surface and scrape skin off with the edge of a knife. A few bits of skin won't hurt the finished sauce.

Place all ingredients except cream, basil, salt and pepper in a blender or food processor and purée until smooth. Transfer to a small sauce pan and heat to a boil. Add cream and basil and cook over medium heat for 4 to 5 minutes. Season with salt and pepper.

Note: For a lighter version of the sauce, substitute game bird stock, game stock or chicken broth for cream.

BÉCHAMEL SAUCE

A basic sauce frequently used as a base or thickener for a variety of sauces. Create your own sauces by adding assorted ingredients such as cheeses, herbs and citrus juices.

Approximately 1 cup

2	tablespoons butter
2	tablespoons flour
1	cup milk
	salt and white pepper to taste

In a medium saucepan over medium heat, melt butter. Add flour while whisking until mixture is bubbly. Cook for 2 minutes, whisking frequently. Do not allow mixture to brown. Reduce heat, if necessary. Gradually blend in milk in a thin stream while whisking and cook until sauce boils and is smooth and thick. Season with salt and pepper.

SAGE-PEPPERCORN SAUCE

Waterfowl, Doves, Antlered Game

Approximately 2 cups

1 tablespoon olive oil
¼ cup shallots, minced
2 garlic cloves, sliced thinly
½ teaspoon freshly ground black pepper
2 ½ cups game stock or beef broth
¼ cup brandy
2 bay leaves
2 tablespoons tomato paste
3 tablespoons butter
½ cup zucchini, diced into 1/4 inch cubes
½ cup carrot, diced into 1/4 inch cubes
1 tablespoon brined green peppercorns
2 tablespoons fresh sage, minced
1 tablespoon flour, sifted
   salt to taste

In a medium skillet over medium-high flame, heat oil and sauté shallots, garlic and black pepper for 2 to 3 minutes. Transfer contents to a medium sauce pan over medium-high heat and add game stock, brandy, bay leaves and tomato paste. Reduce liquid to about 1 1/2 cups. Add butter to skillet over medium heat and sauté zucchini, carrot, peppercorns and sage for 3 minutes. Sift flour over skillet, stirring in with vegetables. Cook for 2 minutes more. Transfer contents of skillet to sauce pan. Stir to blend, bring to boil, season with salt and remove from heat.

BALSAMIC BLUEBERRY SAUCE

for Montana Mallard

For One Duck

⅓ cup balsamic vinegar
2 garlic cloves, minced
½ teaspoon fresh rosemary leaves (or substitute a pinch of dried leaves)
1 tablespoon blueberry preserves
3 tablespoons chilled butter
   salt and freshly ground black pepper to taste
1 cup fresh or frozen blueberries

Start by placing the duck in a pan, crispy skin side down.

Combine sauce ingredients and add to the pan

PISTACHIO PESTO CREAM SAUCE

For use with Game Birds

Approximately 2 cups

  1   cup unsalted California pistachios, shelled & roasted in oven until lightly browned
  ½   cup Parmesan cheese, grated
  6   garlic cloves, roasted until golden brown, but not burned
  1   cup fresh basil, chopped
  ¼   cup olive oil
  1   cup heavy cream
     salt and white pepper to taste

In a blender or food processor, blend 1/2 cup of pistachios, cheese, garlic, basil and olive oil. Transfer to medium sauce pan over medium-high heat and add cream and remaining pistachios. Reduce liquid by one-half and season with salt and pepper.

SWEET-HOT BARBECUE SAUCE

All game meats

Approximately 3 1/2 cups

  1   tablespoon butter
  1   medium onion, diced fine
  2   garlic cloves, minced
  2   tablespoons lemon peel, diced fine
  1   cup packed brown sugar
  ½   teaspoon chili flakes
  ½   teaspoon cayenne pepper
  ½   teaspoon salt
  ¼   teaspoon freshly ground pepper
  ¼   cup tomato paste
  2   8 ounce cans tomato sauce
  ½   cup cider vinegar
  2   tablespoons Worcestershire sauce

In a medium sauce pan over medium heat, heat butter and sauté onions, garlic and lemon peel until onions become translucent, but not brown. Add sugar and cook for 3 more minutes, stirring often. Add remaining ingredients, bring to boil, reduce heat to low and cook for 30 minutes.

PORT WINE SAUCE

Big Game, Waterfowl, Doves

Approximately 1 cup

3 cups port wine
2 shallots, minced
3 3 inch fresh rosemary pieces
1 tablespoon sugar
½ cup heavy cream
  salt and pepper

In a medium sauce pan over high heat, bring first 3 ingredients to boil. Reduce heat to medium and cook, uncovered, until liquid is reduced to 1 cup. Strain out shallots and rosemary. Add sugar and cream, cook until liquid is reduced again to 1 cup. Season, as desired, with salt and pepper.

LEMON CREAM SAUCE

Duck Ravioli, Game Birds

Approximately 1 cup

2 cups dry white wine
1 shallot, diced fine
2 garlic cloves, minced
1 ½ cups heavy cream
¼ cup fresh lemon juice
2 tablespoons sugar
  salt and white pepper to taste

In a medium sauce pan over high heat, add first 3 ingredients. Reduce liquid to 1/2 cup. Strain out shallots and garlic. Add cream, lemon juice and sugar and reduce to 1 cup liquid. Season with salt and white pepper.

MUSTARD DIPPING SAUCE

An extremely simple and low-fat sauce for all game.

Apprximately 2 cups

1 cup whole grain mustard
1 cup red currant preserves
2 tablespoons freshly squeezed lemon juice
2 tablespoons fresh basil, minced

In a bowl, mix all ingredients. Use as a baste or dipping sauce for game dishes. You can substitute your favorite preserves for red currant preserves.

PICO DE GALLO SALSA

Salads, Upland Game, Boar

Approximately 2 cups

2 cups fresh tomato, coarsely chopped
¼ cup red onion, diced
1 garlic clove, minced
2 tablespoons fresh lime juice
1 teaspoon red wine vinegar
1 tablespoon jalapeño pepper, seeded and diced fine
¼ cup fresh cilantro, chopped fine
1 teaspoon sugar
¼ teaspoon ground cumin
¼ teaspoon chili powder

Combine above ingredients and refrigerate for at least 30 minutes. Can be stored in a covered container in the refrigerator for up to 5 days.

MANGO SALSA

Game Birds, Wild Pigs

Approximately 2 cups

1 ½ cups mango, peeled and diced into 1/2 inch cubes
⅓ cup red bell pepper, diced fine
2 tablespoons red onion, diced fine
¼ cup fresh cilantro, chopped
¼ teaspoon chili flakes
¼ cup green onions, diced
dash cumin
dash Tabasco sauce
  juice of 1 lime

Combine above ingredients and refrigerate for 1 hour.

SWEET AND SOUR ZINFANDEL SAUCE

Waterfowl, Doves and Big Game

Approximately 2 cups

2	tablespoons olive or peanut oil
4	garlic cloves, minced
⅓	cup yellow onion, diced fine
¼	cup brown sugar
2	cups zinfandel
2	tablespoons Balsamic vinegar
1	cup game stock or beef broth
1	tablespoon Worcestershire sauce
3	tablespoons tomato paste
4	ounces butter, cut into 5 pieces
	salt and pepper to taste

In a medium sauce pan over medium-high heat, sauté garlic and onion for 2 to 3 minutes. Add brown sugar and cook until the sugar liquefies and caramelizes the onion and garlic. Add the remaining ingredients except butter, salt and pepper. Reduce contents by boiling, uncovered, until there is approximately 1 1/2 cups of liquid. Remove pan from heat and whisk in butter pieces, one at a time, until sauce is thickened. Season sparingly with salt and pepper. If you need to heat the sauce at a later time, do so over low heat. Do not boil or sauce will separate.

SUNDRIED TOMATO PESTO

Upland Game

Approximately 1 cup

⅓	cup pine nuts, lightly browned in an oven at 350° F.
1	cup basil leaves
2	garlic cloves
⅓	cup sundried tomatoes in oil
⅓	cup olive oil
	salt and pepper to taste

Place all ingredients in a food processor and blend to make a coarse paste. Season with salt and pepper. To store, cover paste with a little additional olive oil, cover and refrigerate.

PLUM SAUCE

Doves, Waterfowl, Game Birds

Approximately 2 cups

1 ½	cups plum preserves
¾	cup applesauce
½	teaspoon ground ginger
2	garlic cloves
1	teaspoon chili flakes
1	tablespoon cornstarch
1	tablespoon soy sauce
2	tablespoons cider vinegar

In a sauce pan over medium heat, cook plum preserves and applesauce until boiling. Combine remaining ingredients and reduce heat until sauce thickens.

ORANGE-BASIL HOLLANDAISE SAUCE

Delicious on all sautéed light-fleshed game birds. If desired, substitute orange juice and fresh basil with your own favorite citrus fruits and fresh herbs.

Approximately 1 1/2 - 2 cups

4	egg yolks
1	teaspoon dijon mustard
2	tablespoons freshly squeezed orange juice
8	ounces clarified butter
2	tablespoons fresh basil, diced
	salt and white pepper to taste

In a double boiler over simmering water, whisk together the first three ingredients. Add butter in a very thin steady stream, whisking constantly until sauce thickens. Season with salt and pepper. Serve immediately.

If you wish to hold sauce and warm at a later time, place in a covered container and refrigerate. To warm, place over double boiler with barely simmering water and whisk constantly until just warm. If sauce gets too hot, it will separate.

BALSAMIC CHERRY SAUCE

All Game Meats

Makes Approximately 1-cup

2	tablespoon Balsamic vinegar
1½	cups dry red wine
2	tablespoons brown sugar
2	teaspoons fresh rosemary, minced
1	cup dried cherries
1	tablespoon cornstarch mixed with 1-tablespoon cold water
	salt and pepper to taste

In a medium saucepan over high heat, add vinegar, wine, sugar, rosemary and 1/2 of the dried cherries.Reduce liuid by one half, transfer mixture to a blender or food processor and process for 15 seconds. Return sauce to pan, add remaining dried cherries, lower heat and simmer for 3 to 4 minutes. Add cornstarch misture, stirring in a little at a time utnil sauce thickens. Season with salt and pepper.

WASABI LIME CREAM SAUCE

For fish, shellfish and upland game.

Makes 2/3 cup

½ cup dry white wine
1 green onion, minced
1 clove garlic, minced
1 teaspoon gingerroot, peeled and minced
1 teaspoon Rose's lime juice (or any other sweetened lime juice)
1-2 tablespoons (or more!) prepared wasabi paste
  pinch granulated sugar
⅔ cup heavy (whipping) cream

Heat wine, onion, garlic and ginger in a small saucepan over medium-high heat until only a tablespoon or two of liquid remains. Stir in remaining ingredients and heat to blend flavors.

WASABI SWEET AND SOUR SAUCE

This is one of my go-to sauces that's great on fish, fowl and large game.

¼ cup soy sauce
¼ cup seasoned rice vinegar
1½ tablespoons apricot preserves
1 teaspoon minced pickled ginger
2 teaspoons freshly squeezed lime juice pinch sugar
1-2 teaspoons prepared wasabi paste (Japanese horseradish)

Combine all ingredients in a small saucepan and bring to a boil.

MUSTARD MARINADE

Makes about 2 cups

- ½   cup red wine vinegar
- ½   cup dry red wine
- ⅓   cup Dijon mustard
- 2   tablespoons ketchup (yep, ketchup)
- 1   tablespoon fresh garlic cloves, minced
- 1   tablespoon Italian seasoning
- 1   teaspoon Kosher salt
- ½   teaspoon cracked black pepper
- ⅔   cup olive oil

Combine all ingredients except oil and whisk together to blend. While whisking, add oil in a thin stream until emulsified. Pour marinade over split ducks or ducks breasts. Refrigerate for 2 to 12 hours, turning often. Grill, broil or pan sear to desired doneness.

BALSAMIC CHIPOTLE VINAIGRETTE

Makes about 1½ cups

- ⅓   cup balsamic vinegar
- ¼   cup Tabasco Chipotle Pepper Sauce
- 2   teaspoons blackberry preserves
- 2   garlic cloves, minced
- ¼   teaspoon salt
- ⅛   teaspoon freshly ground black pepper
- 1   cup olive oil

In a bowl, whisk together vinegar and next 5 ingredients. While whisking vigorously, drizzle in oil in a thin stream. To use as a marinade, pour over whole birds or breasts, cover and refrigerate for 2 to 24 hours. Can also be used as a finishing sauce…just drizzle over just before serving. Serve with Mexican rice and warm flour tortillas.

ALABAMA WHITE
BARBECUE SAUCE

If you grew up in Alabama, this version of barbecue sauce probably seems perfectly normal. To the rest of the country, it might look more like a recipe for salad dressing. At a recent barbecue I attended outside of Huntsville, Alabama it appeared that the guests preferred the white stuff over the traditional barbecue sauce two to one. Don't be afraid. It kinda grows on you. Baste meat just before serving and have some extra on hand for dipping.

Makes about 2 cups sauce

1	cup mayonnaise
1	cup cider vinegar
1	tablespoon lemon juice
1½	tablespoons black pepper
½	teaspoon salt
¼	teaspoon cayenne
	sugar to taste

MUSHROOM SAUCE

Makes about 3 cups

2	cups fresh sliced mushrooms
¼	cup butter
1	tablespoon butter
1	tablespoon shallots, minced
½	cup chopped mushrooms
½	teaspoon dried thyme
1	bay leaf
¼	cup red wine
2	cups beef broth
1	tablespoon arrowroot powder
	salt to taste
	freshly ground black pepper

Saute all ingredients over medium heat and serve immediately.

SOUTH CAROLINA BARBECUE SAUCE

Makes about 1½ cups

⅓ cup apple cider vinegar
½ cup yellow mustard (prepared)
½ cup brown sugar
2 tablespoons water
1 tablespoon chili powder
½ teaspoon black pepper
   dash Tabasco sauce
½ teaspoon soy sauce
1 tablespoon butter

In a medium saucepan, combine the vinegar, mustard, sugar, water, chili powder, pepper, and Tabasco. Simmer for 25 minutes. Whisk in soy sauce and butter.

APRICOT-BERRY GLAZE

for Ducks

Here's a recipe that combines apricots with any berry in season. It'll remind you of a sweet glaze for ham. This is a finishing sauce that should be brushed over the duck just before serving. If you brush it on too early, the brown sugar in the glaze will burn. For a twist, add a shot or two of brandy or rum to the sauce.

Makes about 2 cups

¼ cup light brown sugar, firmly packed
2 tablespoons cornstarch
1½ cups orange juice
2 tablespoons lemon juice
1 cup dried apricots, thinly sliced
1½ cups fresh or frozen berries

In a small saucepan, combine brown sugar with next 3 ingredients. Cook over medium heat, stirring often, until mixture starts to thicken. Add apricots, reduce heat and simmer for 3 to 4 minutes. Stir in berries and brush over ducks before serving.

JERKY MARINADE FOR WATERFOWL

For 2 pounds of meat.
When your meat needs a little help, try this marinade.

1½	teaspoons Kosher salt
1	teaspoon cracked black pepper
1	teaspoon red pepper flakes
1	teaspoon garlic powder
1	teaspoon onion powder
1	teaspoon Tabasco sauce
½	teaspoon Liquid Smoke
¼	cup water
¼	cup soy sauce
2	tablespoons Worchestershire sauce

Combine all ingredients and marinade sliced meat for 12 to 24 hours in the refrigerator. Remove meat from marinade and allow to air-dry on a rack for 1 hour before drying.

ARTICHOKE AND BASIL SAUCE

This is a simple sauce for fish that can be prepared in the blender in just a few minutes. You can heat it slowly in a saucepan, but, if you do, don't bring it to a boil. I just spoon it over just-cooked fish. I also add a dash or two of a green hot sauce. If you use a red hot sauce, it may give the Artichoke and Basil Sauce an unflattering brown color.

Makes about 1 cup

⅔	cup marinated artichoke hearts
1	cup fresh basil leaves
1	lemon, juice only
2	garlic cloves, minced
2	tablespoons almonds, lightly toasted in a 325 degree oven
3	tablespoons grated Parmesan cheese
¼	cup olive oil
	salt and pepper to taste

Combine artichoke hearts and the next five ingredients in a blender or food processor. Pulse to process until mixture is almost pureed, but still a little chunky. While motor is running, add oil in a thin stream until emulsified. Season with salt and pepper to taste.

HOLLANDAISE SAUCE

Hollandaise sauce is a natural accompaniment for fish, shellfish and vegetables. The problem is, many folks have tried to make it the traditional way – with a double-boiler and a lot of whisking. Even then, the sauce can separate. The other option is to use the dry hollandaise mix in the packet. Works great, but doesn't taste like hollandaise. Here's my road-tested, no-fail hollandaise that won't separate and tastes great. Feel free to add your own touches with some orange zest or with some fresh tarragon and a dash of vinegar to make béarnaise – great on filet mignon. The traditional Leysath Christmas breakfast requires champagne and Dungeness Crab Eggs Benedict. Substitute a mound of fresh crab meat for the usual Canadian bacon and top with hollandaise sauce. Sounds pretty good, doesn't it?

Makes about 1 1/2 cups sauce

3	egg yolks
½	teaspoon Dijon mustard
1	tablespoon lemon juice
1	cup butter, melted and hot

Place egg yolks, mustard and lemon juice in a blender or food processor and process until well blended. While motor is running, add hot butter, a few drops at a time and then increasing to a slow, steady stream until all butter is incorporated and sauce is smooth. Keep sauce at room temperature until ready to serve. You can heat it over low heat while stirring, but only to warm. *DO NOT BRING TO A BOIL!*

HORSERADISH CREAM SAUCE

Great on waterfowl and antlered game.

Makes 1 cup

1	tablespoon olive oil
2	green onions, diced
1	garlic clove, minced
1	teaspoon fresh rosemary leaves, minced
	(or substitute pinch dried rosemary leaves)
¼	cup dry white wine
½	teaspoon Worcestershire sauce
2 - 3	tablespoons prepared horseradish
¾	cup heavy (whipping) cream

Heat olive oil in a small saucepan over medium heat. Add green onions, garlic and rosemary and cook for 1 minute. Add white wine and Worcestershire sauce and reduce liquid by one-half. Stir in horseradish and cream and bring to just below boiling while stirring.

ORANGE CITRUS BUERRE BLANC

This recipe is great for impressing company. The flavors are rich and buttery, but not so much that it overpowers the taste of the fish or game. Try it with any fish, shellfish or upland game. Drizzle a couple of tablespoons over the cooked fish, etc.

Makes about 1 cup sauce (6 – 8 servings)

1	cup orange juice (preferably fresh squeezed)
1	cup dry white wine
2	tablespoons lemon juice
2	tablespoons lime juice
1	tablespoon shallot, minced (or sub white part of a green onion)
1/2	pound chilled butter, cut into small pieces
	salt and white pepper to taste

In a medium saucepan over medium-high heat, combine first five ingredients and bring to a boil. Reduce heat to medium and simmer, uncovered, until the liquid is reduced to about 3 – 4 tablespoons. Add butter pieces, a couple at a time while whisking continuously. When all butter has been melted, immediately remove from heat. Season with salt and pepper and serve at once.

To reheat sauce, do so over very low heat while whisking constantly. Do not bring sauce to a boil or it will break!

PARMESAN CREAM SAUCE

For all upland game birds. Great with pasta!

1 cup sauce

3	tablespoons butter
3	tablespoons yellow or white onion, minced
3	garlic cloves, minced
1	tablespoon all-purpose flour
½	cup dry white wine or chicken broth (cold)
1	lemon, juice only
⅔	cup heavy (whipping) cream
½	cup shredded parmesan cheese

Melt butter in a large saucepan over medium heat. Add onions and garlic and cook until onions are translucent. Sprinkle flour over onions and garlic, stir and cook for another 1 – 2 minutes. While stirring, slowly add in wine or chicken broth and lemon juice. Simmer for 5 minutes. Stir in cream and cheese and stir until cheese is melted and sauce is hot and bubbly.

CALYPSO SAUCE

I discovered this sauce at a restaurant in Tamarindo, Costa Rica. It's from the West Indies was served over pan-seared fresh dorado and very large shrimp. The recipe may have lost something in the translation and may not be exactly the same one I was served, but it's pretty darn good. The original recipe calls for 25 fresh habaneros. I cut it in half and there's still plenty of heat. If you're feeling tough, throw in a dozen or so more habaneros. Try it with jalapeño peppers, too.

Makes about 1 pint

1	tablespoon vegetable oil
1	large onion, slice into rings
4	garlic cloves, mashed
2	tablespoons sugar
13-15	fresh habanero peppers, stem and seeds removed
¼	cup white vinegar
¼	cup limeade concentrate
2	tablespoons rum or vodka
3	tablespoons dry mustard
3	teaspoons salt

Heat oil in a large skillet over medium-high heat. Add onion rings and sauté until translucent. Add garlic, sugar and peppers and sauté 2 – 3 minutes more. Allow to cool and transfer to a food processor or blender. Add remaining ingredients and blend until smooth. Refrigerate.

Spoon over cooked fish, shellfish and chicken.

MUSTARD AND DILL SAUCE

Great with Fish

½	cup mayonnaise
1	tablespoon brown sugar
2	tablespoons Creole mustard
2	tablespoons fresh dill, minced
	dash Tabasco
	pinch salt

Combine all ingredients and refrigerate.

WATERMELON AND TOMATO SALSA

I know it sounds a little goofy, but you've got to give this one a try. It's great with any grilled fish. Since the salsa is fairly mild, I like to rub the fish with olive oil, salt, pepper and a little cayenne pepper. Just before serving, squeeze some fresh lime over the fish. I know that it's a crap shoot when buying a whole melon since you can't look inside, but chose one that's firm and not grainy.

Makes about 2 cups salsa

1	cup seedless watermelon, cut into 1-inch cubes
1	cup cherry tomatoes, halved
2	tablespoons red onion, finely chopped
1	jalapeño pepper, seeded and minced
2	garlic cloves, minced
2	tablespoons fresh basil or cilantro, chopped
	pinch cumin
1	tablespoon olive oil
1	tablespoons lime juice
	pinch sugar
	salt and pepper to taste

Toss all ingredients gently. Let rest at room temperature for 30 minutes. Spoon over grilled fish.

MY FAVORITE BLOODY MARY MIX

This will make a batch of Bloody Mary mix for the perfect after-the-hunt beverage. Always fill the glass with ice, add a couple ounces of vodka, a fresh squeeze of lime and shake before using.

1	quart tomato juice
¼	cup prepared (not cream-style) horseradish
⅓	cup Worcestershire sauce
¼	cup freshly squeezed lemon juice
2	tablespoons freshly squeezed lime juice
2	teaspoons celery salt
2	teaspoons coarse ground black pepper

Combine all ingredients and stir to blend.

ROASTED GARLIC AND LEMON COMPOUND BUTTER

Compound butters like the one below are great on any fish. Play around with the ingredients and make your own version.

- ½ pound butter, softened at room temperature
- 1 cup fresh basil leaves, chopped
- 2 tablespoon lemon zest (the outside yellow skin), minced
- 8 8 cloves whole garlic cloves, roasted and chopped
     pinch each salt and white pepper

Blend together in a medium bowl. Lay a 1 foot square piece of waxed paper or plastic wrap on a flat surface. Spread butter onto the center, about 2 inches wide by 6 inches long. Roll the butter up with the paper or plastic wrap so that it is shaped into a loaf, either square or round, about 6 inches long. Place in the refrigerator or freezer until firm.

ALL-PURPOSE MARINADE

Great on just about anything including vegetables, upland game, waterfowl and any other antlered game. Save some to serve on the side for dipping.

- ¾ cup olive or vegetable oil
- ½ cup soy sauce
- 3 tablespoons cider vinegar
- 3 tablespoons honey
- 1½ teaspoons garlic powder
- 1½ teaspoons ground ginger
- 1½ teaspoons salt

Mix ingredients together. Pour over meat in plastic bag or non-reactive container. Cover and marinate several hours or overnight. Drain meat and pat with paper towels before adding to the 'cue. Excess oil from the marinade may cause the meat to flame up and burn your whiskers.

BASIC DUCK MARINADE

Makes about 1 quart

- 2 cups dry red wine
- ½ cup soy sauce
- ¼ cup balsamic or red wine vinegar
- ¼ cup vegetable oil
- 1 medium onion, diced
- 6 garlic cloves, minced
- 1 tablespoon cracked black pepper

Combine all ingredients in a container with a tight fitting lid. Shake well and pour over game. Cover and refrigerate for 6 to 24 hours, turning occasionally. Before cooking, let game drain and pat dry with paper towels.

CHILI-LEMON-LIME MARINADE

It's hard for me to make anything with chilies and not use the juice of freshly squeezed lemons and limes. The lime really perks up the flavors of this spicy marinade that's great on salmon, tuna and just about any wild game. You don't need to smother the fish or meat with this marinade. A little goes a long way! This marinade is perfect for grilled foods. Because of the acidic lime and lemon juices, light colored meats and fish should only marinate for about an hour or so or else the marinade will "cook" the fish or meat and make it mushy.

Makes 2 cups

5	garlic cloves, minced
1	or more jalapeno peppers, seeded and minced (or leave some seeds in for heat)
2	teaspoons kosher salt
1	teaspoon chili powder
¼	cup granulated sugar
1	teaspoon freshly ground black pepper
½	cup freshly squeezed lemon juice
¾	cup freshly squeezed lime juice
¼	cup red onion, minced
5 - 6	sprigs fresh cilantro, chopped
¼	cup olive oil

Combine first 6 ingredients and mash together with the back side of a large spoon. Add remaining ingredients except oil and mix well. Add oil to mixture while stirring.

CHIPOTLE TOMATO SAUCE

First, a word of caution about chipotle peppers. They're smoky and flavorful, but can also run a bit hot, especially when packed in adobo sauce. Adobo is a paste made from ground chiles, herbs and vinegar and a little goes a long way. Start with a little and add as much more as you can handle. During the off-season when store-bought tomatoes lose all flavor, you can substitute a 14 1/2 ounce can of diced tomatoes.

Makes 2 cups

1	tablespoon olive oil
½	cup onion, chopped
2	garlic cloves, minced
1	tablespoon brown sugar
3	cups fresh tomatoes, peeled and diced
2	canned chipotle chiles, minced (with 1 tablespoon adobo sauce)
½	teaspoon dried oregano flakes
2	tablespoons balsamic or red wine vinegar
	salt to taste

In a medium saucepan, heat oil over medium heat. Add onions, garlic and brown sugar and sauté for 3 – 4 minutes or until onions soften. Add remaining ingredients except salt and simmer for 10 minutes. Season with salt.

AVOCADO CITRUS SALSA

A San Diego area grower just sent me a box of the creamiest Hass avocados and I just can't get enough. He also sent along a very special avocado variety called Sir Prize. These babies weigh about 20 pounds apiece (OK, slight exaggeration). A normal Hass avocado has about 65% flesh, the rest is seed and skin. Sir Prize avocados have 83% flesh. Spoon this salsa over just-cooked fish.

Makes 1 ³/₄ cups

½	cup orange segments
½	cup grapefruit segments
¾	cup avocado - peeled, seeded and cut in 1/2 in cubes
2	tablespoons lime juice
	pinch sugar
¼	cup red onion, minced
¼	cup chopped fresh basil or cilantro leaves
1	pinch red pepper flakes
	salt to taste

Gently toss all ingredients. Let stand at room temperature for 20 minutes before serving.

HERB VINAIGRETTE

For all fish, shellfish and game.

Makes about 1 cup

¾	cup olive oil
¼	cup red wine or white wine vinegar
2	cloves garlic, minced
1	teaspoon Dijon mustard
1	lemon, juice only
	pinch granulated sugar
1	tablespoon dried Italian seasoning (or substitute fresh herbs)
	salt and pepper to taste

Combine all ingredients in a jar with a tight-fitting lid and shake vigorously until blended.

CAPER DILL VINAIGRETTE

Makes 1 cup

4 tablespoons white wine vinegar
1 garlic clove, minced
½ teaspoon Dijon mustard
¼ teaspoon sugar
¾ cup olive oil
1 tablespoon fresh dill, chopped
1 tablespoon capers, drained and chopped
½ teaspoon lemon zest, minced (use a zester or vegetable peeler to remove the thin yellow skin, not the white part, of the lemon)
salt and pepper to taste

In a medium bowl, whisk together first 4 ingredients. While whisking vigorously, drizzle in olive oil until emulsified. Stir in remaining ingredients and season with salt and pepper.

BALSAMIC BLACKBERRY GLAZE

When balsamic vinegar is reduced, it intensifies the sweetness and oaky flavors. You can simplify the process by substituting a pinch or two of brown sugar for the berries. I keep this syrup on hand year around for a quick finishing touch for salmon and grilled meats.

Makes about 1 cup syrup

3 cups balsamic vinegar
1 cup fresh or frozen blackberries
1/2 teaspoon cornstarch mixed with 1 teaspoon balsamic vinegar

Add vinegar and berries to a medium saucepan and bring to a boil. Reduce heat and simmer until liquid has been reduced to about 1 1/2 cups. Strain berries out through a strainer and return liquid to pan. Make sure all berry seeds have been removed. Bring liquid to a boil and stir in cornstarch mixture, a little at a time, until liquid thickens. Allow to cool and transfer to a squeeze bottle. Syrup will thicken as it cools

GRILLED TOMATO-ROSEMARY VINAIGRETTE

1	large tomato
¼	cup white wine vinegar
1	teaspoon Dijon mustard
1	teaspoon granulated sugar
½	cup olive oil
¼	cup fresh basil, chopped
1	teaspoon capers
	salt and pepper

Cut tomato in half and rub with olive oil, salt and pepper. Place on a white-hot grill and grill for a couple of minutes or until tomato is charred. Allow to cool and removed skin. Dice cooled tomato and place in a medium bowl.

To prepare vinaigrette, whisk tomato with next 3 ingredients. Slowly add oil while whisking. Whisk in tomato, basil and capers. Season with salt and pepper.

HERB PAN SAUCE FOR FISH

This is a quick sauce to make in the same pan in which you cooked the fish. Cook the fish in the pan and transfer fish to a warm pan or oven, but make sure you don't continue to cook the fish. This sauce takes about 5 - 6 minutes to prepare. If you don' have access to a variety of herbs, just use parsley. I know you can find parsley!

Makes about 1/2 cup sauce

5	tablespoons chilled butter
¼	cup onion, finely diced
2	garlic cloves, minced
½	cup fish or chicken broth
1	tablespoon lemon juice
3	tablespoons fresh herbs (dill, basil, thyme, parsley – preferably a combination), chopped
	salt and pepper

Add 2 tablespoons butter to pan over medium heat. Add onion and garlic and saute until onions are softened, but not brown. Add the stock and lemon juice, increase heat to high and bring to a boil, reducing liquid by half. Remove pan from heat and whisk in herbs and remaining 3 tablespoons of butter until melted. Season to taste with salt and pepper. Spoon over fish immediately.

MANGO WASABI SWEET AND SOUR SAUCE

Makes 1 1/2 cups

- ⅔ cup rice vinegar
- ¼ cup low-sodium soy sauce
- 3 tablespoons apricot preserves
- 2 cloves garlic, minced
- ½ teaspoon sesame oil
- 2 teaspoons pickled ginger, minced
- 2 green onions, chopped
- 2 limes, juice only
- 1 - 2 tablespoons prepared wasabi (you can always add more)
- 1 - 2 tablespoons cornstarch mixed with equal part cold water
- 1 mango; peeled, seeded and diced

Combine first 6 ingredients in a sauce pan over medium heat and bring to a boil. Reduce heat to low and simmer for 2 – 3 minutes. Stir in green onions, wasabi and simmer until wasabi is incorporated into the sauce. Increase heat to medium and stir in cornstarch, a little at a time, until sauce is thickened, but not pasty. Remove from heat and stir in mango. Adjust flavors to suit you taste. Too sweet? Add more vinegar. Too sour? More sugar. Not enough wasabi?

MANGO PUREE

For the past year or so, mangoes have been plentiful and cheap, often less than a buck each. If the mango you purchase is hard, stick it in a paper bag for a day or two until the skin just starts to shrivel. Also, next time you're at Trader Joe's, pick up a bag of frozen mango chunks. They're great for last minute mango sauces, purees and salsas.

This puree is great with any cooked fish. To serve, put some puree on the center of the plate and set the cooked fish on top. Garnish with something green, like a sprig of fresh cilantro leaves.

1½ cups puree (4 – 6 servings)

- ¼ cup yellow onion, diced
- 1 teaspoon fresh gingerroot, peeled and minced
- 1 jalapeño pepper, seeds and ribs removed, minced
- 1½ cups ripe mango chunks
    juice of 2 limes
- 3 tablespoons olive oil
    salt and pepper

Sauté onion, ginger and jalapeño pepper in half of the olive oil over medium heat until softened, but not browned. Add mango and cook for 2 – 3 minutes. Transfer to a blender or food processor, add lime juice and process until smooth. While motor is running, drizzle in remaining olive oil to emulsify. Season with salt and pepper.

RAW TOMATO SAUCE

Don't mistake this sauce for Mexican salsa. Uncooked tomato sauces have been around many cultures forever. Although you can make this sauce anytime of the year, it's best with summertime vine-ripened "real" tomatoes. Don't let the anchovy throw you off. The flavor is subtle and, if you prefer, you can leave them out.

Makes about 3 cups

2   cups ripe tomatoes; cored, seeded and diced (cut them in half and squeeze out the seeds before chopping)
1   cup zucchini, peeled, seeded and diced into 1/4-inch cubes
2   anchovy fillets, minced
3   tablespoons black olives, chopped
1   tablespoon capers, drained
⅓   cup fresh mixed herbs, chopped
2   green onions, chopped
1   tablespoon freshly squeezed lemon juice
1   tablespoon balsamic vinegar
⅓   cup extra virgin olive oil
    salt and pepper to taste

Combine all ingredients in a non-reactive bowl and set aside at room temperature for 1 hour, stirring occasionally

BEER BARBECUE SAUCE

Makes about 2 cups

2   tablespoons butter
1   medium yellow onion, finely diced
2   tablespoons brown sugar
2   garlic cloves, minced
1   ounce Budweiser beer
1   lemon, sliced into rings
3   tablespoons Worcestershire sauce
1   cup tomato purée
½   teaspoon liquid smoke
¼   up cider vinegar
    salt and freshly ground pepper to taste

Prepare sauce. Melt butter in a saucepan over medium heat. Add onion and cook until translucent. Add brown sugar and garlic and cook for 2 to 3 minutes. Add remaining ingredients except salt and pepper. Stir well, bring to a boil and then simmer until sauce thickens. The sauce should be the consistency of thick tomato sauce.

GAME FISH

As one of the millions of Americans who grew up with a fishing rod in hand, my passion for catching a variety of game fish grew with every outing. As a young boy, I carved bass plugs out of broom handles and fished local farm ponds for monster-sized largemouth bass. As an adult, I am no more or less successful with expensive commercially-made lures. Our summer family vacation included the long drive down Interstate 95 to Daytona Beach, Florida, where my father taught my brothers and me the art of flounder fishing off a crowded pier. Once I received the coveted driver's license, my spring and summer weekends were spent trout fishing in the Blue Ridge Mountains. Since moving west, I have had the opportunity to fish some of the most pristine and productive trout streams in the country.

During my years as an independent restaurateur, my fishing time was limited, but I was able to improve my culinary skills by preparing fresh-caught striped bass, salmon and sturgeon that others brought to the restaurant for me to prepare for them. One of the most important lessons that I learned about preparing fish for others is that the presentation of the dish is almost as important as the taste of the finished dish. Complementary colors and flavors combined with artfully arranged ingredients can make the difference between a great dish and a mediocre one.

I am firmly committed to the catch and release philosophy of fishing. Not only will this insure that future generations will have the opportunity to catch wild game fish, but I really don't have much of a desire to fill my cooler with fish, only to pack them into my freezer and prepare them at a much later time. Freshly caught fish taste infinitely better than those fish that have been frozen. Although I am primarily a fly fisherman and use barbless hooks, occasionally a fish will get hooked in such a manner that survival after release is questionable. Those are the fish I save for the dinner table.

It is important to keep your fish cold before preparation. The sooner it is on ice, the less opportunity it will have to take on unpleasant "fishy" flavors and aromas. Your nose will give you the best indication of the condition of any fish or shellfish. If your fish smells "fishy," it is difficult to mask the smell and taste when cooked. If you must prepare your improperly stored or handled fish, do so by baking or poaching in aromatic liquids. Should you choose to freeze your catch, make certain that it is cleaned, cooled and tightly wrapped. When freezing your fish, take a permanent marker and note the type of fish and date caught on the outside of the package. As an alternative to freezing, share your catch with friends and neighbors when the fish is still fresh.

FRIED CATFISH
WITH A SPICY PUMPKIN SEED CRUST AND CILANTRO TARTAR SAUCE

I prefer a couple of small fish to one large one. Flavors are usually delicate and sweet, and they make an attractive presentation when shingled atop one another. If you are unable to locate shelled pumpkin seeds, substitute shelled sunflower seeds or any crushed roasted nuts.

4 servings

8	small catfish, skin and heads removed
1	cup flour, seasoned with 1 tsp salt and 1/2 tsp freshly ground black pepper
	vegetable oil for frying

Batter

2	large eggs
⅔	cup flour
1	teaspoon salt
⅓	cup cornmeal
1	cup flat beer
2	jalapeño peppers, seeded and finely diced
⅓	cup red bell pepper, finely diced
1	cup shelled pumpkin seeds
1	teaspoon chili flakes

Cilantro Tartar Sauce

1	cup mayonnaise
2	tablespoons capers, drained
2	tablespoons pitted black olives, chopped
¼	cup fresh cilantro, chopped
1	tablespoon freshly squeezed lemon juice
1	teaspoon dijon mustard

To prepare batter, beat eggs in a medium bowl. Add flour and salt to blend. Add cornmeal and beer, a little of each at a time while whisking lightly to blend. Batter should be a little lumpy. Let stand at room temperature for 1 hour. Lightly fold in remaining ingredients.

To prepare tartar sauce, mix all ingredients well and season with salt and pepper.

Heat oil to about 375° F in a deep fryer or deep, heavy stock pot. Dust fish with seasoned flour and then place in batter to coat. Fry for 3 to 4 minutes each or until medium-brown.

LARGEMOUTH BASS
IN A POTATO SHELL

Thin-sliced potatoes, lemon and fresh basil leaves add a protective shell to seal in moisture and flavor. Serve on a bed of lightly sautéed spinach and red bell peppers for a colorful main dish.

4 servings

2	cups dry white wine
1	shallot, minced
1	tablespoon lemon juice
4	6-ounce largemouth bass fillets, about 4 inches long, 3 inches wide and 1 inch thick
4	large baking potatoes
1	cup fresh basil leaves
1	lemon, sliced into 8 thin slices
¼	cup vegetable oil
	salt and freshly ground black pepper
4	ounces butter, cut into 4 pieces

In a small saucepan over medium-high heat, bring wine and shallots to a boil and reduce liquid to about 1/3 cup. Add lemon juice and set aside.

Wash the potatoes, do not remove skin. Using a sharp vegetable peeler, electric slicer or a very sharp, thin knife, slice the potatoes lengthwise into long paper-thin slices. Slicing the potato as thinly as possible is critical. Thicker slices will break or split when folded. You need to make the potato crust quickly while the just cut slices are still sticky. For each serving lay out potato slices, overlapping edges by 1 inch as you lay them out to form an area approximately 9 inches by 9 inches square. Place the fillet on the center of the potatoes. Season the potatoes and bass with salt and pepper. Place basil leaves and then 2 slices of lemon on top of the fillet. Fold potato slices around fillet and seal top with additional potato slices. Brush top and sides with oil and season with additional salt and pepper. Place in a 425° F oven for 8 to 10 minutes or until potato shell is lightly browned.

Return wine mixture to heat and bring to boil. Remove from heat and whisk in butter pieces, one at a time, until thickened. Season with salt and pepper. Place one portion of bass on each plate and drizzle wine sauce over each.

SMOKED SALMON
WITH GINGER-WASABI SAUCE

Moist salmon fillets are marinated with Asian flavors, seasoned with smoke and served with a enticing sauce.

4 servings

1	cup low-sodium soy sauce
½	cup seasoned rice vinegar
½	cup brown sugar
2	tablespoons sesame oil
2	tablespoons freshly squeezed lemon juice
1	teaspoon ground ginger
½	teaspoon freshly ground black pepper
2	garlic cloves, minced
4	6 to 8 oz salmon fillets, skin intact
2	cups white wine
2	tablespoons fresh ginger, peeled and minced
2	tablespoons prepared wasabi (Japanese horseradish)
4	ounces butter, cut into 4 pieces
	salt and white pepper to taste

To make marinade, combine first 8 ingredients in a medium saucepan over a medium flame and heat to blend flavors. Let cool. Place salmon fillets in a shallow container and pour marinade over fillets. Cover and refrigerate for 12 hours, turning occasionally. Remove fillets, place on a rack skin side down, and air-dry in a well ventilated location for 2 hours.

In a small saucepan over medium-high heat, bring wine and ginger to a boil. Reduce liquid to about 1/2 cup. Remove from heat and whisk in wasabi and butter pieces, one at a time, until sauce is thickened. Season with salt and pepper. Keep warm over very low heat. Do not allow sauce to get too hot or it will separate or "break." Place fillets, skin side down in a medium-hot smoker and smoke until fish is just-cooked and still moist. Place one fillet on each plate and spoon sauce over each.

Note: When using smaller fillets, you can stack them on top of each other, forming the stacked fillets into the appropriate size.

POACHED STEELHEAD
WITH PEPPERCORN VINAIGRETTE

I'll never forget the day I witnessed a five-pound steelhead trout caught on fresh salmon roe in a small stream above Chico, California. Unfortunately, the fish was not my catch, but I was fortunate enough to enjoy the fish that night prepared in the following manner.

6 servings

1	quart cold water
2	cups dry white wine
2	cups white wine vinegar
1	large onion, chopped
1	carrot, chopped
2	celery stalks, diced
2	fresh rosemary sprigs
1	tablespoon salt
¼	teaspoon freshly ground black pepper
2 ½	pounds steelhead fillet(s), skin and head removed

In a large stock pot, combine first 9 ingredients and heat to boil. Reduce heat to low, cover and simmer for 30 minutes. Let cool and strain liquid into a large baking dish, long enough to accommodate the fish. Cover and place in a 450° F oven for approximately 15 minutes or until meat is opaque in the center and bones can be easily removed. Remove dish from oven, remove skin and pull skeleton out carefully. Place equal portion of fish on each plate and top with warmed vinaigrette.

Peppercorn Vinaigrette

⅓	cup white wine vinegar
1	garlic clove, minced
2	teaspoons dijon mustard
1	tablespoon pink peppercorns, crushed
1	tablespoon green peppercorns, crushed
¼	teaspoon freshly ground black pepper
⅓	teaspoon salt
1	tablespoon sugar
1	cup olive oil

In a food processor or blender, process all ingredients except olive oil for 30 seconds. While motor is running, add oil in a very thin stream until emulsified and vinaigrette thickens. Warm in a saucepan over very low heat to serve.

BAKED RAINBOW TROUT
IN PARCHMENT PAPER

*The parchment paper allows the fish to steam in white wine, butter, lemon and fresh
herbs. Serve the fish in the paper, hot out of the oven and watch your guests as they
open up the package and take in the unbelievable aroma.*

4 servings

4	12 to 14 inch rainbow trout, skin and heads removed
½	cup dry white wine
6	ounces butter, softened
1	red onion, sliced into thin rings
4	garlic cloves, cut in half
1	lemon, sliced into 8 slices
2	tablespoons fresh basil, minced
2	tablespoons fresh sage, minced
2	tablespoons fresh thyme, minced
	salt and pepper to taste
4	14 inch circles of parchment paper

In a medium bowl, combine wine and butter, whisking to blend. Place blended butter
in refrigerator to firm up mixture. For each serving, lay out one parchment paper
circle. Place fish across the center of the paper. Spread 1/4 of the butter-wine mixture
over fish. Combine fresh herbs and sprinkle over fish. Set onion rings over fish. Lay
2 garlic clove halves and 2 lemon slices over onion. Season with salt and pepper.
Fold paper over, overlapping edges. Fold bottom edge up and over top edge, towards
center of the paper. Staple edges securely. Carefully place fish on a shallow baking
sheet in a 400° F oven for 10 to 12 minutes. Remove from oven and serve immediately.

FRESH TROUT
WITH CITRUS

A great way to prepare just-caught trout either streamside or in the kitchen. Fillet fish by first placing on a firm surface. Make a knife cut below the head with a sharp fillet knife. Hold onto the head while running the knife blade along the backbone, angling the blade slightly downward, until the side is excised at the tail. Flip the fish over and repeat the process for the other side.

4 servings

4-6	fresh trout, cleaned and filleted and lightly seasoned with salt and freshly ground black pepper
2	tablespoons olive oil
3	garlic cloves, mashed
½	cup white wine
1	lemon, quartered
1	lime, quartered
1	orange, quartered
½	red onion, cut into rings
2	tablespoons butter, chilled

Heat olive oil in a large skillet over medium heat. Add garlic and sauté for 2 to 3 minutes. Place trout, skin side down, in skillet and cook for 3 minutes. Add wine and cook until wine reduces by one-half and meat begins to get firm. Add onion rings. Squeeze citrus fruits into pan and sauté until meat is thoroughly cooked, about 3 minutes more. Remove trout to serving plates. Remove pan from heat and whisk in butter until sauce thickens. Pour sauce over fillets and serve immediately.

BARBECUED STURGEON
WITH RED PEPPER RELISH

A simple preparation of my favorite game fish that tastes as much like a delicate piece of pork as it does fish. Sturgeon is now raised commercially in many areas. If you are not able to catch one, ask your grocer to order some for you.

4 servings

4	4 to 6 oz. sturgeon fillets, cartilage and skin removed
	cup freshly squeezed lime juice
¼	*salt and freshly ground black pepper to taste*
1	cup red bell pepper, diced
½	cup black olives, chopped
¼	cup slivered almonds
1	garlic clove, minced
2	tablespoons fresh basil, chopped
1	tablespoon red wine vinegar
2	tablespoons olive oil

Sprinkle lime juice over fillets, season with salt and pepper and let stand at room temperature for 1 hour. Combine remaining ingredients in a small bowl and let stand until ready to serve. Place the sturgeon fillets on a lightly greased grill in a medium-hot barbecue. Cover and cook for 3 to 4 minutes per side or until grill marks appear on both sides. Garnish each with red pepper relish.

SALMON GRAVLAX
WITH HERBS AND PEPPER

A real treat when prepared with firm, fresh salmon fillets. the preparation may seem a bit unorthodox if you've never made gravlax-style salmon before, but I am certain that you'll want to try it more than once. Serve as a first course with toast points or crackers with Creole mustard.

8 - 10 Appetizer Servings

⅓	cup Kosher salt
⅓	cup light brown sugar
2	tablespoons each, white, black and pink peppercorns, crushed.
1	tablespoon mustard seeds, crushed
½	cup fresh dill, chopped
½	cup fresh basil, chopped
½	cup fresh parsley, chopped
1	lemon
2	1 pound salmon fillets, skin intact, all bones removed

Combine first 6 ingredients and mix well. Squeeze one-half of each lemon on the flesh side of each fillet. In a long, deep glass or ceramic dish, sprinkle one fourth of the herb mixture on the bottom of the dish. Place one of the fillets, skin side down in dish over herb mixture. Distribute one-half of the herb mixture evenly over the salmon flesh. Place the second fillet skin side down, matching head to head with first fillet. Sprinkle remaining mixture over exposed skin side of second fillet. Cover with a double layer of heavy foil and place two bricks on top of foil. Place in refrigerator for 3 days, turning the salmon 2 to 3 times daily.

Prior to serving. wipe off the herb mixture and pat dry with paper towels. Place the fillets, skin side down, on a cutting board and slice thin slices diagonally across the grain.

MARYLAND
FISH CHOWDER

Growing up in Northern Virginia, I had the opportunity to spend some quality time on Maryland's Eastern Shore feasting on oysters, crabs, scallops and a variety of fresh fish. The following simple chowder recipe can be used with an assortment of freshwater and saltwater game fish.

6 servings

¼   cup salt pork, diced
1   large yellow onion, diced
2   carrots, diced
3   celery stalks, diced
½   cup dry white wine
     dash Worcestershire Sauce
     water
2   cups potatoes peeled, diced into 1/2 inch cubes and cooked firm
¼   cup fresh parsley, minced
1   quart half and half milk
2   cups skinless fish fillets
     salt & freshly ground black pepper to taste

In a medium stock pot over medium heat, cook salt pork until lightly browned. Stir in onions, carrots and celery. Increase heat to medium-high and cook for 3 to 4 minutes. Add clam juice, white wine, Worcestershire, fish, and enough water to barely cover fish. Cover and simmer for 10 minutes. Reduce heat to low medium, add potatoes, parsley and half and half, and fish. Cook until fish is just cooked and potatoes are warmed throughout. Season to taste with salt and pepper.

GRILLED STRIPED BASS
WITH AVOCADO CREAM SAUCE

Place a piece of lightly greased foil over the barbecue grate and place the fish on the foil to keep It from sticking.

4 servings

4	6 to 8 ounce striper fillets, skin removed
½	teaspoon ground coriander
½	teaspoon paprika
½	teaspoon freshly ground black pepper
⅔	cup dry white wine
2	garlic cloves, minced
1	medium, ripe avocado, skin and seed removed
½	cup heavy cream
2	teaspoons freshly squeezed lemon juice
1	dash Tabasco
	salt and freshly ground black pepper to taste

Season fillets on both sides with coriander, paprika and pepper. Let stand for 15-20 minutes while barbecue is warming and coals are getting white-hot. When coals are ready, move them to the outside edges of the barbecue. For gas units, set heat at medium. Grill each side of the fillets only until grill marks appear. Total cooking time should not exceed 3 -4 minutes per side.

To prepare sauce, add wine and garlic to a small saucepan, bring to a boil and cook uncovered for 3 to 4 minutes. Transfer to a food processor or blender. Add avocado and process until puréed. Add remaining ingredients, process for 3- seconds to blend, then transfer contents to saucepan, season with salt and pepper and warm before serving. Place one cooked striper fillet on each plate and drizzle sauce over half of each fillet.

SIMM'S SWEET-HOT
GLAZED SALMON

Bob Simms, host of The Outdoor Show on KFBK in Sacramento CA, likes his salmon crispy on the edges. This marinade and glaze will do the trick. Keep in mind that the reason the fish is crispy is because the honey is burning along the outside edges. It's good.

4 servings

4	6 – 8 ounce salmon steaks or fillets (skin on or off)
⅓	cup honey
¼	cup soy sauce
¼	cup rice vinegar
3	tablespoons hoisin sauce
1	tablespoon Asian chili sauce (or sub any hot sauce)
3	tablespoons water
1	tablespoon fresh ginger, peeled and minced
3	cloves garlic minced

Combine honey with remaining ingredients (not the salmon!) in a small saucepan. Heat to blend flavors and then cool mixture/glaze. Place salmon in a shallow container and brush glaze over both sides, saving at least half to use a glaze when cooking. Cover and refrigerate for 2 hours. Fish can be either broiled or grilled. I prefer the grill. To broil, place on a baking pan under a preheated medium-heat broiler, about 6 inches from the heat source. After 4 – 5 minutes, remove from oven and baste with additional glaze. Return to oven and cook 3 – 4 more minutes or until just cooked. Check often to make sure that the fish is getting a little crispy, but not "burnt to a crisp." When grilling, place fish on a well-greased medium-high heat grill. Grill until grill marks appear on the bottom and fish moves easily on the grill, about 5 minutes. Flip over, baste liberally with glaze and cook 4 minutes more.

CATFISH
WITH PECAN CREAM CHEESE

I've used this recipe on a variety of both freshwater and saltwater fish. The key is to make sure that the fillets are thin enough to roll up without a struggle and thick enough to keep from tearing.

2 servings

2   6 to 10 ounce catfish fillets (about 1/4 inch thick), skin removed
1   teaspoon Cajun spice
⅔   cup cream cheese, softened
1   teaspoon freshly squeezed lemon juice
1   green onion, white and green part, minced
¼   cup roasted pecans, chopped
2   tablespoons dry cornbread stuffing, smashed
    salt and pepper to taste

Season fillets with Cajun spice. In a small bowl, combine remaining ingredients. Lay fillets flat on surface. Spread cream cheese mixture evenly over each fillet. Starting at one end, roll each fillet snugly and secure with a wooden skewer. Sprinkle additional cornbread stuffing over top and bake in a preheated 400 degree oven for 15 minutes. Remove skewer and serve.

LEMON-LIME TARTAR SAUCE

Use a vegetable peeler or zester to remove the outside or yellow and green part of the lemon and lime. Don't go deep into the white part!

Makes 1 1/4 cups

1   cup mayonnaise
1   tablespoon sweet pickle relish
1   teaspoon capers
1   tablespoon yellow mustard
1   teaspoon each lemon and lime zest, minced
1   tablespoon lime juice
1   teaspoon lemon juice
2   garlic cloves, minced
1   tablespoon fresh parsley, minced

Combine all ingredients in a bowl, cover and refrigerate for 1 – 3 hours before serving.

HOT AND CRUSTY
LARGEMOUTH BASS

The fiery flavor and crunchy texture of this simple fish dish makes it one of my favorites. You can serve this either as an appetizer or as a main dish. Serve with your favorite dipping sauce such as tartar, cocktail or honey-mustard. Try not to put too much spice into your accompanying sauce since the fish is plenty hot by itself. This recipe works equally well with any fish with a moderate to low oil content. When frying fish, make certain that your fish and batter are both very cold before beginning the process. Cold batters and seasonings adhere to cold fish more readily than to warm or room temperature fish.

4 – 6 servings

2	pounds bass fillets, cut into chunks
¾	cup milk
2	eggs
	Tabasco
½	cup red onion, minced
⅔	cup yellow cornmeal
½	cup flour
½	teaspoon cayenne pepper
½	teaspoon salt
	canola or peanut oil for frying

Lightly whisk together milk, eggs and several dashes of Tabasco. It's your funeral, so use as much of the hot stuff as you think you can handle. In a wide bowl, combine remaining ingredients except oil. Heat oil over medium-high heat until hot but not smoking.

Dip fish in milk mixture and then cornmeal mixture. Drop carefully into hot oil with tongs, one piece at a time. Remove and place on paper towels to drain when fish is golden brown.

201

POOR MAN'S SHRIMP

OK, here's the deal. This is one of Donny Mac's favorite recipes for a few good reasons. First of all, it's country. Just the name implies that you're going to make something like bluegill taste like shrimp. It's like saying that monkfish is Poor Man's Lobster. I'll buy that if you believe that a hot dog, prepared just the right way, can be called Poor Man's Pork Tenderloin. Second, it's easy to prepare. Finally, it tastes good. We ate a pile of them following the taping of our HuntFishCook Shellcracker show. I hate to admit it, but it really does taste like shrimp.

    bluegill, shellcracker, etc fillets - cut into finger-width strips
    Old Bay Seasoning
    Lawry's Seasoned Salt
    vegetables steamer basket
    cocktail sauce
    saltine crackers

Heat an inch or two of water in a steamer basket in a medium to larger pot. Lay the fish strips in the basket without overcrowding. Season with Old Bay and Lawry's. Cover and steam for 3 - 4 minutes or until fish is firm. Remove basket from pot and allow to cool. Place "shrimp" on cracker and top with cocktail sauce.

PICKLED SHRIMP

The Marinade

1¼	cup canola oil
¾	cup white vinegar
1½	teaspoons Kosher salt
2½	teaspoons celery seed
2½	tablespoons capers, with juice
1	tablespoon Tabasco sauce

The Pickled Shrimp

2½	pounds shrimp
¼	cup pickling spice
2	quarts water for boiling shrimp
1	medium onion, quartered
3-4	bay leaves
1	lemon, cut into 5 – 6 slices
1	cup artichoke hearts (optional)
1	cup button mushrooms (optional)

Heat marinade ingredients in a medium saucepan over medium heat. Bring to boil to blend flavors. Remove from heat and thoroughly cool marinade.

Bring water and pickling spice to a boil over high heat for 4 – 5 minutes. Add shrimp and cook until just pink. Drain shrimp through colander. Place in large jars or a container with onion, bay leaves, lemon slices, artichoke hearts and mushrooms. Pour marinade over. Refrigerate for 12 hours before eating. Keep refrigerated.

SAUGER AND SHRIMP CAKES

If you like crab cakes, you'll really like these sauger and shrimp cakes. There are two things to remember when making fish cakes. First, they have to be just moist enough to hold together, but not so moist that they fall apart when cooked. Second, you can't mess with them when they're in the pan or they'll break apart. Now that we've got that straight, let's get started. I use any light white fish that will flake easily, like crappie, halibut, rockfish, etc.

4 servings (8 large cakes)

8	large shrimp; tail-on, peeled, deveined and butterflied
2	tablespoons butter
½	cup onion, finely diced
1	jalapeno pepper, seeded and finely diced
¼	cup fresh cilantro, chopped
4	cups fish fillets, flaked and pressed dry with paper towels (really important!)
1	tablespoon red pepper flakes
2	garlic cloves, minced
2	tablespoons flour
3	tablespoons Japanese breadcrumbs (or any breadcrumbs)
½	teaspoon salt
⅛	teaspoon pepper
1	teaspoon Old Bay Seasoning
3	tablespoons mayonnaise
2	egg whites, beaten
	oil for frying

Heat butter in a medium skillet over medium-high heat. Add onion and pepper and sauté for 4 – 5 minutes. Make sure that fish has been patted dry thoroughly with paper towels. In a large bowl, add cilantro, fish, pepper flakes, garlic and cooled onion/pepper from pan. Dust shrimp thoroughly with flour. Sprinkle remaining flour, breadcrumbs salt, pepper and Old Bay Seasoning over while tossing, making sure to coat fish evenly. Fold in mayonnaise and egg whites. Take some of the mixture and form into a ball, about 3 inches in diameter. If it holds together, you're in business. If it's too dry and flaky, add some more breadcrumbs. It should be moist, but not soggy. Form mixture into 8 equal sized patties. Hold shrimp flat and build the fish cake around the shrimp. The idea is to have a normal looking fish cake with a shrimp tail sticking out of the side.

Add enough oil to just cover the bottom of a large skillet and heat over medium heat. When oil is hot, add cakes and cook until medium brown on one side, about 5 - 6 minutes. Carefully flip over and brown other sides, about 5 minutes more. When cakes are just cooked, remove from pan and top with your favorite sauce.

PARMESAN BAKED HALIBUT

This one's not for the heart-healthy set, but it sure does taste good! It's better with a good quality freshly grated Parmesan cheese, but the pre-shredded stuff will do. Serve with a fresh vegetable and a glass of Kunde Chardonnay.

4 servings

4	6-ounce halibut fillets
	salt and freshly ground pepper
3	tablespoons butter
1	cup heavy cream
¾	cup shredded Parmesan cheese
½	teaspoon Italian seasoning
2	green onions, chopped
2	garlic cloves, minced
1	cup tomato, seeded and diced

Season fish with salt and pepper. Rub a 9-inch (or similar sized) baking dish with 1 tablespoon of the butter and arrange fish in dish. In a saucepan, melt remaining butter over medium heat. Stir in cream and bring to a boil. Stir in cheese, Italian seasoning, onions and garlic. Pour sauce over fish and place dish in a preheated 400 degree oven. Cook until top is lightly browned, about 18-20 minutes. Top with tomato before serving.

BASQUE-STYLE BAKED DORADO

Basque cuisine is simple and straightforward, taking advantage of fresh seasonal herbs and vegetables. The Basque region of Spain is a rugged land of sea, mountains and wine. Hey, that sounds like California!

4 servings

1½ - 2	pounds dorado fillet
	tablespoons olive oil
3	salt and pepper to taste
1	medium red onion, chopped
2	garlic cloves, minced
2	anchovy fillets, chopped (optional, but great)
¼	cup dry red wine
2	cups tomatoes, peeled, seeded and chopped (canned is OK)
¼	cup chopped black olives
2	tablespoons fresh parsley, chopped
	pinch dried thyme

Preheat oven to 450 degrees. Rub fillets with 1 tablespoon of the olive oil and season with salt and pepper. Arrange in a heavy-duty baking dish. Combine remaining ingredients in a bowl. Season with salt and pepper. Spoon tomato mixture over fish and bake, uncovered, for about 20 minutes or until the fish is just cooked.

GRILLED HALIBUT
with NECTARINE AND CHERRY SALSA

If your halibut has a habit of sticking to the grill, it's a good idea to leave the skin on while cooking and then remove the skin before serving. For best grilling results, pray some pan spray on the grates before lighting, set skin side down on grates and don't flip it unless you're sure it will work. Close the lid on the 'cue and the fish will cook throughout.

4	6 to 8 ounce halibut fillets, skin removed
	salt and freshly ground pepper
2	medium nectarines; flesh chopped into 1/2 inch cubes
1	cup cherries, seeded and halved
½	jalapeño pepper, seeded and minced
2	tablespoons fresh mint, chopped
2	green onions; white part and about half of the green part, minced
½	teaspoon fresh ginger, grated
2	garlic cloves, minced
1	tablespoon lime juice
1	teaspoon lemon juice

Season fish liberally with salt and pepper. Place on a medium-heat grill until just cooked. Flip fish over half way through cooking if you are confident that it will remain intact.

To prepare salsa, combine all ingredients and let stand at room temperature for 30 minutes. To serve, place fish on plate and spoon salsa over middle half. Do not smother fish with salsa.

TUNA
WITH SESAME GINGER DIPPING SAUCE

Buy your sesame seeds in the Asian or Hispanic section of your market. Sesame seeds are much cheaper there than in the spice section.

4 - 6 appetizer servings

1½   pounds fresh tuna loin, cut into 2-inch thick strips
¼   cup Creole mustard
1   tablespoon sesame oil
¼   cup soy sauce
⅔   cup sesame seeds
2   tablespoons vegetable, olive or peanut oil

Combine Creole mustard, sesame oil, soy sauce and sesame seeds in a large bowl. Add tuna and toss to coat. Cover and refrigerate for 1 – 6 hours. Heat oil over medium-high heat in a large skillet and lightly brown tuna, but not past medium-rare. Slice into 1/4-inch thick slices and arrange on platter. Serve with dipping sauce.

Sesame Ginger Dipping Sauce

½   cup soy sauce
2   tablespoons lemon juice
1   teaspoon sesame oil
2   green onions, chopped
1   teaspoon fresh gingerroot, minced
2   cloves garlic, minced
2   tablespoons olive oil
1   tablespoon Asian chili-garlic sauce or Tabasco

Combine all ingredients in a container with a tight-fitting lid and shake vigorously to blend flavor

OVEN "FRIED" CRAPPIE
with MUSTARD DILL SAUCE

4 servings

1½   pounds crappie fillets
1   cup flour
1   teaspoon onion powder
½   teaspoon garlic powder
½   teaspoon salt
¼   teaspoon white pepper
2   eggs
1   cup flat beer
1½   cups seasoned breadcrumbs
½   cup cornmeal
     pan coating spray
6   lemon wedges

Preheat oven to 425 degrees. Combine flour with next 4 ingredients. In a medium bowl, beat eggs well with beer. Combine breadcrumbs and cornmeal and spread out on a plate. For each fillet, first dredge the fish with the seasoned flour. Dip the fillets into the egg mixture and then roll in the breadcrumbs. Spray fish lightly with pan coating spray. Place each fillet on a lightly oiled baking pan and bake uncovered for 5 to 7 minutes or until golden brown. Serve with lemon wedges and mustard and dill sauce on the side for dipping.

Mustard and Dill Sauce

½   cup mayonnaise
1   tablespoon brown sugar
2   tablespoons Creole mustard
2   tablespoons fresh dill, minced
     dash Tabasco
     pinch salt

Combine all ingredients and refrigerate.

FLOUNDER
with MANGO MARGARITA SAUCE

The basic deal here is to make a margarita, less the ice, dump it onto your fish. It won't hurt to drink a margarita in the process.

4 servings

4	6 – 8 ounce flounder fillets
¼	cup all-purpose flour
¼	cup masa flour (or sub additional 1/4 cup flour)
1	teaspoon kosher salt
2	tablespoons butter
1	tablespoon olive oil
¼	cup tequila
¼	cup sweet and sour mix
2	teaspoons sweetened lime juice (like Rose's)
2	tablespoons orange liquor
2	garlic cloves, minced
1	tablespoon freshly squeezed lime juice
½	cup fresh mango, peeled and cut into 1/4-inch cubes
4	tablespoons butter, chilled
1	tablespoon fresh cilantro leaves, chopped

Combine flour, masa and salt. Lightly dust fish with mixture. Heat 2 tablespoons butter and oil in a large skillet over medium heat. Add fish and lightly brown on one side. Flip over and cook for 2 – 3 minutes. Combine tequila and next 5 ingredients.

CAUTION!
Adding any liquid that contains alcohol to a hot pan is dangerous and it may ignite. Remove the pan a safe distance away from the heat and slowly add liquid while keeping the pan away from your face or anything you don't want to burn.

Add 1/4 cup to pan with fish. Remove fish when just cooked and keep warm. Add remaining liquid (see DANGER) and reduce liquid to a few tablespoons. Whisk in chilled butter and mango until butter melts. Take skillet off the stove immediately and stir in cilantro. Spoon sauce over fish.

CRUNCHY CATFISH
with LEMON LIME TARTAR SAUCE

The special ingredient, besides really fresh catfish, is masa flour. It's the treated corn flour used to make tamales. It's probably in your market, but you may not know it's there. Look for a bag in the Hispanic or baking sections of your store. A $4 bag will last you a long time, unless you get the urge to make a batch of tamales. If you don't feel like hunting down the masa, substitute regular old flour. Lemon Lime Tartar Sauce is on page 200.

4 servings

1½   pounds catfish fillets, cut into 1-inch wide strips

The Wet Stuff

3   eggs, beaten
2   tablespoons yellow mustard
2-3 garlic cloves, minced
1   teaspoon salt
½   teaspoon black pepper
     dash (or more) regular or Chipotle Tabasco
⅓   cup milk

Combine all ingredients in a medium bowl. Keep cold.

The Dry Stuff

1   cup masa harina flour
1   cup corn meal
1   tablespoon salt
1   teaspoon black pepper
     oil for frying

Combine in a medium bowl.

Dredge fish first into The Wet Stuff, then coat with The Dry Stuff. Using tongs, carefully place each piece, one or two at a time, into 360 degree oil in a deep, heavy-duty pot or fryer.

Fry until golden brown and then drain on paper towels. Season with additional salt and pepper as desired while fish are still hot. Serve with Tartar Sauce on the side.

SESAME CRUSTED FISH

Take a hunk of firm fleshed fish, like yellowtail, tuna or wahoo and give it a crispy sesame crust...sounds pretty good doesn't it? Buy your sesame seeds in the Asian or Hispanic section of the market. They're much cheaper than in the spice section.

4 servings

4	6 – 8 ounce firm fish fillets, skin removed
2	tablespoons sesame oil
3	tablespoons soy sauce
1	tablespoon Dijon mustard
½	cup sesame seeds
3	tablespoons vegetable or peanut oil
2	tablespoons freshly squeezed lime juice
2	tablespoons freshly squeezed lemon juice
1	tablespoon fresh gingerroot, minced
3	green onions, chopped

Combine sesame oil, 1 tablespoon of the soy sauce and Dijon mustard. Rub mixture over both sides of fish fillets. Cover with sesame seeds and lightly press seeds into both sides. Heat oil in a large skillet over medium heat. Add fish and cook until sesame seeds are lightly browned on one side. Carefully flip over and cook other side for 1 minute. Add remaining soy sauce, lemon and lime juice and gingerroot to pan and cook until fish is just a tad underdone. Remove from pan and transfer to plates. Top with chopped green onion

PACIFIC NORTHWEST SALMON
with bok choy

This recipe is from Don Gazzaniga's No Salt, Lowest Sodium Internatonal Cookbook. It is made with fresh, wild Pacific salmon; the fresh vegetables make it a real taste treat. A serving has only 93.9 mg of sodium. Timing with the preparation is essential, but easily done.

4 servings

- 4   5-ounce fillets of Pacific wild (Coho) salmon fillets* (254.2 mg)
- 4   ounces mushrooms, sliced (4.2 mg)
- ½   medium size red bell pepper, cut into about 12 strips (1.19 mg)
- ½   pound red cabbage thinly sliced or shredded to equal 4 cups (75.6 mg)
- 2   small bok choy cleaned and cut vertically into 1/4ths (38 mg)
- ½   cup filtered low-sodium water (trace)
- 1   cup uncooked rice, steamed (makes about 2 to 3 cups steamed rice (2 mg)

  Sauce:
- 1   tablespoon filtered low-sodium water (trace)
- 2   tablespoons natural rice vinegar (.30 mg)
- 1   tablespoon sesame oil (trace)
- 1   tablespoon sugar or Splenda substitute (trace)

You will need a nonstick fry pan and a nonstick** griddle or grill.

Prepare rice according to package directions. Usually takes 15 to 25 minutes depending on the method used. Prepare the salmon for grilling. Especially nice done on a bar-b-que. Grilling time varies with thickness of fillets, but figure on at least 10 to 15 minutes.

Prepare the vegetables and separate them. You will cook them individually using a large 12-14 inch nonstick fry pan with lid. They will cook in approximately 10 minutes.

Make sauce by whisking all the ingredients together in a small bowl. When the rice is just about ready, put the salmon on the grill.

Heat ½ cup of filtered watered in the fry pan over medium heat and cook the mushrooms and red pepper until they begin to soften about 3 – 4 minutes stirring frequently, remove them to a small bowl and keep warm. Pour the sauce into the fry pan (most of the water from the mushrooms will be evaporated), and heat over medium heat.

Add the cabbage and sauté until it begins to wilt about 4 minutes, put the lid on the pan for the final 2 minutes. Remove to a second bowl and keep warm. Last, when the fish and rice are ready, add ¼ cup of water to the same pan, heat and add the bok choy. Cover with lid. It will steam rapidly in about 2 – 3 minutes. The variance in time accounts for keeping the vegetables from overcooking and the cabbage from turning the others red.

Serve each plate individually by putting ½ cup rice on a plate and arranging a bed of vegetables next to it. Lay the grilled salmon on top of both and serve with a wedge of lemon.

FISH CREOLE

Of the dozens of Creole-style fish recipes I've tried, this one is the easiest and best tasting. The beauty of the dish is that you can use either one type of lean, firm fish or an assortment of fish and shellfish, depending on what is available. Try this dish with halibut, sea bass, cod, snapper, drum and dorado. Serve with white rice.

6 - 8 servings

1½	pounds fish fillets, cut into bite-sized pieces
15-20	large shrimp, peeled and deveined
15-20	medium fresh oysters with oyster liquor
	juice of 2 lemons
1	teaspoon Old Bay Seasoning (optional)
	salt and freshly ground black pepper
⅓	cup peanut oil
⅓	cup flour
1	cup yellow onion, finely chopped
¾	cup green bell pepper, finely chopped
1	jalapeño pepper, seeded and finely chopped
1	cup celery, chopped
6	garlic cloves, minced
1	6-ounce can tomato paste
2	cups tomatoes, fresh or canned, diced
1	cup fish stock
¼	cup Cajun spice mix

Place fish, shrimp and oysters in a bowl, squeeze lemon juice over, season liberally with salt and pepper and set bowl aside. In a heavy-duty large saucepan (preferably cast iron), heat oil over medium-high heat. Add flour a little at a time and stir constantly until medium brown in color. Reduce heat to medium-low and add onions, peppers, celery and garlic and cook for 7 minutes, stirring often. Reduce heat to low and stir in remaining ingredients and juice from fish, shrimp and oysters. Cook for an additional 10 minutes. Adjust seasonings with salt and freshly ground black pepper.

Place the fish, shrimp and oysters in a large baking dish. Pour sauce over and bake, uncovered, for 20 minutes or until fish is firm, but flaky.

GRILLED
OR PAN-SEARED GROUPER
with TOMATO RELISH

When it comes to cooking on a warm day, I'll always choose the 'cue. The tomato relish is especially good with real vine-ripened summer tomatoes, not the ones from the grocery store that claim to be vine-ripened. Who are they kidding?

4 servings

4   6 – 8 ounce fish fillets or steaks

The Rub

2   garlic cloves, minced
1   tablespoon fresh rosemary leaves
1   lemon, juice only
    pinch each salt and pepper
⅓   cup olive oil

Tomato Relish

1   cup ripe tomato, seeded and diced
⅓   cup red onion, finely diced
⅓   cup black olives, chopped
1   garlic clove, minced
1   tablespoon balsamic vinegar
½   teaspoon capers, chopped
½   teaspoon sugar
¼   cup olive oil
    salt and pepper to taste

To prepare the rub, combine all rub ingredients in a small bowl and let stand at room temperature for 30 minutes to 1 hour. Brush mixture on both sides of the fish. Place over medium coals or a medium-hot gas grill and cook on 1 side for 4-5 minutes without moving the fish. Flip fish over and baste with more of the rub. Remove fish when done, about 3 – 5 minutes more.

To prepare the relish, combine all ingredients and season with salt and pepper. Let stand for 30 minutes at room temperature. Spoon relish over fish.

JAKE'S FIRST HALIBUT

July 11, 2005 - Santa Cruz, CA Eight year old Jake Leysath landed his first halibut today, a 21-pounder, after an exhausting morning of fishing off the coast of Northern California. Using fresh anchovies and the skill of a seasoned fisherman, Jake boated the beauty after nearly 10 minutes of a hard-fought battle.

4 servings

4	halibut fillets, about 6 - 8 ounces each
	olive oil, lemon juice, salt and pepper
½	cup red onion, thinly sliced
⅓	cup pitted kalamata olives, chopped
1	cup fresh basil leaves, loosely packed
1	teaspoon Dijon mustard
2-3	tablespoons balsamic vinegar
2-3	garlic cloves, thinly sliced
1	cup diced tomato
2-3	handfulls fresh spinach leaves
⅓	cup crumbled feta cheese

Rub fish with olive oil and lemon juice. Season with salt and pepper. Heat a couple of tablespoons of olive oil in a large skillet over medium-high heat. Add fish and brown on one side, about 4 - 5 minutes. Flip over and cook for 2 minutes more. Move fish to one side of pan. To other side, add onion and next 5 ingredients. Cook for 2 minutes more. Remove fish from pan before overcooking. To pan, add spinach, tomato and 2 - 3 tablespoons more olive oil. Heat until spnach starts to wilt.

Mound spinach mixture on center of plates. Top with fish. Sprinkle feta cheese over fish.

HALIBUT
with HERB AND CHIVE OIL

Fresh halibut is on my Top Ten list of favorite fish, especially the smaller "local" variety from California. This blended oil will complement any fish, even if you do insist on overcooking it. You can prepare the fish any way you please – grill, broil, sauté, bake or pan-sear. When not grilling the fish, I like to dust it with a 50/50 blend of flour and masa (the stuff you make tamales with) and then season with salt and pepper. Serve this with warm buttered pasta.

4 servings

4	halibut steaks or fillets, about 6 – 8 ounces each
	salt and pepper

Herb and Chive Oil

½	cup fresh parsley leaves
½	cup fresh basil leaves
1	tablespoon fresh oregano leaves
1	tablespoon fresh thyme leaves
1	tablespoon orange zest
½	teaspoon whole peppercorns
⅔	cup canola oil

In a blender or food processor, combine parsley with next 5 ingredients. Add to a saucepan with oil and heat over low heat for 2 – 3 minutes, but do not boil! Remove from heat. Allow to cool at room temperature for 2 – 3 hours. Place in a jar with a tight-fitting lid and shake vigorously before serving.

Season fish with salt and pepper. Lightly brown on both sides until just cooked. Drizzle oil over fish.

BOURBON GLAZED FISH

4 servings

4	6 to 8 ounce fish fillets, skin removed
	freshly ground black pepper
⅓	cup dark brown sugar
⅓	cup bourbon
¼	cup soy sauce
1	teaspoon hoisin sauce
4	garlic cloves, minced
2	tablespoons fresh gingerroot, peeled and minced
⅓	cup orange juice (preferably freshly-squeezed)
1	lemon, juice only

Season fish with pepper. Combine remaining ingredients. Place fish in a glass or plastic container or large zip-lock bag. Reserve 1/2 cup of the marinade. Pour remaining marinade over fish and refrigerate 2 to 4 hours, turning occasionally. Remove fish from marinade (discard marinade). Pat fish down with paper towels and air dry in the refrigerator for 30 minutes. Grill fish over white-hot coals until just cooked…a little rare in the center is perfect! Just before removing from the grill, brush with reserved marinade.

ASIAN SLAW

AND SPICY SHRIMP

4 large servings

The Slaw

4	cups shredded cabbage
½	red bell pepper, thinly sliced
½	orange, yellow or green bell pepper, thinly sliced
4	green onions, chopped
1	cup dry roasted peanuts
1	cup mayonnaise
½	cup rice vinegar or white wine vinegar
1	lime, juice only
2	tablespoons sugar
½	teaspoon gingerroot, peeled and minced
2	tablespoons soy sauce
	salt and pepper to taste

In a large bowl, combine cabbage with next 4 ingredients. In a medium bowl, combine mayonnaise with next 5 ingredients and whisk together until smooth. Season with salt and pepper. If dressing is too sweet for your taste, add more vinegar or lime juice. Too sour? Add more sugar. Add dressing to slaw and toss to coat evenly.

The Spicy Shrimp

1	pound large shrimp, peeled and deveined
2	tablespoons blackening spice or your favorite Cajun spice
2	tablespoons olive oil
2	limes, juice only

Season shrimp with blackening or Cajun spice. Heat oil in a large skillet over medium-high heat. Add shrimp and cook quickly, about 1 – 2 minutes per side. Squeeze lime juice over shrimp and add to slaw.

BROILED CALICO BASS
with TOMATO AND CUCUMBER SALSA

This is a light, crunchy salsa that won't overpower the mild flavor of calico bass. You can also sauté, pan sear or grill the fish. The skin can be left on or off. I like to toss the tomatoes gently in a colander and let rest for a few minutes to drain off some of the tomato liquid before making the salsa.

4 servings

4	6 – 8 ounce calico bass fillets
¼	cup melted butter
2	tablespoons lemon juice
¼	teaspoon garlic powder
	salt and pepper

Combine butter, lemon juice, garlic powder and a pinch each of salt and pepper. Place fish in a greased baking dish and brush butter mixture over fish. Place fish under a broiler, about 10 inches from the flame or coil. Broil for 6 – 8 minutes or until fish is lightly browned on top and just cooked. Top with salsa.

Tomato and Cucumber Salsa

1	cup red grape tomatoes, halved
½	cup cucumbers - peeled, seeded and diced
2	tablespoons black olives, chopped
2	tablespoons red onion, minced
1	tablespoon lime juice
1	tablespoon olive oil
2	tablespoons fresh cilantro leaves, minced
	dash Tabasco
	pinch ground cumin
3	tablespoons slivered almond, lightly toasted
	salt and pepper to taste

Combine all ingredients in a bowl and toss gently. Allow to rest at room temperature for 15 minutes before serving.

BROILED FISH
with ROASTED GARLIC SAUCE

This recipe works well with just about any type of fish, but I use it most often with striped bass and halibut. In addition to broiling, the fish can be cooked over smoky barbecue coals or in a sauté pan with some butter and white wine. The recipe calls for fillets, but smaller whole or halved fish work well also. To roast the garlic, place the whole garlic cloves in a pan, uncovered, and bake in a 325-degree oven until evenly golden browned, but not burnt. If you get distracted and burn the garlic, start over. Burnt garlic tastes bitter, not better.

4 servings

4	6 to 8 ounce fish fillets
	salt and pepper
¼	cup white wine vinegar
¼	cup whole garlic cloves, roasted (see above)
1	lemon, juice only
½	teaspoon Dijon mustard
½	teaspoon granulated sugar
⅓	cup olive oil

Season fillets with salt and pepper and place them in a lightly greased shallow baking dish. Broil about 8 to 10 inches away from the heat source until lightly browned. To prepare sauce, process the vinegar with the next 4 ingredients in a food processor or blender until well blended. While motor is running, add oil in a thin stream until emulsified. Season to taste with additional salt and pepper. To serve, drizzle room temperature sauce over warm fish.

GRILLED STUFFED FISH

Use this recipe with firm, fish like swordfish, yellowtail, tuna, shark or wahoo. Play around with the stuffing ingredients and create your own signature dish.

4 servings

Marinade

4	6 – 8 ounce fish fillets
¼	cup low-sodium soy sauce
1	teaspoon fresh ginger, peeled and minced
3	garlic cloves, minced
1	teaspoon sesame oil
3	tablespoons olive oil
2	tablespoons freshly squeezed lemon juice

Stuffing

3	cups fresh spinach; washed, dried and chopped
½	cup fresh basil leaves, chopped
2	green onions, chopped
1	cup fresh tomato, diced
2	garlic cloves, minced
2	tablespoons olive oil
2	tablespoons white wine vinegar
	pinch or two salt and pepper

Combine marinade ingredients. Pour over fish, cover and marinade for 1 to 4 hours. Remove fish from marinade and pour marinade into a saucepan. Simmer marinade over medium heat until liquid reduced by one-half.

Combine stuffing ingredients in a bowl and toss to combine. Cut a pocket into the fillets and stuff mixture into pockets. If desired, you can seal the pockets with toothpicks or you can be extra careful when grilling.

Rub stuffed fillets with olive oil and place on a medium-hot well-oiled barbecue grill. Cook for about 4 minutes per side or until just cooked. To serve, place fillets on plates and drizzle reduced marinade over.

SAUTEED FISH
with ARTICHOKES, BLACK OLIVES AND PARMESAN

This recipe works well with any fish - firm or flaky, dark or light.

4 servings

4	6 – 8 ounce fish fillets
2	tablespoons olive oil
	salt and pepper
3	tablespoons butter
1	cup canned artichoke bottoms, quartered
2	tablespoons roasted red pepper (from jar is fine), diced
1/4	cup pitted Kalamata olives, chopped
3	tablespoons red onion, finely minced
2	garlic cloves, minced
1	tablespoon lemon juice
1/3	cup shaved or shredded Parmesan cheese

Rub fish with olive oil and season with salt and pepper. Melt butter in large, oven-safe skillet over medium heat. Add fish and sauté on one side until lightly browned. Flip fish over and sauté 2 – 3 minutes more. Combine remaining ingredients except cheese in a bowl and spoon equally over fish. Put cheese over artichoke mixture and place skillet in a preheated 400 degree oven until cheese is melted. Serve immediately

GRILLED SPINY LOBSTER
with TOMATO BASIL BUTTER

Nothing messes up a delicious lobster more than an overpowering recipe that covers up the mild flavors of the meat. It's imperative that you cook and eat your lobsters at their freshest, not frozenest. Once they die, the meat degenerates and bacteria grows quickly. Whack 'em on the back of the head or place the live lobsters in boiling water to send them to lobster heaven. Save those spiny lobster legs and shells and make a lobster stock with cold water, celery, carrots and onion. Bring to a boil, simmer for 30 minutes, strain through a colander and simmer for 30 minutes more to concentrate flavors. You can also grind up the shells, heat with butter and strain through a sieve into ice water to make lobster butter. It's good.

I don't know how big your rock lobsters are, so I can't tell you how many lobsters to use for the recipe. About 3/4 cup of cooked lobster meat equals 1 pound.

1. Boil lobsters for 3 - 5 minutes, depending on the size of the lobster. Remove from water and place on a firm surface.

2. While lobster is boiling, prepare the Tomato Basil Butter Sauce

Tomato Basil Butter

Makes approximately 1 1/2 cups

¼	cup dry vermouth
2	tablespoons lemon juice
3	garlic cloves, minced
1½	sticks salted butter, cut into chunks
⅓	cup seeded and diced tomato
2	tablespoons fresh basil, chopped

Heat vermouth, lemon juice and garlic in a saucepan over medium-high heat. Reduce liquid to 2 tablespoons. Reduce heat to low and add butter, a chunk or two at a time, while whisking constantly. Keep heat low enough so that butter does not boil and separate. Keep whisking in butter until all is emulsified. Immediately remove pan from heat and stir in tomato and basil.

3. When lobsters are cool enough to handle, split lengthwise from head to tail and place on hot grill. Whether you remove the coral, liver, etc is your choice. While grilling, baste tail meat with Tomato Basil Butter. When meat is white or opaque, remove from grill and spoon additional Tomato Basil Butter over.

HONEY ORANGE STIR-FRIED FISH

Needless to say, you have to be a little careful when you stir-fry fish, especially the flaky varieties. How you cut your fish prior to stir-frying depends on the fish. If you plan on using light, flaky fish like halibut or sea bass, use larger pieces. Chances are good that they're going to break up when cooking. With sturdier fish like tuna or yellowtail, go with smaller pieces. The recipe calls for "1 hot pepper, seeds in or out, thinly sliced". I'm not big on sweet flavors unless they have a spicy counterpart. If you're OK with sweet stuff, leave it out. If you like it spicy, don't hold back. Use your favorite hot pepper – jalapeno, serrano, habanero.

4 servings

1/4	cup honey
1/3	cup soy sauce
1 1/2	tablespoons cider vinegar
1	tablespoon cornstarch
1	tablespoon orange rind, grated
1	tablespoon lime juice
1	tablespoon vegetable or peanut oil
4	cloves garlic, minced
2	teaspoons fresh gingerroot, grated
3	cups fish fillets, cut into bite-sized pieces (see above)
1	sweet red pepper, seeded and thinly sliced.
1	cup snow peas
1	hot pepper, seeds in or out, thinly sliced
3	green onions, chopped
1	cup orange segments
4	cups warm cooked noodles

Combine first 6 ingredients in a bowl and whisk to blend thoroughly. Set aside. Heat oil in a large skillet or wok over medium-high heat. Stir-fry garlic and gingerroot for 1 – 2 minutes. Add fish, peppers and snow peas. Cook until fish is translucent, but not overcooked. Add honey mixture and heat until sauce thickens. Stir in onions and oranges. Serve over noodles.

FISH CHOWDER

This chowder takes less than 30 minutes to prepare, however, you may want to take a little longer and make your own homemade fish stock. See next page.

6 servings

1	cup potato, peeled and diced into 1/4 inch cubes
½	1cup carrot, peeled and diced into 1/4 inch cubes
½	cup celery, diced into 1/4 inch cubes
3	garlic cloves, minced
½	cup onion, peeled and diced into 1/4 inch cubes
4	tablespoons butter
2	tablespoons flour
1	quart cold fish stock, clam juice or chicken broth
2	cups heavy cream, half and half or milk
2	tablespoons cornstarch mixed with equal part cold water
2	cups fish fillets, cut into 2 inch pieces (you can also add shrimp, scallops, etc.)
	salt and freshly ground pepper to taste
2	tablespoons fresh parsley, minced

1. Heat butter in a stock pot over medium heat and add potato, carrot, celery, garlic and onion. Cook for 5 minutes or until onions are translucent, but not brown.

2. Sprinkle flour over vegetables and stir. Continue cooking for another 5 minutes, stirring often.

3. Stir in fish stock, a little at a time and bring to a boil. Reduce heat and simmer for 5 minutes.

4. Add cream and bring to a boil again. Simmer for 5 minutes more. If thickness is to your liking, do not use the cornstarch mixture. If you would like the chowder a little thicker, add some of the cornstarch mixture, a little at a time, until you reach your desired thickness. If you are using heavy cream, you shouldn't need much, if any. If you are using milk, especially skim milk, you may want to thicken it up a bit.

5. Once you have the thickness of the chowder under control, add the fish. Cook for just a few minutes, stirring only gently a time or two. Add salt and pepper as desired.

6. To serve, ladle chowder into bowls and garnish with chopped parsley.

Pour sauce over fish in baking dish. Place baking dish under a pre-heated broiler and broil until sauce is lightly browned and bubbly.

HOW TO MAKE FISH STOCK

The next time you clean a mess of fish, preferably light-fleshed white fish, thoroughly rinse off the heads and skeleton and toss them into a large pot.

Chop up an onion, some celery, carrot, garlic, bay leaves and any herbs you may have handy and add them to the pot on top of the fish parts.

Add a cup or two of dry white wine and then cover the stuff in the pot with cold water.

Bring to a boil and then simmer for 30 – 45 minutes, skimming any foam as you go.

Pour the liquid through a strainer lined with cheesecloth and you have a great tasting fish stock.

You can freeze the fish stock and use for soups, stews, chowders and sauces.

If you're not up to the task of making your own stock, use fish bouillon (Knorr makes a decent one), clam juice or chicken broth. You can also dice up some bacon, leaving the grease and the browned diced bacon in the stockpot, to replace the butter.

Just don't blame me if you can't fit into your waders.

TEMPURA BATTERED FISH
with SPICY HONEY MUSTARD SAUCE

Use this recipe with any light-fleshed, flaky fish fillets. Great with rock fish, halibut, crappie and catfish. Make sure fish is chilled before dipping. For extra-crunchy fish, dust fish with flour before dunking in the batter.

4 servings

Tempura Batter

½   cup flour
½   cup cornstarch
1   teaspoon baking soda
1   teaspoon baking powder
1   teaspoon sugar
½   teaspoon salt
1   egg
⅔   cup ice water
    oil for frying

Sift together the dry ingredients in a bowl. Beat egg slightly and mix with water. Add the dry ingredients. Stir only until mixed; mixture will be slightly lumpy. Use immediately. Dip fish into batter and deep fry until golden brown. Drain on paper towels.

Honey Mustard Sauce

⅓   cup honey
1½ cups mayonnaise
¼   teaspoon freshly ground black pepper
    dash Worcestershire sauce
⅓   cup prepared yellow mustard
    pinch salt
    dash or two Tabasco

Mix ingredients together to blend.

HERBED KOKANEE
with ROASTED GARLIC and LEMON BUTTER

4 servings

> 2   pounds Kokanee salmon fillets, skin on or off
> 1   cup flour
> 1   tablespooon l salt
> 2   tabalespoon Italian seasoning
> 2   tablespoon olive oil
> 2   tablespoon butter

Combine flour, salt and Italian seasoning. Lightly coat fish with flour mixture. Heat oil and butter in a skillet and sauté fish, skin side up until golden brown, about 4 – 5 minutes. Flip over and cook 2 minutes more. Slice off 1/4 inch thick pieces of the chilled butter and place over hot fish.

Roasted Garlic and Lemon Butter

> ½   pound butter, softened at room temperature
> 1   cup fresh basil leaves, chopped
> 2   tablespoon lemon zest (the outside yellow skin), minced
> 8   cloves whole garlic cloves, roasted and chopped
>   pinch each salt and white pepper

Blend together in a medium bowl. Lay a 1 foot square piece of waxed paper or plastic wrap on a flat surface. Spread butter onto the center, about 2 inches wide by 6 inches long. Roll the butter up with the paper or plastic wrap so that it is shaped into a loaf, either square or round, about 6 inches long. Place in the refrigerator or freezer until firm.

BARBECUED FISH WRAP

We used to call these things burritos before the marketing people decided that they could call it a "wrap" and make a big splash in the fast food market. Call it what you like. This recipe works great with any kind of fish. Don't feel like you need to stick to the listed ingredients for this recipe. Anything you like in a burrito or taco will work great in this recipe. If you cannot locate very large flour tortillas, allow two regular flour tortillas per person. Be careful not to overstuff your wrap or it will probably split when rolled.

4 servings

1½	pounds firm fish fillets
¼	teaspoon kosher salt
3	tablespoons olive oil
2	tablespoons lime juice
3	garlic cloves, minced
½	teaspoon, or to taste, hot sauce
1	red bell pepper, quartered
1	yellow onion, sliced into thick slices
1	cup pepper-jack cheese, shredded
1	cup cooked black beans, warm
1	avocado, peeled, pitted and sliced
4	tablespoons sour cream
4	extra-large flour tortillas, warm

Combine salt, olive oil, lime juice, garlic and hot sauce. Pour over fish in a plastic, glass or ceramic container, cover and refrigerate for 2 hours. Grill fish, bell pepper and onion over ash-white coals until lightly browned. For each wrap, spread a tablespoon of sour cream across tortilla. Layer equal portions of fish, pepper, onion, black beans and avocado in a rectangular mound on the tortilla. Fold the bottom edge over and roll the wrap from one side, leaving one end open.

BEER POACHED FISH
with PARMESAN CREAM SAUCE

Poaching is a great way to keep cooked fish moist and flavorful. Food is gently cooked in liquid just below the boiling point. You can poach fish in a covered pan on the stovetop or in the oven as in this recipe. I've used this recipe with whole dressed fish and fillets of halibut and sea bass.

4 Servings

1	12 oz. beer, flat
1	carrot, chopped
1	onion, chopped
2	celery stalks, chopped
3	garlic cloves, chopped
2	bay leaves
4	6 – 8 ounce fish fillets, about 1-inch thick
2	tablespoons butter
2	tablespoons all-purpose flour
1/4	cup whipping cream
1/2	cup grated Parmesan cheese
	salt and pepper
2	tablespoons fresh parsley, chopped

Heat beer and next 5 ingredients in a large skillet over medium-low heat. Simmer for 10 minutes. Add fish fillets in a single layer and simmer for 10 minutes (or a minute or two less for fillets less than 1-inch thick). Transfer fish to a well-greased baking dish.

Increase heat under skillet to medium-high and cook until liquid is reduced to about 1 cup. Strain contents of pan, reserving liquid. Cool liquid in the freezer, stirring often. Melt butter in a skillet over medium heat and stir in flour, a little at a time, until blended with the butter. Continue stirring until it is smooth. Add cooled broth, a little at a time, to the flour and butter mixture, while stirring. Slowly add cream while stirring. Add cheese and salt and pepper to taste. Reduce heat to medium-low and continue stirring until sauce is hot and smooth.

SWEET AND SOUR FISH

The idea is to create a dish that is flavorful, colorful and low in calories. If you don't have the exact ingredients, don't hesitate to make substitutions with whatever looks good in the market. Either a wok or a decent large non-stick skillet will work for this dish. Adjust the flavor of the sauce to your liking by adding more apricot preserves or rice vinegar - the sweet and sour parts. This recipe works best with firmer fleshed flesh like yellowtail, tuna, swordfish, sturgeon and marlin.

4 servings

4	6 to 8 ounce fish fillets
1	tablespoon peanut or vegetable oil
2	green onions, diced
1	teaspoon fresh ginger, peeled and minced
2	garlic cloves, minced
1	medium carrot, peeled and thinly sliced
2	medium zucchini, split lengthwise in half and then cut into 1-inch pieces
1	red bell pepper, sliced into rings
2	tablespoons low-sodium soy sauce
¼	cup fish or chicken broth
3	tablespoons seasoned rice vinegar
2	tablespoons apricot preserves
1	teaspoon cornstarch mixed with equal part cold water
1	cups fresh pineapple, cut into 1-inch cubes
4	cups warm cooked rice

Heat oil in a wok or skillet over medium-high heat. Add green onions, ginger and garlic. Cook for 1 minute. Add fish fillets and lightly brown on both sides, about 3 minutes per side. Add cut carrots, zucchini and bell pepper. Cook for 1 minute. Add soy sauce, fish or chicken broth, vinegar, apricot preserves and cornstarch mixture. Add pineapple and return fish to the pan to warm. To serve, place fish, vegetables and sauce over rice.

GRILLED SALMON
with BOURBON GLAZE

When it's my time to cash in my chips, I want my last meal to be at Billy's Oyster Bar in Panama City Beach, Florida. I just returned from my second visit in about fifteen hours. I just could not control myself. This funky joint came highly recommended not for the ambiance, but for the food. The atmosphere is remarkably similar to my previous last meal location, Al's Place (Al the Wop's) – located in the Sacramento River town of Locke, California. Al's has the most sinfully delicious (i.e. greasy) cheeseburger on earth. They also con visitors into giving up dollar bills so that the bartenders can stick them to the ceiling. At Billy's, both the ceiling and walls are plastered with singles, but it looks likes the bills are there to stay. I spotted one with a 1987 date inscribed with permanent marker. If you find yourself east of the Mississippi, stop by Billy's. The Select Steamed Florida Blue Crabs are damn good. The raw oysters are the best I've had, even in July, and the steamed shrimp are perfectly seasoned, hot and delicious. I did not want to stop eating!

So, west of the Mississippi...Al the Wop's – east of the Mississippi...Billy's Oyster Bar. It doesn't have anything to do with this recipe, but it's worth remembering.

4 servings

4	6 to 8 ounce salmon fillets, skin removed
	freshly ground black pepper
1/3	cup dark brown sugar
1/3	cup bourbon
1/4	cup soy sauce
1	teaspoon hoisin sauce
4	garlic cloves, minced
2	tablespoons fresh gingerroot, peeled and minced
1/3	cup orange juice (preferably freshly-squeezed)
1	lemon, juice only

Season salmon with pepper. Combine remaining ingredients. Place salmon in a glass or plastic container or large zip-lock bag. Reserve 1/2 cup of the marinade. Pour remaining marinade over salmon and refrigerate 2 to 4 hours, turning occasionally. Remove salmon from marinade (discard marinade). Pat fish down with paper towels and air dry in the refrigerator for 30 minutes. Grill fish over white-hot coals until just cooked...a little rare in the center is perfect! Just before removing from the grill, brush with reserved marinade.

FISH TACOS

Bring the hot summer months, I probably eat more fish tacos than any other single dish. Firm-fleshed fish such as salmon, swordfish, snapper and striped bass may be easily grilled outdoors. The more delicate and smaller fish may either be pan-seared in a hot skillet with a tablespoon or two of olive oil or broiled in the oven. This is a great recipe to try on someone who prefers not to eat fish. The flavor is not unlike a taco made from seasoned chicken. The recipe specifies warm soft flour tortillas, but crispy corn tortilla shells work well also. Do be careful not to overcook your fish. Overcooked fish always tastes dry and often rubbery.

4 servings/ 8 tacos

3	tablespoons fresh cilantro leaves, chopped
2	garlic cloves, minced
	juice of 2 limes
½	cup orange juice
2	ounces tequila
½	teaspoon ground cumin
½	teaspoon ground chili powder
1	pound fresh fish fillets
¼	cup red onion, diced
8	medium flour tortillas, warmed
2	cups romaine or iceberg lettuce, shredded
1	cup jack cheese, grated
1	ripe avocado, diced
1	cup fresh tomato, diced

In a large bowl, combine first 7 ingredients. Cover and refrigerate for 30 minutes. Remove fish from marinade and discard marinade. Cook fish either on barbecue, in skillet or under broiler. Break cooked fish apart into small chunks. Place an equal portion of fish into each tortilla. Top with remaining ingredients.

FISH, TOMATO, AVOCADO
AND BASIL BEURRE BLANC

If you don't have any fresh basil handy, use any other fresh herb you like or leave out the herb part altogether. The type of fish you use is not critical. The recipe works with just about any fresh fish. Obviously, this recipe is better when the tomatoes are home-grown, not the ones in the stores. If your tomatoes are store-bought, slice them and then sprinkle a little bit of salt, a pinch of sugar and a splash of balsamic or white wine vinegar on them and let them sit for 15 minutes before assembling the dish. You'll be amazed at how much better they taste. I've allowed half an avocado per person. I like avocado. If you don't like avocado, you should pick a different recipe anyway.

4 servings

8	3 – 4 ounce fish fillets, skinless; about 1/2 inch thick
1	teaspoon salt and pepper
2	tablespoons butter
1	tablespoon olive oil
¼	cup dry white wine
2	large just ripe avocados, peeled, seeded and sliced about 1/4 inch thick
1	lemon, juice only
2	large tomatoes, sliced about 1/4 inch thick (see note about tomatoes above)

Basil Buerre Blanc

2	cups dry white wine
2	tablespoons shallot, minced (or substitute the white part of a green onion)
1	lemon, juice only
½	pound butter
2	tablespoons fresh basil, minced
	salt and white pepper to taste

To make the sauce, bring the wine, shallot and lemon juice to a boil in a sauce pan over medium-high heat. Reduce liquid to 1/4 cup. Strain out shallots. Remove pan from heat and whisk in butter and basil until butter is melted and sauce is smooth. Season with salt and white pepper to taste. Do not bring to a boil again. If you need to rewarm to sauce, do so over very low heat while gently whisking until warm, not hot. If it gets too hot, it will separate and look bad.

Season the fish on both sides with salt and pepper. Heat the butter and oil in a large skillet over medium heat. Lightly brown fish on both sides and then add the white wine to pan. Cook for a few minutes more. When you slice the avocado, sprinkle the lemon juice over so that the slices will not brown. To serve, place a piece of fish on the plate, top with sliced avocado and then tomato. Repeat layer. Drizzle sauce over fish, avocado and tomato.

BLACKENED CATFISH

Catfish has a fairly high fat content and it's even better with bacon grease, but then, aren't most recipes? It's best to prepare this one outdoors. Whenever you pepper-coat something and burn it in a pan, it will create fumes that make it difficult to breathe when you're in close quarters. Add to that a mess of splattering bacon grease and you've got trouble. If you decide to cook it indoors, open the windows, rank up the fans and be listen for the smoke detector alarm. Might be a good time to check the batteries! This recipe is best with thick fillets from large catfish. You can substitute commercial blackening seasoning or Cajun spice. If you make your own and are missing an ingredient or two, nobody will notice.

4 servings

4	catfish fillets, 6 – 8 ounces each
2	tablespoons olive oil
2	tablespoons bacon grease
4	tablespoons sour cream
2	teaspoons lime juice
	pinch sugar

Blackening Seasoning

2	teaspoons paprika
¼	teaspoon basil leaves
¼	teaspoon ground oregano
¼	teaspoon thyme
¼	teaspoon ground black pepper
½	teaspoon onion powder
½	teaspoon garlic powder
½	teaspoon white pepper
½	teaspoon cayenne pepper
3	3 teaspoons salt

Combine Blackening Seasoning ingredients in a bowl and mix well. Rub fish with olive oil and then coat evenly with spice mixture. Cover and refrigerate for 30 – 60 minutes. Heat bacon grease in a heavy skillet, preferably cast iron, over high heat. Add fish and sear on one side until blackened. Flip over and sear other side, but only until fish is just cooked and not overcooked.

Place fish on plates, blackest side up. Combine sour cream, lime juice and sugar and spoon over fish.

SNAPPER
with MARGARITA CREAM CHEESE

This recipe works well with any type of fish that either fairly thin, yet sturdy or that can be butterflied to about 1/4 inch thick. I first used the recipe on speckled trout and it was fantastic!

4 servings

4	snapper fillets, butterflied so that the meat is about 1/4 inch thick
1	tablespoon salt and pepper
⅔	cup softened cream cheese
2	tablespoons tequila
1	tablespoon sweet and sour mix
1	teaspoon sweetened lime juice
1	lime, juice only
2	garlic cloves, minced
2	tablespoons fresh cilantro leaves, minced
¼	cup crushed cracker crumbs

Season fish with salt and pepper. In a bowl, combine remaining ingredients. Lay fillets flat on a work surface. Spread cream cheese mixture evenly over fillets. Roll fillets up snugly, but try and keep the filling from squeezing out. Place the fillets, seam side down in a lightly buttered baking dish. Place in a 375° F oven for 15 minutes or until fish is just cooked.

BLACKENED SNAPPER

You've got to have a really hot skillet to make this work. It also helps if you cook it outdoors since searing three kinds of pepper in a hot skillet is a lot like breathing in pepper spray. If you have to do it inside, make sure you allow for plenty of ventilation. There's a decent chance that you smoke alarm may go off! Try this with salmon also.

4 servings

4	6 to 8 ounce fish fillets
3	tablespoons melted butter
1	teaspoon garlic powder
1	teaspoon onion powder
½	teaspoon each dried thyme, cayenne pepper, black pepper, white pepper
1	teaspoon paprika
½	teaspoon salt
4	sandwich rolls
4	tablespoons mayonnaise
8	slices cooked bacon
	sliced tomato
	shredded lettuce

Coat fillets with melted butter. Combine seasonings and dust fish in seasonings. When skillet is very hot, carefully add fillets to pan. Cook for about 2 minutes, depending on the thickness of the fillets, or until charred. Flip fish over and char other side. Spread mayonnaise on sandwich rolls, add sliced tomato, bacon, lettuce and blackened fish.

BIG SQUID
With Tortellini Pasta and Basil Vinaigrette

To process the squid, take the cleaned tube pieces and lay the outside part on a cutting surface. This works best if the squid is at least partially frozen. Make sure that the membrane is removed. With a very sharp fillet knife, slice the squid as thinly as you can, cutting at a slight angle. When you're done, you should have the squid sliced into very thin (and I mean very thin) pieces, about 1-2 inches wide and paper thin. Cook the squid until it just barely changes color, just a few seconds per side. If you cook it too long, plan on gnawing on it for awhile. If you want to make things easier on yourself, lightly brown the seasoned squid and toss with warm pasta and Italian dressing. This dish can also be served chilled as a salad.

4 servings

1½	cups sliced squid (see intro above)
⅓	cup flour seasoned with salt and pepper
⅓	cup diced prosciutto (or bacon)
2	tablespoons olive oil
1	cup diced tomato
3	tablespoons chopped black olives
4	cups cooked tortellini pasta
¼	cup freshly grated Parmesan cheese

Basil Vinaigrette

2	garlic cloves, minced
2	lemons, juice only
1/3	cup seasoned rice vinegar
1/2	teaspoon Dijon mustard
	pinch granulated sugar
1	cup fresh basil leaves, chopped
1/3	cup olive oil
	salt and pepper to taste

To make vinaigrette, combine all ingredients except olive oil, salt and pepper in a bowl and whisk together. While whisking, add oil in a thin stream until emulsified. Season with salt and pepper.

Toss sliced squid in seasoned flour to lightly coat. In a large skillet over medium-high heat, lightly brown prosciutto in olive oil. Add squid and cook until it just starts to change color and is lightly browned. Remove squid from pan. Add tomato, black olives and tortellini pasta to pan, along with 1/2 of the vinaigrette. Heat to warm pasta and vinaigrette. Return squid to the pan and toss to warm slightly. Serve in wide bowls, drizzle additional vinaigrette over and top with Parmesan cheese.

BARBECUED TROUT

When it's summertime and you really don't feel like heating up the kitchen, the logical place to cook your dinner is outdoors on the barbecue. The recipe specifies trout, but this preparation works well with most fish. When cooking whole fish, figure on about 1 pound per person after cleaning and removing the head. If you are lucky enough to have caught a big one, place the fish farther away from the heat and take your time cooking it.

2 servings

2	whole trout, about 1 pound each
	salt and black pepper
	juice of 2 lemons
½	bunch fresh basil
2	garlic cloves, minced
3	thinly-sliced onion rings
6	slices tomato
2	pieces butcher string, each about 2 feet long.
2	tablespoons vegetable oil

Season fish inside and out with salt and pepper. Squeeze the juice of 1 lemon into each cavity. Pack equal portion of basil, garlic, onion and tomato into cavity. Tie a loop around one end of each fish and make a few more loops around the fish, securing the stuffing. Brush fish with oil. Place on a medium-low heat barbecue grate for 5 to 7 minutes then flip over cook other side about 7 minutes more or until skin is crisp and fish is just-cooked throughout. To serve, cut string and place fish on plate.

GRILLED ORANGE MARINATED TROUT

The sweet flavors of freshly squeezed orange juice and honey are balanced with just enough vinegar so that the marinade doesn't overpower the fish. Trout has a delicate flavor so you don't want to bury it in strong flavors. The marinade is great chicken, pork and shellfish as well.

4 servings

4 1-pound trout (weight after cleaning)
 salt and freshly ground black pepper

Marinade

½ cup orange juice
2 teaspoons honey
¼ cup white wine vinegar
¼ cup olive oil
2 cloves garlic, minced
¼ cup red onion, minced
1 tablespoon Italian seasoning

Season trout evenly with salt and pepper. Place trout in a plastic, ceramic or glass container and pour marinade over. Cover and refrigerate for 2 – 4 hours, turning occasionally.

Place marinated trout over medium-hot coals. Cook for 6 – 8 minutes per side or until

SPICY STEELHEAD
with PICKLED CUCUMBERS

These sea-run rainbow trout are excellent when cooked on the barbecue, but you can grill, pan-sear or broil the fish as well. A four-pound fish, before cleaning, is perfect for a meal for four adults. The flesh is firm and the flavor is similar to trout and salmon. Fillet large fish for grilling. For smaller fish, you may choose to leave the bones intact until after grilling. The spicy part is easy. Just lay out a few thin lines of Asian chili-garlic sauce (sambal, sriracha, etc.) over the top of the fish before serving. If you can't find the Asian stuff, use your favorite hot sauce.

4 servings

Lay fillets, skin side down, in a shallow tray or dish. Squeeze lemon juice over fillets. Rub oil over fillets then season with pepper and salt. Cover and refrigerate for 1 hour. Place fillets, skin side down, on a medium-low temperature barbecue grate. Cover and cook for 6 to 7 minutes. Carefully turn fillets one quarter turn on grate, keeping skin side down. Replace cover and cook 4 to 5 minutes more. Actual cooking time will depend on thickness of fillets and temperature of barbecue. Cooked fish will be firm to the touch and light pink in color.

Allow cucumbers to stand at room temperature for 30 minutes. Drain well. Arrange cucumbers on individual plates or platter. Remove fillets from barbecue. Carefully remove skin and place fillets on cucumbers. Top with some chili-garlic sauce, but be careful!

Pickled Cucumbers

½	yellow onion, peeled and thinly sliced
1	large cucumber, thinly sliced
½	teaspoon salt
½	cup water
¼	cup white vinegar
¼	cup sugar
1	teaspoon toasted sesame seeds

In a saucepan over medium heat, combine all ingredients except onion and cucumber. Heat for a few minutes dissolve sugar, but do not boil. Place cucumber and onion in a bowl, pour liquid over and chill in refrigerator for 2 to 3 hours.

PAN-ROASTED STRIPED BASS
with ROSEMARY, VEGETABLES and TOMATO

4 servings

2   tablespoons olive oil
4   1-inch thick striper fillets, dark flesh removed
    salt and pepper
4   sprigs rosemary
4   tablespoons unsalted butter
2   tablespoons dry vermouth
    seasonal vegetables, sliced 1/4 inch thick and 2 inches long
    salt and pepper
3   tablespoons freshly grated Parmesan cheese
    fresh tomato, peeled and diced

Heat oil in pan. Season fish with salt and pepper. Add fish to pan with rosemary. Brown on one side, flip. Cook for 2 minutes more. Add butter, vermouth and vegetables to pan. Season veggies with salt and pepper. Place in a 400° F oven for 5 – 6 minutes. Arrange vegetables on plate. Top with fish. Top fish with parmesan and tomato.

POTATO CRUSTED STRIPER

Take a little extra time to clean up your striper fillets. Remove the skin and any of the dark, fatty areas along the center of the fillet. Make 'em pretty and they'll taste better once cooked.

4 servings

4	6 to 8 ounce striped bass fillets
1	cup flour, seasoned with salt and pepper
2	cups red potato, skin-on; grated
	salt and pepper
1	large egg, lightly beaten
3	tablespoons vegetable oil
¼	cup chicken stock
½	cup dry white wine
2	green onions, minced
1	lemon, juice only
3	tablespoons chilled butter

Dust fish with seasoned flour. Add some salt and pepper and the egg to the shredded potatoes and mix well. Press a 1/2-inch layer of potatoes onto the top of each fillet. Heat oil in a large non-stick skillet over medium-high heat. Carefully place the fillets, potato side down, into the hot oil. Cook for 3 to 4 minutes or until medium-brown. Carefully flip fillets over and add remaining ingredients except butter to pan. Cook for another 3 to 4 minutes or until fish is just cooked. Transfer fish to plates and increase heat in pan to high. Reduce liquid in pan to a few tablespoons, remove pan from heat and whisk in chilled butter until melted. To serve, drizzle sauce over fish.

STURGEON
with BRANDY ORANGE SAUCE

Sturgeon ranks near the top of my list of favorite fish. The flavor and texture is unlike any other fish. It is firm to the bite and somewhat neutral in flavor. The texture is reminiscent of a cross between pork and fish. As an added bonus, there are no bones to mess with - just the cartilage. Filleting is a snap and you can grill, pan sear, broil or sauté this strange looking creature. It looks prehistoric. It tastes out of this world.

4 servings

4	6 ounce sturgeon steaks
	salt and pepper
1	tablespoon olive oil
1	tablespoon butter
½	teaspoon fresh ginger, grated
¼	cup brandy
½	cup freshly squeezed orange juice
1	lemon, juice only 1 lime, juice only
¼	cup dried nectarines, peaches or apricots
¼	cup dried cherries or cranberries ("Craisins" work fine)
2	additional tablespoons chilled butter
	salt and pepper to taste

Season fish with Lawry's Lemon Pepper. Heat olive oil and 1 tablespoon butter in a skillet over medium-high heat. Add fish to pan and sear on one side, about 3 minutes. Flip fish over and sear 2 minutes. Add brandy and ginger to the pan.

But First:

CAUTION - DON'T PUT YOUR FACE ANYWHERE NEAR THE PAN When you add brandy it will probably flme up and burn something like your face, the drapes, etc. Check the area around the pan before adding any alcohol.

You can *reduce the risk of flames* by combining the brandy with the next 3 ingredients and adding slowly to the pan.

Or…after adding the brandy, add orange, lemon and lime juices. Add dried fruits. Remove fish and keep warm. It's done. Reduce liquid to 1/4 cup. Stir in butter until melted. Season with salt and pepper.

To serve, place sturgeon on plate and spoon sauce over

SOUTHWESTERN TROUT
and Green Chili Grits

Unless you live in the Southeastern U.S., you may not get too worked up over a recipe that includes "grits." Grits is coarsely ground corn. Or is it, grits are coarsely ground corn. Either way you say it, it's pretty much the same as polenta, its Italian cousin. If you don't want to go to the trouble of filleting your trout, cook it whole and remove the skeleton after it's cooked. The recipe calls for Quick Grits. You can take your time and use the regular variety, but I'm not a big fan of Instant Grits.

4 servings

The Grits

2	cups chicken broth
1	cup half and half
	pinch salt
1	cup quick grits
½	cup roasted green chilies, diced
	pinch ground cumin
1	cup shredded jack cheese
¼	cup fresh cilantro leaves, minced

Bring chicken broth and half and half and salt to a boil in a medium saucepan over medium-high heat. Slowly stir in grits. Reduce heat to medium-low, cover. Cook 5 -7 minutes, stirring occasionally. Stir in green chilies, cheese and cilantro. Keep warm.

The Trout

½	cup all-purpose flour
⅓	cup masa flour
1	teaspoon salt
½	teaspoon black pepper
4	trout fillets, about 8 – 10 ounces each
3	tablespoons olive oil
¼	cup dry white wine
⅓	cup red onion, finely diced
3	garlic cloves, minced
2	Anaheim peppers, sliced into rings
1	jalapeno pepper, seeded and minced
½	cup chicken broth
½	cup canned or fresh diced tomato
1	teaspoon freshly squeezed lemon or lime juice
4	tablespoons butter, chilled

Combine first 4 ingredients and dust fish fillets with seasoned flour. Heat olive oil in a large skillet over medium heat. Add trout and lightly brown on both sides. Remove trout from pan and keep warm. Add wine to pan and stir to loosen bits. Add onion, garlic and peppers. Saute for 3- 4 minutes. Add broth, tomatoes and lemon juice. Bring to boil and reduce liquid by one-half. Whisk in chilled butter until melted.

To serve, place a mound of grits on the center of each plate. Arrange trout around grits and spoon sauce over.

GRILLED ALBACORE
with PEACH SALSA

Southerners might be surprised to learn that California, not Georgia, produces more peaches than any other U.S. state. This recipe works well with any fruit in season – whatever looks good in market. The salsa is great on any fish, but I'm partial to pairing it with freshly caught grilled albacore or yellowfin tuna. I like my tuna cooked rare to medium-rare.

4 servings

4	6 - 8 ounce albacore steaks
	olive oil
	salt and freshly ground pepper
3	medium peaches; skin removed and flesh chopped into 1/2 inch cubes
1	jalapeño pepper, seeded and minced
2	tablespoons fresh cilantro, chopped
2	green onions; white part and about half of the green part, minced
½	teaspoon fresh ginger, grated
2	garlic cloves, minced
1	tablespoon lime juice
1	teaspoon lemon juice
2	tablespoons olive oil

Rub fish with olive oil and season liberally with salt and pepper. Place on a medium-hot grill for 3 -4 minutes, flip over and cook 1 – 2 minutes more. To prepare salsa, combine remaining ingredients and let stand at room temperature for 30 minutes. To serve, place fish on plate and spoon salsa over middle half.

YELLOWTAIL, SHRIMP, AVOCADO And CHIVES

Shrimp, avocado and fresh chives contribute to this delectable treat featuring fresh-caught yellowtail. When avocados are plentiful and of good quality, use them, otherwise, use prepared guacamole.

4 servings

4	6 to 8 ounce yellowtail fillets, skin removed
	salt and freshly ground pepper
⅓	cup flour
4	tablespoons butter
2	tablespoons oil
3	tablespoons yellow onion, minced
¼	cup dry white wine
¾	cup heavy cream
1	cup uncooked shrimp, roughly chopped
3	tablespoons fresh chives, chopped (or substitute green onions)
1	ripe but firm avocado, peeled and diced into 1/2 inch cubes
	juice of 1 lemon

Season fillets with salt and pepper and then dust with four. Heat 2 tablespoons of the butter and all of the oil in a large skillet over medium heat. Sauté fish on each side for 3 to 4 minutes or until just firm. Remove fillets and place on a warmed plate or platter. Add remaining butter and onions to skillet and sauté for 2 minutes. Increase heat to medium-high and add wine. Scrape the bottom of the pan to loosen any bits. Reduce liquid to 1 tablespoon. Add cream and cook until sauce thickens. Season with salt and pepper. Stir in shrimp and chives and return fish to skillet to warm.

Gently toss diced avocado with lemon. Place one warmed fillet on each plate and drizzle shrimp and chive sauce over fish. Top with diced avocado.

YELLOWTAIL, ASPARAGUS and MUSHROOM STIR-FRY

Just spicy enough to get your attention, but not so much that it buries the flavor of the fish, this recipe is quick and easy. The sauce has just a hint of sweetness to balance the heat of the chili flakes. Serve over steamed rice or Asian noodles.

4 servings

2	tablespoons peanut oil
1	teaspoon fresh gingerroot, peeled and minced
2	garlic cloves, minced
½	red onion, chopped
2	cups fresh asparagus spears, chopped diagonally into 2 inch pieces
2	cups button mushrooms, quartered
1½	pound yellowtail fillet, cut into ½ to 1 inch cubes
½	cup fish or chicken broth
2	tablespoons soy sauce
¼	cup seasoned rice vinegar
1	tablespoon brown sugar
1	teaspoon dried chili flakes (or sub fresh minced hot peppers)
2	green onions, chopped
2	teaspoons cornstarch mixed with equal part cold water

Heat oil, gingerroot and garlic in a wok or skillet over high heat for 1 minute. Add onion and asparagus and stir-fry for 2 – 3 minutes. Add mushrooms and yellowtail and lightly brown fish pieces evenly. Add remaining ingredients and bring to a boil, stirring until thickened, about 1 – 2 minutes.

GRILLED YELLOWTAIL
with JALAPEÑO JELLY GLAZE

Here's a recipe that's so easy, you'll use it over and over. Great in a pinch when you want something that's fast and delicious.

4 servings

4	6 – 8 ounce yellowtail fillets
¼	cup jalapeño jelly
2	tablespoons rice or white wine
½	vinegar
¼	teaspoon Dijon mustard
	teaspoon salt

Combine jelly, vinegar, mustard and salt in a small saucepan over medium-low heat. Heat while stirring until jelly is dissolved. Allow to cool. Brush a coating over fish. Grill fish until just done, basting 2 – 3 times with glaze while cooking.

GRILLED YELLOWTAIL
with SPICY PEPPERCORN OIL

This Spicy Peppercorn Oil is best made a day ahead, so plan accordingly. In a pinch, you can make a fast batch and just slap it on your fish, but it's mo' betta after a day or two.

4 servings

4	yellowtail fillets, 6 – 8 ounces each
3	tablespoon whole peppercorns, any color or mixed
1	cup olive oil
2	teaspoons red pepper flakes
5	garlic cloves, crushed
¼	cup red or yellow onion, chopped
1	lemon peel
1½	teaspoons Kosher salt

Place peppercorns in a medium-hot dry skillet and lightly toast for 3 – 4 minutes while stirring(releases flavor!). Add peppercorns to a small saucepan with oil, pepper flakes, garlic and onion. Bring to a boil while stirring. Remove from heat, stir in lemon and salt and allow to cool. Place in a jar and let stand at room temperature for 12 – 24 hours. Strain through coffee filter (optional). Brush fish with peppercorn oil and place on a white-hot grill for 3 – 4 minutes each side or until just a tad undercooked. Drizzle additional oil over and serve.

TROUT WITH HERB VINAIGRETTE

You can bake it, broil it, sauté it, pan-sear it, blacken it or throw it on the grill.
Personally, I prefer to cook it on the grill to smoky fruit wood coals along with some
sweet bell peppers and red onions, but you do what you want. If your trout is dry, don't
blame it on the fish - you've overcooked it. If you have trouble with fish sticking to the
grill when you barbecue, make sure that the grate is clean and hot. The fish is much
more likely to stick to a grill that is not very hot. If that still doesn't work, dust the fish
with a little seasoned flour before grilling. If that doesn't work, give up and put the
fish under the broiler.

To butterfly your trout, use a sharp boning knife and, starting at the head, run the
knife between both sides and the spine. This will separate the bones from the spine
and fish can be opened up flat. After cooking, the bones can be easily removed.

4 servings

4	one pound trout (weight after cleaning, head-on), butterflied
½	teaspoon freshly ground black pepper
	pinch salt
½	cup white wine vinegar
1	teaspoon Dijon mustard
2	garlic cloves, minced
1	tablespoon lemon juice
½	teaspoon sugar
½	cup olive oil
⅓	cup fresh herbs, chopped

Season fish with salt and pepper. Combine remaining ingredients in a jar with a tight-
fitting lid and shake vigorously. Baste the fish with the stuff in the jar and let stand at
room temperature for 30 minutes. Place fish, skin-side down on a medium heat barbecue. Cover with lid or foil for 5 minutes, baste again and give the fish a quarter turn
with a spatula. Cover again and cook for 5 minutes more. Fish should be done throughout. Remove bones and serve with vinaigrette on the side.

BACON-WRAPPED GRILLED TROUT

Fish and game cooks love to wrap stuff in bacon. "OK, here's the deal, you take your goose and cut it into little strips. Then, you soak it in a combination of Worcestershire, ketchup, Italian dressing, garlic, onion and Coca-Cola for... oh, about 3 days. Then, you wrap 'em up in jalapeño pepper and bacon and toss them on the grill. They don't even taste like goose!" Whether you go to extreme measures to make your fish and game edible or not, the bottom line is – most things taste better wrapped in bacon, and freshly caught trout is no exception.

2 servings

2	whole dressed trout, about 1 pound each
	salt and black pepper
	juice of 2 lemons
½	bunch fresh basil
1	garlic cloves, minced
2	thinly-sliced onion rings
6	slices tomato
4	strips bacon
	short skewers soaked in water for 30 minutes

Season fish inside and out with salt and pepper. Squeeze the juice of 1 lemon into each cavity. Pack equal portion of basil, garlic, onion and tomato into cavity. Wrap each with 2 strips of bacon and secure with skewers. Place on a medium-low heat barbecue grate for 5 to 7 minutes then flip over cook other side about 7 minutes more or until bacon is browned and fish is just-cooked throughout. Remove skewers and serve fish whole.

Cooking Tip: When wrapping fish and game in bacon, try cooking the bacon half way first and then wrap around the meat, etc. This is especially good with things that cook quickly, like dove breasts, since the bacon is crispy, not limp, when the meat is cooked.

WALLEYE, CAPERS and LEMON

4 servings

4	6 – 8 ounce walleye fillets
½	cup all-purpose flour
1	teaspoon salt
¼	teaspoon white pepper
½	teaspoon garlic powder
1	tablespoon Italian seasoning
2	tablespoons butter
3	tablespoons olive oil
2	tablespoons freshly squeezed lemon juice
¼	cup dry white wine
	pinch sugar
1	tablespoon capers
3	additional tablespoons butter
2	green onions, chopped
½	cup tomato, seeded and diced

Pat fillets dry with paper towels. Combine flour with next 4 ingredients. Dust fish with seasoned flour. Heat 2 tablespoons butter and olive oil in a large skillet over medium heat. Add fish and brown lightly on both sides until just cooked. Transfer to a dish or pan, cover and keep warm in a 200 degree oven.

Wipe pan out with a paper towel and return pan to a medium-hot stove. Add lemon juice, wine, sugar and capers. Bring to a boil and reduce liquid to 1 or 2 tablespoons. Remove pan from heat and whisk in butter and onions until butter is melted. Stir in tomato and spoon sauce over warm fish.

GLOSSARY

Al Dente: Firm to the bite, usually referring to vegetables or pasta.

Baste: To brush with a basting liquid or marinade.

Blanch: To cook for a minute or two in boiling water, stock or fat. Blanching is used to prepare vegetables, fruits and nuts for recipes or to heighten the color of vegetables.

Blend: To mix thoroughly two or more ingredients until smooth.

Braise: To cook with low to moderate heat with a small amount of liquid in a covered pan.

Broth: A liquid derived from simmering meats, bones and/or vegetables in liquid.

Brown: To sear an ingredient with a small amount of fat until browned on all sides. Used to seal in juices and enhance appearance.

Caramelize: To melt brown sugar over low heat until golden brown or to cook vegetables in caramelized sugar until browned.

Cube: To cut into small, approximately 1/2 inch, cubes.

Dash: Less than 1/8 teaspoon.

Deglaze: To add a moderate amount of liquid to a pan to dissolve or loosen cooked food particles, usually done while pan is over heat.

Dice: To cut into very small pieces, about 1/8 to 1/4 inch.

Dredge: To place food in a dry seasoning mixture, usually seasoned flour turning to coat with mixture.

Drizzle: To pour a liquid in a fine stream over food.

Emulsify: To mix usually unmixable liquids. Emulsion is accomplished by adding one liquid to the other, a little at a time, while whisking vigorously or processing in a food processor or blender until liquids become one uniformly consistent liquid.

Julienne: To cut food into matchstick-thin strips.

Knead: To work dough with hands by folding and pressing.

Marinate: To immerse food in a liquid to impart the flavor of the liquid to the food. To rub food with a dry seasoning and let stand for a period of time to enhance the flavor of the food.

Mince: To cut or chop into very fine pieces.

Pan-fry: To cook over medium or higher heat in a pan in a small amount of fat.

Poach: To cook gently with low heat in liquid, usually seasoned with vegetables, herbs and stocks.

Purée: To make a pulp by mashing, straining or processing food in a blender or food processor.

Reduce: To decrease the volume of a liquid by cooking over medium to high heat, uncovered. The water content of the liquid will evaporate, the liquid will thicken and flavors will be more concentrated and pronounced.

Roux: A cooked mixture of fat and flour used for thickening sauces and soups.

Sauté: To cook quickly in a small amount of butter, margarine, oil or other fats.

Stir-Fry: To cook quickly in a hot wok or skillet seasoned with oil and/or ginger, garlic, soy sauce and other vegetables and seasonings. Cooking is done while stirring constantly to cook evenly.

Whisk: To stir a liquid or batter vigorously with a wire whisk.

Index

Calypso Sauce 180
Caper Dill Vinaigrette 185
Catfish, Crunch, with Lemon Lime Tartar Sauce 209
Catfish with Pecan Cream Cheese 200
Chili-Lemon-Lime Marinade 183
Chipotle Tomato Salsa 183
Curried Duck Stir-Fry 58
Deer Burger, Horseradish 122
Dove Hors D'Oeuvre, Sesame w/Bacon 34
Dove, Jalapeno, Brochette 83
Dove Ravioli with Tomato-Basil Vinaigrette 80, 89
Dove Stroganoff 81
Duck Breast with Spiced Apple and Dried Cherries 54
Duck Breasts with Orange and Mint Sauce 55
Duck Egg Rolls 30
Duck Legs, Cajun 161
Duck Ravioli, Monster 160
Duck Wellington 53
Elk Loin with Asian Barbecue Sauce 120
Elk Tostada 127
Elk with Barley Soup 128
Fish, Barbecued Wrap 228
Fish, Beer Poached 229
Fish Chowder 224
Fish Creole 212
Fish, Honey Orange Stir-Fry 223
Fish Rub 157
Fish, Sautéed 221
Fish Stock, How To Make 224
Fish, Stuffed, Grilled 220
Fish, Sweet and Sour 230
Fish Tacos 232
Fish, Tomato, Avocado & Basil Buerre Blanc 233
Flounder with Mango Margarita Sauce 208
Garlic Bread, Really Good 158
Goose Breast Supreme 57
Goose, Saskatchewan Snow, Marinade 48
Green Goddess Dressing 94
Grilled Doves with a Balsamic-Cherry Glaze 82
Grilled Halibut w/ Nectarine and Cherry Salsa 205
Grilled Tomato-Rosemary Vinaigrette 186
Grilled Venison with Balsamic Syrup 124
Grouper, Grilled or Pan-Seared 213
Halibut, Jake's First 214
Halibut with Herb and Chive Oil 215
Herb Pan Sauce for Fish 186

C

Duck, Peppercorn with Horseradish Sauce 45
Duck Ravioli 44
Duck Ravioli, Monster 160
Duck Sausage 159
Duck, Sesame Crusted 49
Duck, Smoked with A Citrus Glaze 145
Duck, Ten Minute 49
Duck Wellington 53
Duck with Raspberry Sauce 37

E

Easy Barbecued Orange-Rosemary Duck 40
Elk Carpaccio 20
Elk Leg Roast, Herb-Crusted 111
Elk Loin with Asian Barbecue Sauce 120
Elk Roast, Stuffed, with Sweet and Sour Zinfandel 113
Elk Steak, Blackened 106
Elk Tenderloin with Crispy Cornmeal Crepes and Fresh Papaya 112
Elk Tostada 127
Elk with Barley Soup 128
Ensalada Ay Caramba 23

F

Fish, Barbecued Wrap 228
Fish, Beer Poached 229
Fish, Broiled 219
Fish Chowder 224
Fish Creole 212
Fish, Honey Orange Stir-Fry 223
Fish Rub 157
Fish, Sautéed 221
Fish Stock, How To Make 224
Fish, Stuffed, Grilled 220
Fish, Sweet and Sour 230
Fish Tacos 232
Fish, Tempura Batter 226
Fish, Tomato, Avocado & Basil Buerre Blanc 233
Flounder with Mango Margarita Sauce 208
Fried Catfish with a Spicy Pumpkin Seed Crust and Cilantro Tartar Sauce 190

G

Game Bird Pie 65
Game Bird Stock 165
Game Fish 189

M

Mallard Stir-Fry with Mandarin Oranges 42
Mango Puree 187
Mango Salsa 170
Mango Wasabi Sweet and Sour Sauce 187
Marinade, All-Purpose (See Saskatchewan Snow Geese 48
Marinated Goose with Citrus and Herb Vinaigrette 22
Maryland Fish Chowder 197
Monster Duck Ravioli 160
Mu Shu Goose 36
Mushroom Sauce 175
Mushroom Sauté 153
Mustard and Dill Sauce 180
Mustard Dipping Sauce 170
Mustard Marinade 174

N

New Mexico Venison Chili 119

O

Orange Citrus Buerre Blanc 179
Orange-Basil Hollandaise Sauce 172
Oven "Fried" Crappie 207

P

Pan-Fried Quail and Nectarine Salad 26
Parmesan Baked Halibut 204
Parmesan Cream Sauce 179
Pecan Pesto Vinaigrette 95
Peppercorn Duck with Horseradish Sauce 45
Pheasant Breast Medallions, Stuffed 71
Pheasant Breast Napoleon 76
Pheasant Breasts, Pan-Fried 68
Pheasant Cobb Salad 94
Pheasant, Crispy Baked 70
Pheasant, Jamaican Barbecued 69
Pheasant, Marinated w/Pecan Pesto Vinaigrette 95
Pheasant Tempura 27
Pheasant Timbales with Lemon Vinaigrette 25
Pheasant w/Cashews & Snow Peas 67
Pheasant with Parmesan Mushroom Cream Sauce 86
Pickled Cucumbers 240
Pico De Gallo Salsa 170
Pistachio Pesto 169

T

U

V

Y

For more fine books from Arrowhead Classics Publishing Company,
please visit www.arrowhead-classics.com

To watch Scott Leysath's current TV shows, check with
www.sportingchef.com

Printed in the United States
95606LV00002B/42/A